Series Editors

W. Hansmann
W. T. Hewitt
W. Purgathofer

R. C. Veltkamp and
E. H. Blake (eds.)

Programming Paradigms in Graphics

Proceedings of the Eurographics Workshop
in Maastricht, The Netherlands,
September 2-3, 1995

Eurographics

SpringerWienNewYork

Dr. Remco C. Veltkamp
Department of Computer Science, University of Utrecht, The Netherlands

Dr. Edwin H. Blake
Department of Computer Science, University of Cape Town,
Rondebosch, South Africa

© 1995 Springer-Verlag/Wien
Printed in Austria

Typesetting: Camera ready by editors
Printing: Druckerei Novographic, A-1238 Wien
Binding: Fa. Papyrus, A-1100 Wien

Graphic design: Ecke Bonk

Printed on acid-free and chlorine-free bleached paper

With 41 partly coloured Figures

ISSN 0946-2767
ISBN 3-211-82788-9 Springer-Verlag Wien New York

# Preface

The papers in this volume are a good sampling and overview of current solutions to the problems of creating graphically based systems. This breadth of scope comes out of the closing discussion at the Fourth Eurographics Workshop on Object-Oriented Graphics. The fifth workshop, on Programming Paradigms in Graphics, set out to provide answers and alternatives to the shortcomings of object-oriented graphics. The presentations investigated the applicability, merits and problems of various programming paradigms in computer graphics for design, modelling and implementation.

This book contains a revised selection of the best papers from the Fifth Eurographics Workshop on Programming Paradigms in Graphics, held 2–3 September 1995 in Maastricht, The Netherlands. All papers at the workshop were subjected to a thorough review by at least three members of the international programme committee. The selection for this book was based on further review and the papers also incorporate the relevant aspects of the discussions at the workshop.

In past Eurographics workshops on Object-Oriented Graphics the prominent trend has been a discovery of the limits of object-orientation in graphics. The limitations of object-orientation were felt to lie in such areas as the expression of relationships between objects. This is an area of particular strength for the declarative languages, such as constraint-based languages. On the other hand, a notion of state has long been a problem in declarative languages and yet it is often seen as an essential aspect of graphical modelling, particularly in simulation and animation.

The lively discussions at the workshop are difficult to summarize. Reading these papers will give an idea of the issues addressed. The workshop was exciting because it brought together researchers whose common interest was graphics but not a particular programming 'ideology'. Some felt that one should not make a "theology" out of object-oriented programming. The need by constraint solvers for global information and the fact that relations cannot be encapsulated in single objects could simply be addressed by relaxing the rules of information hiding and being a bit less strict about encapsulation. The purist camp felt that if violations of good practice were allowed on an *ad hoc* basis then the benefits conferred by object-oriented practice would simultaneously evaporate. In this connection there was some concern expressed about potential directions of the new distributed virtual reality standard for the world wide web — VRML. There might be a danger of VRML unlearning a number of the lessons learnt in developing graphics standards that have culminated in the formulation of object-oriented standards such as PREMO.

The discussion sessions seemed to be good at issuing challenges. Here are a few:

- Is there one paradigm for graphics or are there several sub-domains each with their own? Tie up subdomains with their corresponding paradigms.

- Conceptually speaking, what are the limitations of object-oriented and functional programming paradigms? Is it as crude as that one cannot deal with relationships while the other leads to rather contorted ways of regarding persistent actors changing over time?

- What, if anything, is special about the requirements that graphics (in the broad sense) imposes on programming methodologies?

- Specifically, please present, at the next workshop,

a useful functional animation system.

a well designed VRML.

with object-orientation as a base, an integration of other paradigms that works "well". *Well* means that the integration confers the sum of the benefits of the individual paradigms and not the lowest common factor. Start by integrating a functional paradigm.

a working prototype for every claim; one that effectively demonstrates the solution. This is a call for constructed proofs.

One of the conclusions of the workshop was that the object-oriented methodology is still the most effective approach that is widely used to construct real computer graphics applications. Leaving its role as an implementation tool aside, practitioners have realized the shortcomings of the object-oriented methodology as a conceptual problem solving paradigm for the design and development of large computer graphics applications. The availability of powerful parallel systems and high-speed networks, the phenomenal popularity of World Wide Web, the advent of global computing, and the promise of information super-highways all allow graphics applications to extend the limits of how computers can impact our professional, personal, and social lives. In this context, concurrency and distribution have been proposed as one of the themes of the next workshop in this series. Deferred processing (related to laziness) is important in large animated systems and it is still an open question. The need for extensibility of graphical systems, particularly by third parties without access to source code, should also be addressed more adequately than at present.

The papers are grouped into four parts: Object-Oriented, Constraints, Functional, and Multi-Paradigm. This essentially takes the reader on a tour of the issues we have addressed. Firstly there are the impressive benefits and power of object-oriented approaches, both as conceptually tools for design and as programming frameworks. In constraints, though, the limitations are exposed, and addressed. Functional programming provides a clear alternative approach with some impressive recent breakthroughs conceptually (e.g., the use of monads to express state) and in practice. Finally we present some approaches to resolving (or at least enumerating) the multiplicity of approaches encountered.

The ERCIM Graphics Network supported the workshop. The workshop was organized by CWI, Amsterdam. We thank Ms. Marja Hegt for assistance and organizing local arrangements.

October 1995                                                                 Edwin Blake
                                                                            Remco Veltkamp

# Contents

VIII

# Part I: Object-Oriented

# Issues on Hierarchical Graphical Scenes

Ekkehard Beier

Technical University of Ilmenau, Department of Computer Graphics
E-mail: ekki@prakinf.tu-ilmenau.de

**Abstract** A hierarchical structuring of graphical scenes corresponds to many real world metaphors and implies an ease of use. But, due to the limited resources of graphical systems, graphical scenes are often created as directed acyclic graphs and, therefore, are loosing the advantages of hierarchies.

This paper explores the requirements of various rendering methods with regard to the organization of the graphical scene, and sets up rendering-independent modelling requirements for a generic graphics kernel. Finally, it describes a solution for a specific graphics kernel that is strongly based on hierarchical structures but avoids redundancies in a high degree.

## 1 Introduction

Most real world metaphors are based on hierarchies. Therefore, the usage of hierarchies in computer graphics is quite natural and implies an ease of use. However, due to the limited resources of graphical systems, scenes are often created as directed acyclic graphs (DAG) and, therefore, are loosing the advantages of hierarchies. Thus, two major paradigms exist for the organization of graphical output, the hierarchy and the DAG.

The usage of hierarchies has several advantages, e.g., clear object locations and parent relations, natural manipulations of the scene and, statically bound objects may be realized. This allows, for instance, an efficient implementation of object-oriented modelling paradigms by using retraversing as described in [2]. Hierarchies do not imply the problems which may be encountered when using the DAG approach, that is, the ambiguity of the parent of a primitive, the restructuring of the DAG into a tree in order to do some specific tasks (e.g., pick correlation or individualization of multiply referenced data).

On the other hand, a hierarchical approach causes a certain amount of redundancy for most application areas.

The DAG-oriented structure is characterized by multiple usage of data, i.e., geometry and attributes. This saves memory needs and start-up time in a degree dependent on the existence of similar data structures. Application fields with a high degree of redundancy are, for instance, circuit design, furniture visualization or virtual reality. Drawbacks of this approach are the needs for traversing processes due to the dynamically bound objects with a certain amount of computing efforts and the limited navigation possibilities within the DAG.

Both approaches correspond to various kinds of rendering in a different degree. This will be shortly explained in the following section. Based on these examinations rendering-independent modelling requirements will be set up that may be inherent to a generic graphics kernel. The question is, is it possible to combine the advantages of both paradigms in a rendering and modelling-independent way?

# 2 Organization of the Graphical Output

Generally, a rendering library is strongly correlated to one kind of rendering and, therefore, implements a specific modelling facility, e.g., DAG, tree, set of trees, etc. The following sections examine different rendering methods and a consequent object-oriented graphics system with respect to the modelling and rendering requirements.

## 2.1 Graphical Output in a Shading System

A typical shading library (such as PHIGS [6], OpenGL [8]) uses a limited set of primitive types that represent geometry and are parameterized by attributes which are set before. Both primitives and attributes are ordered in containers[1] (so-called display lists) that can be nested to form a DAG. The output is done by a traversal process that is carried out as follows.

- The traversal starts on a selected display list that acts as root of subgraphs.

- If an attribute is found in the display list it changes the global attribute context of the system in case of OpenGL, or changes a display-list-local attribute context in case of PHIGS. A special attribute is the spatial modelling. Normally (e.g., in PHIGS), a global and local modelling matrix will be concatenated for each display list. In OpenGL this is left to the application for performance reasons.

- If a primitive is found, a temporary primitive will be created in dependence of the current state (attribute context, global and local modelling matrix) and will be put into the rendering pipeline to generate a visible representation by transformation and clipping processes.

Consequently, display lists may be multiply referenced and parameterized by external attributes that, however, may be overwritten by display-list-local attributes. In this way, a memory efficient mechanism is provided. Furthermore, the data for concrete instances of multiple references are found out for each display request. There is no persistent storage of this data. The traversal is at least conceptually necessary for each display update.

## 2.2 Graphical Output in a Ray-Tracing System

A ray-tracer may request the parameters of a primitive (geometry, material) very often when rendering an image, normally several times for one pixel. Ray-tracing a DAG-based graphical scene would imply traversing processes including matrix concatenations for each pixel, even for each ray (subpixel ray or non-primary ray). A run-time efficient

---

[1]OpenGL supports an immediate mode besides the display-list mode. The operation in the immediate mode does not essentially differ from the described display-list mode. Display lists offer the advantage to be hold completely in hardware in an optionally pre-compiled form.

solution would cache data to avoid the permanent traversal processes. This would result in a tree-oriented organization of the graphical scene with more or less data multiply referenced.

Therefore, most ray-tracers use a hierarchical organization and do not support multiple references. However, most primitives are represented as implicit surfaces and not in a tesselated form. This reduces memory redundancies. All data should exist in the form that is needed by the ray-tracer, e.g., modelling matrices (M.C. to W.C.), and bounding boxes in world coordinates are computed. There are no traversing processes necessary for each display/pixel/ray. However, a global or adaptive traversal of the scene may be necessary to update the above-mentioned data.

### 2.3 Graphical Output in an Object-Oriented Graphics System

The design of object-oriented systems focuses mainly on communications between related objects and on realizing the principle of locality. Furthermore, the state of the objects reflects the assigned attributes. This means that a (temporary) assignment of an attribute may cause (computing-intensive) changes of the object (e.g., creating a new object discretization).

Therefore, hierarchical structures are used, at least logically. However, a limited usage of multiple references is possible. Object-oriented implementation languages provide suitable techniques for that, e.g., reference counters, overloadable assignment operators and copy constructors. Thus, multiple references are not primarily supported to provide a more comfortable and intuitive access to graphical scenes. However, several strategies are known to take advantage of shared data (attributes, modelling matrices, geometries). There are no traversing processes necessary for each display/pixel/ray. A global or adaptive traversal of the scene may be necessary to update the state of the objects, however.

## 3 Evaluation

On the one hand, there is a difference between *pipeline-oriented* rendering architectures which generate new data, representing the existing ones with a possible loss of information and geometrical dimensionality[2], and *message-passing* architectures as realized in ray-tracers[3].

On the other hand, a distinction exists between *temporary* primitives that will be generated for immediate processing, and *state-based* primitives that exist for more than one rendering process. In most cases, states are used for performance reasons, e.g., primitive-local intersection caches or display lists, or to represent some kind of modelling.

Furthermore, there are certain modelling-specific differences. For instance, in most applications the primitives are independent of a concrete location in the world coordinates. Thus, a single geometry may be mapped to different spatial places. In contrast,

---

[2] This kind of rendering architectures is formally represented by the reference model CGRM [7].

[3] Note. Ray-Tracing is characterized by a point-by-point sampling of graphical primitives which is the base for implicit representations of graphical primitives and generic implementation of solid textures.

the representation of the data glyphs described in [9] strongly depends on their world location.

Considering these contradictory aspects, there does not seem to be a single paradigm for the organization of the graphical output that matches the various kinds of rendering. This, of course, does not simplify the task of defining graphics kernels which are open to various kinds of rendering[4]. However, for the design of a graphics kernel, that should realize an object-oriented modelling of graphical scenes, but should be independent of a concrete kind of rendering, the following requirements could be summarized.

- A hierarchical structure is necessary to achieve the goals of object-oriented graphical modelling (e.g., retraversing in the hierarchy, delegation of method requests to the parent primitive [2]) and matches all described rendering methods.

- The modelling should be inherited inside the hierarchy. While in most cases, a simple down transferring of attribute values is used, a specific semantics should be implementable as well (e.g., computing a new transformation matrix in dependence on inherited and local modelling).

- A distinction between data that are specific to a node or leaf of the hierarchy and data that may be multiply referenced, is necessary. Examples for the first kind of data are identification information or the transformation matrix.

- Different kinds of rendering have various requirements for both of the above-mentioned kinds of data. One way to integrate these different needs is to use multiple inheritance. The access to rendering-specific data (e.g., display lists) should be possible in a flexible way.

- The multiple usage of data should be completely hidden from the application programmer. However, the programmer of primitives should have full access.

- The primitives should represent the attributes valid for them. Normally, this means that some data of the primitive (e.g., a vertex list or a display list) depend on the assigned or inherited attributes.

The following section will describe some concepts that match the above-mentioned requirements in different degrees.

## 4 Existing Work

Wisskirchen [11] conceptually described an object-oriented extension to a display-list library (GKS/PHIGS) that hides multiple references from the application programmer. Arbitrarily complex graphical primitives consisting of geometry and attributes may be multiply referenced from leaves of a hierarchically organized graphical scene. The system (GEO++) provides various copy methods and an automatic individualization of a multiply referenced geometry, if needed. However, the approach requires permanent traversing processes and, therefore, its applicability is limited to the typical shading

---

[4]one of the major requirements of the up-coming ISO multimedia standard PREMO [5]

method (as realized in GKS/PHIGS). Furthermore, the geometry must not be influenced by the assignment of an attribute. This is guaranteed in GKS/PHIGS, but not in general.

The system described in [1, 2] uses a hierarchical organization, too. Based on this fundamental design decision, physically existent attributes could multiply be used by primitives that logically *inherit* these [2]). Furthermore, primitives were characterized by their state that depends on the assigned attributes in a high degree. For instance, surface, resolution and fillstyle attributes were the appropriate attributes for analytical primitives and, therefore, influence the generated geometry to approximate the analytically defined geometry and the generated display list. While reaching nearly native performance for relatively static scenes, the approach implied a high degree of memory redundancy for various application areas and a certain amount of start-up time.

A quite different concept is explained in [3]. Following a functional approach, graphical output is generated by an arithmetic concatenation of attributes and predefined primitives (values). Thus, visible primitives are created just temporarily from stateless graphical scenes. This offers possibilities for constrainable primitives (e.g., time-dependent geometry or colour). The obviously time-consuming evaluation of the arithmetic expressions is optimized in the underlying graphics layer. For instance, display lists could be used and externally parameterized for analytical primitives such as sphere or cube. However, XGL [12], the porting platform of the system, does not support display lists. Nevertheless, the lack of the state may cause drawbacks for interactively modelled scenes and for certain application areas, e.g., scientific visualization. For instance, data sets, as used in scientific visualization, represent a certain state that cannot be generated explicitly, e.g., after manipulation.

# 5 Multiple References

Multiple references to data allow to share these data for a number of objects. Normally, reference counters are used to manage the data. Especially object-oriented implementation languages provide sufficient possibilities to hide the internal usage of multiple references from the application programmer. An interesting alternative is to store the data common to all objects of a given class as persistent data of this class. For instance, an object of class *X29* may use the class-invariant OFF data set of the X29 as long as it will not modify it. In the case of modification a cloning of the data set has to be provided by the class. A further application of class-invariant data may be the creation and storage of a fixed number of representations with a varying level of detail (LoD). These are normally created at an initial time (e.g., when loading the data set from the data base) and will be used by objects of the class in a dynamic way.

Multiply referenced data may even be parameterized temporarily. For instance, for a geometry that is independent on the material properties and the modelling transformation, both properties may be set to create a temporary primitive. By the way, this is the essence of the *external parameterizability* that is a basic principle of the above-mentioned display-list libraries. A display list containing geometry is called immediately or from other display lists with a current modelling context. However, the parameterization should not affect the shared data in a computing-intensive way. For instance, calling a shared sphere geometry with different values for the tessellation would imply the re-generation of the sphere's approximation for each new resolution value. This reduces the applicability of approaches basing on dynamic re-parenting of multiply referenced primitives.

# 6 Invariant Modelling in the Generic Graphics Kernel

In contrast to most existing graphics kernels that implicitly prescribe the set of (basic) primitives, the kind of rendering and the modelling facility, the generic kernel, that is in implementation at our university, is open, meaning that these things may (and have to) be explicitly specified in the derived graphics kernel. However, following modelling specification is valid for the generic graphics kernel and, therefore, invariant for the derived kernels.

The graphical scene consists of primitives[5] which may be ordered arbitrarily.

A primitive $P$ is created by parameterizing a geometry $G$ with a specific modelling $M$. While there is exactly one geometry, the modelling consists of elementary orthogonal modelling entities $M_1, M_2, ..., M_n$ called attributes. In an object-oriented system the class of a given primitive is derived from abstract or concrete classes representing the specific geometrical, modelling and rendering behaviour.

Both geometry and attributes may be set and got for a given primitive without regarding the (internal) usage of multiple references and the organization of the scene (e.g., hierarchies of primitives). For a given attribute type $M_i$ this could mean an accumulative processing of the $M_i$, beginning from a root primitive. For instance, the modelling transformation of a given primitive $P$ is created by recursive concatenating inherited and local modelling matrices.

At each time the consistency of the graphical scene has to be guaranteed. In a multiple referencing scene this means that the references have to be updated after changes (insertion/deletion of primitives or attributes into the scene). However, the internally-stored data (e.g., display lists) may be created at a later time.

Abstract modelling types have to provide sufficient hook functions (i.e., overloadable, initially empty methods) to implement retraversing or other inquiring functionality in the concrete derived primitive.

In the following section these specifications will be refined in an evolutionary fashion with respect to the needs of the GF kernel. GF is a semantic graphics kernel for furniture modelling and visualization and is derived from the Generic kernel. Deriving, of course, means the creation of specific subclasses. But, it includes the refinement of the generic modelling paradigm, too.

# 7 An example: A Furniture Graphics Kernel

### 7.1 Analysis

A furniture scene consists of a number of primitives that are identified by a specific type and are recursively hierarchically organized. Spatial and other modelling attributes have

---

[5]Light sources are beyond the scope of this paper.

to be inherited inside a hierarchy. For the spatial modelling this means that inherited modelling matrices have to be concatenated with local modelling matrices. The material will be inherited by all primitives which do not explicitly set a material. This is useful because furniture is mainly made of one material except for some specific parts which are made of glass or metal, for instance.

The hierarchical structuring is necessary to delegate (spatial) manipulations in the responsibility of the parent primitive. Furthermore, it is necessary to perform an intuitive modelling, i.e., translations or rotations in the same direction as the user moves the mouse or spaceball, of a primitive independent of its inherited or local modelling.

There is a need for dynamic parent-child relations, i.e., children of a primitive may be removed or additional primitives of given types may be added. The set of types of primitives that may be added to a primitive as children is specific to the type of this primitive.

Most pieces of furniture are created from a small number of solid primitives, made from a homogeneous material. These are frequently used for a given furniture or a set of pieces of furniture. The homogeneity of the material allows the external parameterizability of basic furniture primitives. There are no dependencies of basic furniture primitives of the spatial modelling. Once again, basic furniture primitives may be parameterized externally by assigning a modelling matrix.

The modelling is realized by

- a specific spatial modelling $M_{Spa}$ restricted to rotations only for toplevel primitives and translations for all primitives,

- a customized material attribute $M_{Mat}$ that handles symbolic names like *white paint*, *glass*, *black ash* instead of concrete reflection coefficients, and

- an attribute $M_{Res}$ that specifies the discretization of analytically defined primitives.

The multiple appearance of basic primitives and their external parameterizability imply the usage of multiple references. The next section will describe a concept how to combine multiple references with a hierarchical scene, as implied by the Generic kernel and needed by the furniture kernel.

## 7.2 Primitives and Renderables

The primitives act as wrapper [4] objects that delegate rendering requests to the wrapped objects, the so-called renderables. The primitives are visible from the API and are clearly located in the hierarchies. Renderables are invisible, may be multiply referenced and may be cached in a data base. A primitive is statically and covariantly associated to a renderable. This association indicates the partition of a traditional graphical primitive into two parts having different data, semantics and life time. Both parts communicate via specific methods invisible to the outside. Both primitives and renderables inherit the same rendering interfaces, while primitives additionally inherit modelling interfaces.

A renderable $R$ realizes a functional mapping of the primitive $P$'s geometry $G$ and attribute values $V_1, ..., V_k$ of the appropriate modelling types $M_1, ..., M_k$, which are a subset of the existing modelling types $M_1, ..., M_n$, to a data structure that is directly renderable by a ray-tracer, shader, etc. Values of further modelling types $M_{k+1}, ..., M_n$ or values specific to a given primitive $P$ may be applied to $R$ if they do not change the real contents of $R$. However, they may change references in $R$.

Now, the correlation between a primitive $P_{Sphere}$ and the appropriate renderable may be specified as follows (The square brackets indicate external parameterization.). $V_{Rad}$ is a scalar specifying the radius:

$$P_{Sphere}(V_{Spa}, V_{Res}, V_{Mat}, V_{Rad})$$
$$\rightarrow R_{Sphere}(V_{Res})[V_{Spa}, V_{Mat}, V_{Rad}]$$

Thus, a multiply referenced sphere depends just on a resolution value. All other values may be specified later via references. To find an appropriate renderable in the cache we must look for a sphere object with the given resolution. From these data (class identifier and resolution value) a hash value may be created.

An orthogonal block is a frequently used basic primitive in furniture applications and may be parameterized completely externally. $V_{Dim}$ is a vector specifying the dimensions.

$$P_{Block}(V_{Spa}, V_{Res}, V_{Mat}, V_{Dim})$$
$$\rightarrow R_{Block}()[V_{Spa}, V_{Mat}, V_{Dim}]$$

Obviously, we need only one renderable of type *GFBlockR*. This should be a class-invariant member of class *GFBlock* and, therefore, has not to be stored in the cache.

For other kinds of primitives (e.g., polygon, polyhedron, polygon set) the geometry is not invariant to all objects of the class. Therefore, for these primitives the geometry has to be considered to identify renderables that may be multiply referenced. This would imply a certain number of comparisons of vertices to check geometrical identity. However, in derived classes additional information may be used to avoid the comparisons. For instance, objects of class *GFOffPolygon* contain a large number of polygons, but may be identified by comparing the string $V_{Nam}$ that specifies the OFF data set. Generally, the elementary polygons are defined in a common coordinate system. Therefore, OFF polygons may be parameterized externally in a very efficient manner.

$$P_{OffPolygon}(V_{Spa}, V_{Res}, V_{Mat}, V_{Nam})$$
$$\rightarrow R_{OffPolygon}(V_{Nam})[V_{Spa}, V_{Mat}{}^6]$$

It is also possible to avoid the geometrical and attribute comparisons when using a copy construction. In this case, only the reference to the renderable will be copied and a reference counter has to be incremented.

The management of the cache is realized via protected, i.e., accessible in subclasses, methods of class *GFRenderable*. The class also defines abstract methods for supplying a hash index and a run-time type information, the latter of which is necessary to perform a safe type conversion when retrieving an object from the cache.

---

[6]A material may be specified externally. However, some OFF data sets contain colour specifications.

## 7.3 Attributes

Objects of derived attribute types represent attribute values and provide methods to access them. According to the object-oriented paradigm the access methods hide the real data values. Hence, certain semantics may be placed inside the attribute object and is not visible to the outside. Examples for this are

- retraversing to get a logically inherited value,

- regenerating a primitive's geometry corresponding to the new attribute value, and

- transferring the new value down to children of the primitive.

Concrete primitive types are derived from attribute types to inherit the access methods. Each primitive contains an initially empty list to which attributes of arbitrary types may be added at the primitive's life time.

The common base type of all attributes (*GAttribute*) implements the handling of a reference that may be used instead of a physically existent value. Derived attribute types define an overloadable specific method that will be called after changing the attribute value. This method may be implemented for a given type of a primitive. For the GF graphics kernel the above-mentioned three modelling types are relevant and provided as subtypes of *GAttribute*. The class *GFPrimitive*, which is the basic primitive of all GF primitives, inherits these types via multiple inheritance. Because this class also defines a hierarchical structuring of the graphical primitives, it implements the specific *changed* methods of the attribute types to perform a down-transfer of the new value to the children of the primitive and, therefore, realizes the attribute inheritance.

# 8 Conclusion

The paper described a rendering-independent general object-oriented modelling paradigm that is inherent to our Generic graphics kernel and how this paradigm can be refined to meet the specific needs of a customized graphics kernel. We are observing a trend in the direction of defining (and standardizing) generic libraries for specific problem domains (e.g., ANSI C++ standard template library STL [10]: sets, arrays, sequences and related iterators) and want to encourage the community to contribute to the project of developing a generic graphics kernel.

# References

[1] E. Beier. Object-Oriented Design of Graphical Attributes. In *4th EuroGraphics Workshop on Object-Oriented Graphics, Sintra, Portugal*, pages 41–50, 1994.

[2] E. Beier. Object-Oriented Modeling of Graphical Primitives. In *Advances in Object-Oriented Graphics IV*. Springer-Verlag, 1995. To appear in Spring 1995.

[3] C. Elliot, G. Schechter, R. Yeung, and S. Abi-Ezzi. TBAG: A High Level Framework for Interactive, Animated 3D Graphics Applications. In *SIGGRAPH'94 Proceedings*, 1994.

[4] E. Gamma. *Objektorientierte Software-Entwicklung am Beispiel von ET++: Klassenbibliothek, Werkzeuge, Design*. PhD thesis, University of Zurich, 1991.

12

[5] I. Herman et al. PREMO - An ISO Standard for a Presentation Environment for Multimedia Objects. In *Proceedings of the '94 ACM Multimedia Conference, San Francisco, CA.*, 1994.

[6] ISO. Information Processing Systems – Computer Graphics – Programmer's Hierarchical Interactive Graphics System (PHIGS). Technical Report ISO/IEC 9592:1989, International Organization of Standardization, 1989. Parts 1 – 3.

[7] ISO. Information Technology - Computer Graphics - Reference Model. Technical report, International Organization of Standardization, 1991. Draft International Standard ISO/IEC DIS 11072.

[8] J. Neider, T. Davis, and M. Woo. *OpenGL Programming Guide*. Addison Wesley, 1993.

[9] J. Nuetzel, E. Beier, and R. Boese. In *5th EuroGraphics Workshop on Visualization in Scientific Computing, Rostock, Germany*. EuroGraphics Seminars, 1994.

[10] A. Stepanov and M. Lee. The Standard Template Library. Technical report, Hewlett-Packard Laboratories, 1995.

[11] P. Wisskirchen. *Object-Oriented Graphics - From GKS and PHIGS to Object-Oriented Systems*. Springer-Verlag, 1990.

[12] Solaris XGL 3.0 Reference Manual. Technical report, Sun Microsystems, Inc., 1992.

# Utilizing Renderer Efficiencies in an Object-Oriented Graphics System

Parris K. Egbert

Computer Science Department
3328 TMCB
Brigham Young University
Provo, Utah 84602, USA
Email: egbert@cs.byu.edu

**Abstract** During the past several years it has become obvious that object-oriented programming techniques provide significant benefits to a wide range of applications. Computer graphics fits this paradigm well, since entities in a computer graphics system are naturally thought of as "objects". However, the object-oriented paradigm imposes restrictions on systems that often lead to efficiency degradation. This paper presents the mechanism employed by the GRAMS object-oriented graphics system for improving efficiency in the rendering phase of the system. This is done by establishing a communication interface between the main system and both the modelling and rendering subsystems. While this approach breaks the strict object-oriented paradigm, substantial efficiency gains are realized and desired object-oriented characteristics, such as system extensibility and object integrity, are maintained.

## 1 Introduction

Interest in the field of computer graphics was sparked in the early 1960's when Ivan Sutherland demonstrated his Sketchpad system [12]. During the 1970's and 1980's most of the work in computer graphics centred on generating higher quality images. Advances in rendering, such as ray-tracing [13] radiosity [7], and hybrid systems [10] have made photorealistic images possible.

In the past few years, we have experienced a shift of emphasis. Much attention has been diverted from just producing high quality images to making graphics more accessible to non-computer graphicists. In particular, a large amount of interest has been shown in combining computer graphics with the object-oriented programming paradigm. Many of the deficiencies inherent in today's graphics systems can be alleviated through the judicial use of this paradigm.

The object-oriented paradigm has a natural fit in computer graphics, since entities in computer graphics are intuitively thought of as "objects". A scene is comprised of multiple modelling objects, a camera object is often used for specifying various viewing parameters, etc. In addition, the object-oriented paradigm provides a mechanism for realizing diverse capabilities in a uniform fashion. This can help make complex operations easily usable by naive users. Through the data abstraction mechanism present in object-oriented languages, many of the underlying details of the graphics system can be hidden from the user, thereby allowing the user to access complex system capabilities without understanding their internal workings. Because of this natural fit, several object-oriented graphics systems have been designed recently. Examples of these systems can be found in [6, 11, 14, 15]

One problem that has been discovered is that adhering strictly to the object-oriented paradigm introduces inefficiencies into the system that can be substantial and are often unnecessary. These inefficiencies are not solely a function of the overhead imposed by the object-oriented programming language, but are introduced due to the fact that there are often inter-object constraints inherent in graphics. A more detailed discussion of these problems can be found in [4].

The work presented in this paper is one part of the Graphical Application Modelling Support System (GRAMS). GRAMS is an object-oriented graphics system designed for ease of use by non-programmers. Section 2 provides an overview of GRAMS as a basis for the research presented in this paper. Section 3 then provides the main topic of this paper, which is a detailed discussion of the mechanism employed by GRAMS for realizing renderer efficiencies. Finally, section 4 summarizes the ideas presented here and provides concluding remarks.

## 2 GRAMS

GRAMS is an object-oriented 3D graphics system designed with the goal of ease of use by end users and by application programmers. This section provides an overview of this system as a precursor to section 4. A detailed discussion of the overall system can be found in [2, 3]. The object-oriented structure and classing scheme used in GRAMS is found in [5].

GRAMS is built in a layered fashion, as depicted in Figure 1. There are three main layers in GRAMS. The Application Layer is the highest layer in the system and is the layer at which the application resides. At this layer, the application creates, manipulates and stores data pertinent to the application. A portion of the data will need to be used by the graphics system, and thus is stored in a form understood by the graphics system as well as the application.

The graphics layer is responsible for reading application data, interpreting that data in a semantically correct fashion, and passing appropriate information about that data to the renderer for image generation. The application owns the data, and thus the graphics layer does not alter any of the application data but has the ability of using pertinent data in the graphics process.

The rendering layer is responsible for image generation. Data is passed to it from the graphics layer in a form understood by the renderers.

When an application desires to graphically visualize its data, it does so by storing its data in an instance of class `ApplicationObject`, then telling the graphics system to begin the image generation process. At that point, the graphics system begins executing its code and the application's work is complete.

The graphics layer is separated into sub-layers corresponding to the abstraction level of the graphic objects. At the lowest level, the system supplies objects such as spheres, cylinders, polygons, etc. The highest level contains objects near the level of abstraction

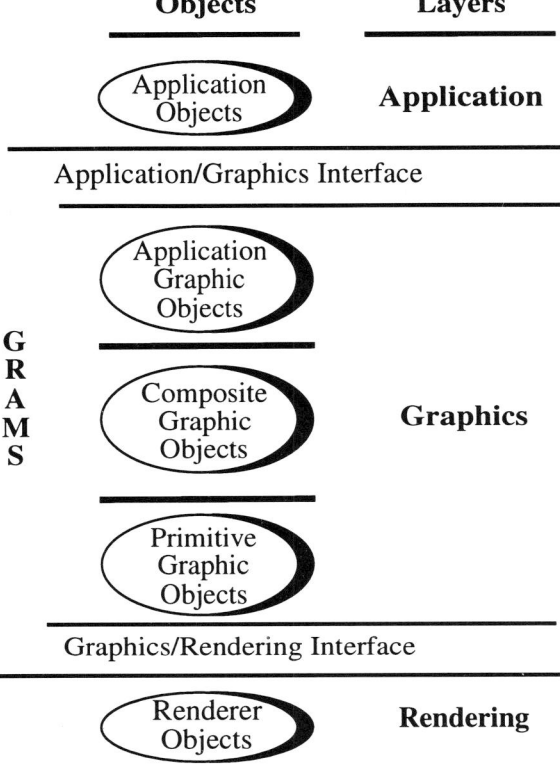

Fig. 1: GRAMS Layers and Interfaces

of the application, such as tables, chairs, trees, etc. The intermediate level bridges the gap between the other two. The graphics layer has been designed to be easily extensible so that new applications can easily add new Application Graphic Objects.

At image generation time, the graphics layer reads the application data. Since the data will probably be at a level of abstraction that is too high for the renderer to understand, the graphics system must transform the data into a form understood by the renderer. Once that is done, the data is sent to the renderer for image generation.

There is a well defined interface between the graphics and rendering layers. Requiring entities to adhere to that interface guarantees that new objects can be easily added to the system at either level. The rules governing the interface are:

1. All renderer objects must be able to accept all objects defined as "primitive graphic objects" (PGOs) by the system.

2. All graphic objects must be able to convert their data into one or more objects defined as PGOs.

Enforcing these two rules guarantees that new graphic objects can be added to the system without knowledge of the internals of the renderer objects, and similarly that new renderer objects can be added to the system without having to know all graphic objects in the system. While this approach addresses the desire for system extensibility, it has the main deficiency that it introduces inefficiencies into the system. In the first place, the graphics layer may have to spend a substantial amount of time in performing the transformation from application data into a data format understood by the renderer. Secondly, this approach by itself does not allow renderer objects to use efficiencies built into them. For example, many ray tracing renderers can handle spherical objects very efficiently. If the graphic object was a sphere, but a sphere object was not included as a PGO, the graphic layer would need to convert the sphere into some other form such as a polygon list, then send that polygon list to the renderer. Thus, time would be expended in performing the sphere-to-polygon list transformation, and in addition the renderer would spend much more time in rendering since a non-optimal object was sent to it. The method employed by GRAMS in solving this problem is the focus of this paper. The following section provides a detailed discussion of our solution.

# 3 Utilizing Renderer Efficiencies

In order to allow renderers to use efficiencies that are built into them there must be a mechanism for the renderer objects to inform the system of the capabilities they possess. In a pure object-oriented system, this is not allowed. Objects must maintain their own internal state and must not share that internal state with other objects. While this is the extreme case, and few (if any) systems adhere to this "pure" object-orientation, this must be enforced to guarantee complete object independence. However, adhering strictly to this notion creates burdens and limitations that are unreasonable. Thus, we adhere to the object-oriented paradigm when it is not unduly limiting (even at times when obvious inefficiencies are introduced), but deviate from the pure object-oriented approach under certain circumstances. Allowing objects to communicate pertinent information about their capabilities was deemed an acceptable exception.

## 3.1 The Graphic Object Conversion Table

The graphics layer is responsible for passing data to the rendering level in a form understood by the renderer objects. Thus, it must read information from the application layer, determine the most appropriate form to put that data into so that the renderer can understand it, then send the data to the renderer. It does this by maintaining a table internally that contains this information. The table is actually a combination of two tables. The first of these maintains information about graphic objects and is called the Graphic Object Conversion Table (GOCT). All graphic objects will be capable of transforming themselves into one of the PGO objects, as discussed in Section 2 above. In addition, there may be other graphic objects into which a particular graphic object can transform itself. The information about which types of graphic objects a particular graphic object can transform into is maintained in this table. This is shown pictorially in Figure 2.

Each graphic object in the system has one entry in the GOCT. Corresponding to

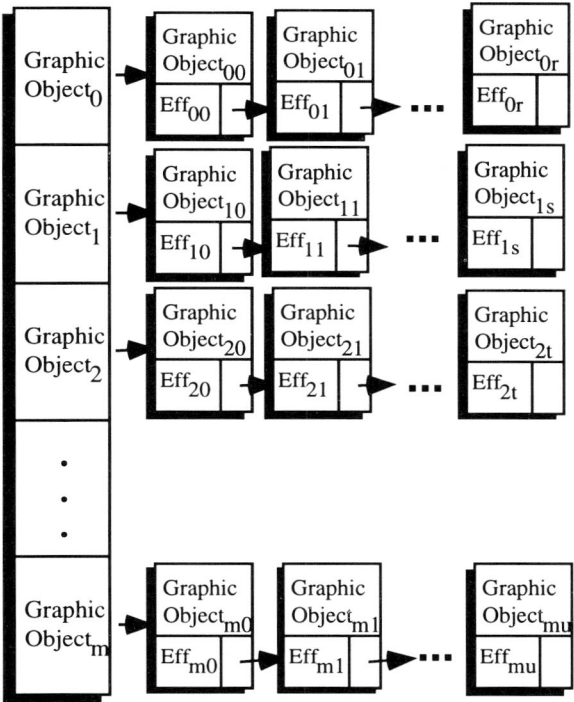

Fig. 2: The Graphic Object Conversion Table

each of those entries is a list of nodes. Each node contains three items: a graphic object, an efficiency rating, and a pointer to the next element in the list. The graphic object represents one graphic object class in the system into which the graphic object in the table can transform itself. Thus, if object A can transform itself into three different other types of graphic objects, there will be four entries in the list that is associated with object A - one for A itself and one for each of the three other object types.

The efficiency rating is an indication of how easily the object can transform into the object on the list, and is a floating point number in the range [0, 1]. Numbers near zero indicate that although the object can be transformed into, it is very time consuming and/or difficult to do so. Numbers near one indicate that it is very easy for the object to transform into the other object type.

Figure 3 gives an example of this. In this case, one graphic object type (sphere) is shown in the table. Corresponding to that object are the objects into which it can transform itself. The sphere can transform itself into polygons or into a sphere, so there are two entries in the list associated with the graphic object sphere. Transforming into a sphere requires no effort, so the efficiency rating for performing that operation is 1.0. Transforming into polygons requires more effort, but is not too difficult. Thus it is given an efficiency rating of 0.7.

Whenever a new graphic object is added to the system, it must send a message to

18

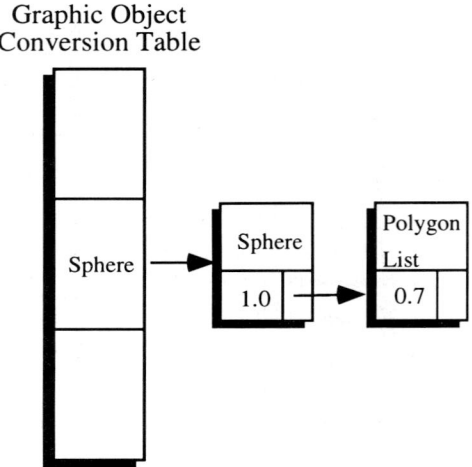

Graphic Object
Conversion Table

Fig. 3: A Sphere Graphic Object in the GOCT

the system stating the objects into which it can transform itself as well as the associated efficiencies corresponding to them. The system then inserts these values into the table for later use.

## 3.2 The Renderer Capability Table

The second table stored by the system is called the Renderer Capability Table (RCT). This table is structured much like the GOCT with the exception that entries in the table are renderer objects, as opposed to graphic objects. Figure 4 shows this table. There is one entry in the table for each renderer object in the system. Corresponding to each entry is a list of graphic objects. A list specifies all of the graphic objects that the associated renderer can understand.

There is also an efficiency rating attached to each graphic object. This efficiency measure indicates the ease with which the renderer can render the particular graphic object. This rating lies within the range [0, 1]. Values near 0.0 mean that although the renderer can render this particular type of graphic object, is does so with difficulty. Values near 1.0 indicate that the renderer can render the graphic object relatively efficiently.

Figure 5 gives a specific example of an entry in this table. One of the renderers in our system is a renderer based on the GL library from Silicon Graphics [9]. This renderer understands how to render spheres, polygons, lines, and points. Thus, each of these graphic object types has been included in the RCT entry corresponding to the GL renderer. Since spheres, lines, and points are rendered very efficiently in GL, they have been assigned an efficiency rating of 0.9. Polygons, while still efficient to render, require slightly more work than the other graphic object types, thus an efficiency rating of 0.8 has been associated with polygons.

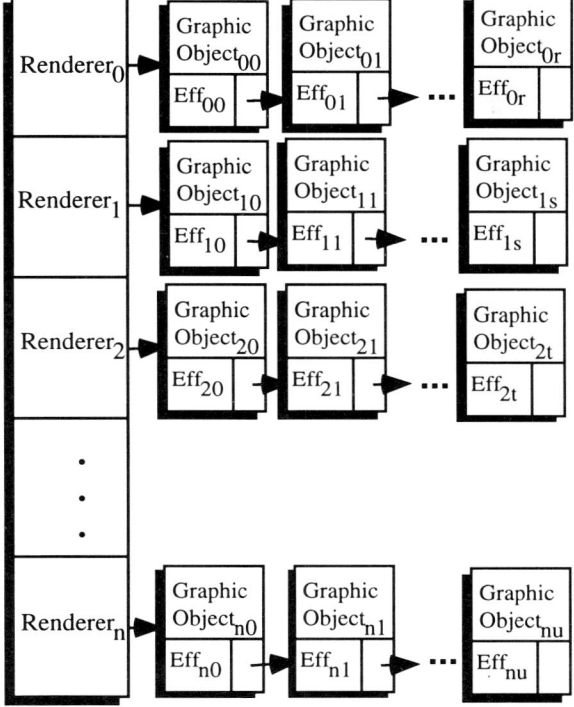

Fig. 4: The Renderer Capability Table

### 3.3 Using the Tables

When a graphic object is to be rendered, the graphics layer must determine the type of data to send to the renderer. This is done in the following manner. The system accesses the GOCT entry corresponding to the graphic object that is to be rendered. For each of the items in the list corresponding to that entry, the RCT is consulted. If the renderer that is to perform the rendering has in its list of understood graphic objects the object that is currently being considered from the GOCT, an overall efficiency rating is determined using the function

$$e = f(E_{GO}, E_R) = E_{GO} E_R (E_{GO} + 10 E_R) \qquad (1)$$

where e is the overall efficiency, f is the efficiency calculation function, $E_{GO}$ is the efficiency rating taken from the GOCT for the object type under consideration, and $E_R$ is the efficiency rating from the RCT for this graphic object type. Since it is assumed that the rendering time will be the dominant time spent in the image generation process, the function places a substantially greater weight factor on the renderer efficiency rating than it does on the graphic object efficiency rating.

Once the efficiency has been calculated for this object type, the next object in the GOCT is examined and the process is repeated. When all entries in the list have been

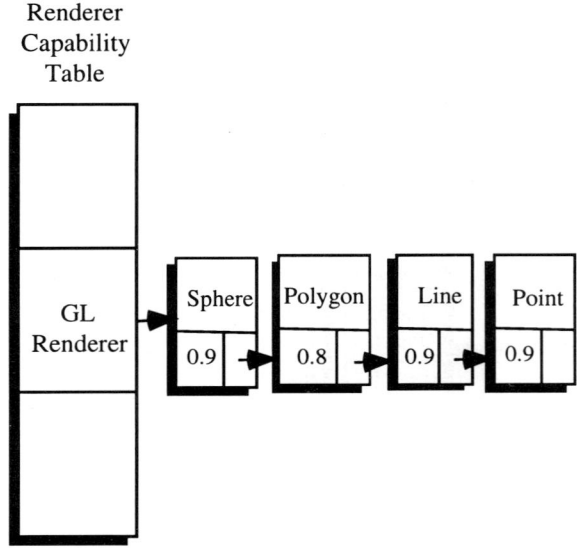

Fig. 5: The Renderer Capability Table Entry for the GL Renderer

exhausted, the calculated efficiencies are compared. The object type with the highest efficiency rating is the one that will be used. The graphics layer converts the graphic object into this new type and sends the new data to the renderer. This ensures that the renderer can understand the data being sent to it, and also that the data is in a form that is deemed most efficient.

### 3.4 Renderer Objects

GRAMS has been designed to allow for any style of rendering desired by the application. Renderers are objects in GRAMS and are used by the graphics system by sending appropriate messages to them. Different applications will desire different rendering techniques based on their desire for realism, the amount of time the application is willing to devote to rendering, cost considerations, and the specific needs of the application. The rendering layer of GRAMS has been designed to accommodate renderers at all levels of the rendering spectrum.

To date we have incorporated three different renderers into GRAMS. The first of these was UIPEX - the University of Illinois implementation of PEX [1]. PEX is a 3D graphics standard designed to support PHIGS PLUS in the X window system. This renderer is a z-buffer style renderer that provides various shading and lighting capabilities.

The second renderer we have used was the GL library from Silicon Graphics. This renderer has provided additional colour capabilities and has reduced rendering time substantially.

The most sophisticated renderer we have incorporated into the system is a hybrid ray trace/radiosity renderer implemented by Peter Shirley [8]. This renderer has allowed us to produce images that are much more realistic than those produced by the prior renderers. The application determines which renderer is appropriate for it to use at a given time. This determination is made by choosing the renderer that provides the appropriate quality/time characteristics. Generally, the higher the rendering quality, the more time is required for rendering. The application has the liberty of changing renderers at any time. Typically, a fast, low-quality renderer will be used to position objects in the scene correctly, then a photorealistic renderer will be used to produce the final image.

# 4 Conclusions

While the object-oriented paradigm has been successfully applied to the field of Computer Graphics, there are instances where this paradigm imposes unnecessary limitations. One of these is in the data sent to renderers. Adhering to the strict object-oriented paradigm requires that objects not know internal capabilities of other objects. In the case of renderers, this means that efficiencies built into the renderer objects cannot be realized. This paper has presented a method for allowing renderers to use their built-in efficiencies. While this approach breaks the strict object-oriented paradigm, the gains in efficiency more than make up for problems caused by not enforcing strict adherence to the paradigm. Substantial savings in execution time were observed after incorporating the technique described here - particularly in the high end renderers. For example, allowing the ray-tracing renderer to have spheres sent to it, rather than polygonizing those spheres prior to render time saved an order of magnitude in rendering time.

The most frequently used arguments for maintaining strict adherence to the object-oriented paradigm are extensibility issues. We have designed the technique described here such that even though it breaks the strict object-oriented paradigm, extensibility is still easily achievable.

# References

[1] Parris K. Egbert. Uipex: Design of the application programmer interface. Master's thesis, Department of Computer Science, University of Illinois at Urbana-Champaign, May 1990.

[2] Parris K. Egbert. *An Object-Oriented Approach to Graphical Application Support.* PhD thesis, Department of Computer Science, University of Illinois at Urbana-Champaign, June 1992.

[3] Parris K. Egbert. Design of the grams object-oriented graphics system. In *IEEE International Phoenix Conference on Computers and Communications*, pages 248–254, April 1994.

[4] Parris K. Egbert and Travis L. Hilton. Mixed paradigm graphics. In *Fourth Eurographics Workshop on Object-Oriented Graphics*, pages 85–100, May 1994.

[5] Parris K. Egbert and William J. Kubitz. Application graphics modeling support through object-orientation. In *IEEE Computer 25(10)*, pages 84–91, October 1992.

[6] Phillip Getto and David Breen. An object-oriented architecture for a computer animation system. *Visual Computer*, 6(2):79–92, March 1990.

[7] Cindy M. Goral, Kenneth E. Torrance, Donald P. Greenberg, and Bennett Battaile. Modelling the interaction of light between diffuse surfaces. In *Computer Graphics (SIGGRAPH '84 Conference Proceedings), 18(3)*, pages 212–222, July 1984.

[8] Peter Shirley. *Physically Based Lighting Calculations for Computer Graphics*. PhD thesis, Department of Computer Science, University of Illinois at Urbana-Champaign, November 1990.

[9] Silicon Graphics Inc. *Graphics Library Programming Guide*, 1st edition, 1992.

[10] F. Sillion and C. Puech. A general two-pass method integrating specular and diffuse reflection. In *Computer Graphics (SIGGRAPH '89 Conference Proceedings)*, pages 335–344, July 1989.

[11] Phillip Slusallek and Hans-Peter Seidel. Vision - an architecture for global illumination calculations. *IEEE Transactions on Visualization and Computer Graphics*, 1(1), March 1995.

[12] Ivan E. Sutherland. *Sketchpad, A Man-Machine Graphical Communication System*. PhD thesis, Department of Electrical Engineering, Massachusetts Institute of Technology, January 1963.

[13] Turner Whitted. An improved illumination model for shaded display. *Communications of the ACM*, 23(6):343–349, June 1980.

[14] Peter Wisskirchen. Towards object-oriented graphics standards. *Computers and Graphics*, 10(2):183–187, 1986.

[15] R.C. Zeleznik et al. An object-oriented framework for the integration of interactive animation techniques. In *SIGGRAPH '91 Proceedings, Computer Graphics Vol. 25, no. 4*, pages 105–112, 1991.

# Object-Oriented Design for Image Synthesis

Philipp Slusallek and Hans-Peter Seidel

Universität Erlangen
IMMD IX - Graphische Datenverarbeitung
Am Weichselgarten 9, D-91058 Erlangen, Germany
E-mail: slusalle@informatik.uni-erlangen.de

**Abstract** The structure of the image synthesis process naturally leads to the use of object-oriented software design and many existing rendering systems are based on some kind of object-oriented approach. However, some areas in image synthesis, such as global illumination, were considered to violate some fundamental principles of object-orientation. In this paper, we suggest a design approach which overcomes this apparent inconsistencies and allows for a uniform use of object-oriented techniques in image synthesis. The second part of the paper discusses attributes in hierarchical scene descriptions using a new object-oriented approach.

## 1 Introduction

Object-oriented techniques have been successfully used in many disciplines of computer graphics, especially in the design and the implementation of rendering systems [13, 25, 21, 8, 17]. However, there have been several areas, in which the application of object-oriented techniques has been unsatisfactory. The problems encountered were mostly related to the problem of expressing relationships between objects.

There are several occurrences of this problem in image synthesis. The most apparent is the calculation of global illumination in a scene. All global illumination algorithms use some kind of global control, which requires access to the participating objects describing the emission and reflection of light at surfaces and volume objects. This problem is closely related to the problem of computing a global solution to constraints in a system, which also requires global access to objects [7, 22].

In Section 3 we propose a solution to this problem, by making the description of reflection and emission passive entities and by introducing a special subsystem that is responsible for the calculation of a global solution. Together with suitably general interfaces to the local descriptions, this approach is not in conflict with object-oriented restrictions. In this paper we concentrate on the object-oriented aspects of this approach [19].

Another problem is the association of attributes with objects. A general rendering architecture requires that arbitrary attributes can be associated with objects. However, it is not immediately clear how such attributes can be managed by objects they apply to.

In this paper, we describe a new and radical approach, where we completely separate all non-geometric attributes from the geometric primitives. Instead of applying attributes to the objects in the scene, we apply the attributes to the operations on primitives and to their results. With this approach attributes are handled uniformly and orthogonal concepts are separated.

The above techniques for object-oriented software design have been used to implement the Vision architecture. This rendering architecture uses the underlying physical description of light propagation to derive an object-oriented decomposition of the rendering process. The Vision architecture has successfully integrated almost all state-of-the-art rendering techniques into a uniform and consistent image synthesis system [19].

# 2 A Physically-Based Rendering Architecture

In this section we give a brief overview of the design of the Vision rendering architecture [18] and its object-oriented decomposition into subsystems. This forms the basis for our later discussions.

A basic idea behind object-oriented design is the modelling of a software system based on real world objects [3]. For image synthesis these real world objects describe the geometric objects in a scene and their optical attributes, such as emission and reflection of light.

A responsibility-driven analysis and design [24] of image synthesis based on the physical process of light propagation in a scene suggests a decomposition into the following set of high-level subsystems. For each of the major subsystems we briefly describe its set of responsibilities. The details of the derivation of this object-oriented decomposition and the interfaces offered by these subsystems can be found in [18]. For the following discussion we use the term "subsystem" [23] instead of the more common term "class" in order to better express that many of these subsystems will be implemented by a set of related classes.

**GeoObject, Surface, and Volume:** The Surface and Volume subsystems describe the geometric objects in our scene based on an abstract base class GeoObject. In contrast to the use of geometric objects in other rendering systems, these subsystems are purely geometric descriptions of the shape of geometric objects and do not contain any optical or other attributes.

**LightSourceShader:** The LightSourceShader subsystem describes the effects of light emitted from a surface or a volume. This description of emission is also completely separated from the geometric description of a surface or a volume. The interface of the LightSourceShader subsystem offers methods to compute the emitted light for a point on a surface or in a volume. Given a common description for these points, the LightSourceShader subsystem does not need to know which kind of geometry it is attached to.

**Shader:** The Shader subsystem describes the interaction of light with a point on a surface. Its main responsibility is to compute the amount of light reflected into a given outgoing direction based on a suitable description of the incoming illumination. In addition it offers access to several other aspects of the interaction of light with a surface.

For Monte-Carlo like global illumination algorithms [11, 16, 1, 14] the Shader subsystem offers the possibility to obtain the importance information for illumination. Thus, the Shader can provide information about how important illumination from different directions is for its computation of the reflected light. This interface is essential in order to implement efficient importance sampling techniques [12].

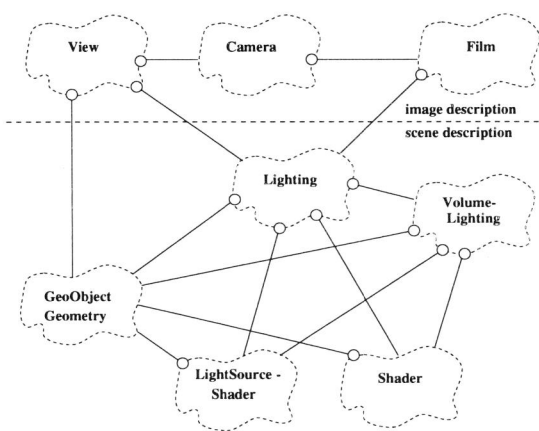

Fig. 1: A class diagram [3] of the subsystems of the major Vision rendering architecture and their "uses"-relation. In addition to the scene description subsystems discussed in this paper, the View, Camera, and Film subsystems use this description for the actual generation of images.

For finite-element style algorithms, such as radiosity [4, 9], the Shader subsystems offers access to the mean reflectance and transmittance of a surface over a given surface element. In order to allow for higher order basis functions on elements it also offers a sampling interface, that provides enough information for a suitable and adaptive sampling of the Shader.

Given the common representation of points on surfaces, this description of the Shader is again independent of the actual representation of the underlying geometric objects.

**VolumeLighting:** The interaction of light with a volume is quite different from the interaction of light with a surface. The subsystem VolumeLighting describes the general interaction of light with a volume. Because volume objects are much more complicated than surfaces this subsystem is further decomposed in several other subsystems. However, we do not further discuss volume objects in this paper.

**Lighting:** The Lighting subsystem is responsible for the global aspect of light propagation in a scene. This is probably the most non-intuitive subsystem in our decomposition and has no counterpart in most other rendering systems. However, it conveniently separates the global aspects of light propagation from the local descriptions provided by the previous subsystems.

Its responsibility is the computation of the global illumination incident at any point in the scene. It uses the other subsystems to find the local description on which the computation of the global illumination is based. The reasons for the introduction of this subsystems are discussed in Section 3.

Figure 1 summarizes the basic subsystems and their relationships in the Vision architecture. The above decomposition of the rendering process into subsystems is basically similar to decompositions in other systems, but has some important differences. For the discussion in this paper we concentrate on two of them, which we describe in the following sections:

First of all, we use purely passive subsystems for the scene description and the optical attributes. This means that, none of these objects actively tries to compute some illuminations values. The computation of the illumination in a scene is the responsibility of the Lighting object.

Secondly, we have strictly separated the description of geometric shapes from the description of their attributes, such as their transformation or their optical properties. This separation is discussed in detail in Section 4.

# 3 Lighting

The problem of global illumination, which is at the heart of a physically-based rendering architecture, is the requirement for global knowledge about participating objects and details about their interaction with light. Using object-oriented design, it is difficult to map the global aspect of illumination to a set of independent and self-contained objects. To compute a solution, global knowledge must be maintained by at least one object in the architecture.

Explicit global knowledge can be avoided when using local propagation methods, in which only direct communication between the entities is allowed. Methods like progressive radiosity [4] seem to use local propagation, because they only propagate radiosity from one patch to another. However, the computation of the exchange coefficients or form-factors involves all other patches in the environment for visibility computation. Furthermore, these algorithms use global control, e.g. for selecting the brightest patch as the next sender of radiosity.

The problem of global solutions is similar to the well-known problem of using constraints in object-oriented systems [7, 22]. There, each constraint is a purely local description of some interaction between two objects, but a solution meeting all constraints over all objects can be computed best if global information about all constraints is available. This global aspect of the problem is often described at a higher level of abstraction, that acts to coordinate the local descriptions of single constraints.

We approach the global aspects of rendering from a similar perspective. The process of global illumination is split into purely local descriptions of emission, reflection, and so on. At a higher level, the Lighting subsystem combines the local descriptions to allow for the computation of the global solution.

## 3.1 Local Descriptions and Global Solutions

At first sight, the introduction of an object with global knowledge might seem like a violation of the object-oriented principle of encapsulation, but it really is not. The crucial point is the definition of the interfaces to the local description of reflection and emission in a scene. If we can find general interfaces to get access to these optical properties that are necessary for implementing global illumination algorithms, we do not break encapsulation. The classes used for the local description are free to use any internal representation or algorithm as long as they implement the general interface.

Another important point we want to make is that this general interface should be based on the underlying physics. This approach ensures that all representations of the local descriptions can support this interface, because they are all approximations to the same underlying physics. Based on the physical description and the requirements of the two basic global illumination techniques, Monte-Carlo and finite elements, we have developed a very general and flexible set of interface methods for these local descriptions [19, 18].

As a result of this design, and in contrast to other statements [5], we believe that it is not necessary to break the object-oriented approach due to the nature of the image synthesis process.

### 3.2 Active Versus Passive Objects

Another aspect of our architecture is that the Lighting object is the only active object in the computation of illumination. This has the advantage that we can easily change the algorithms for computing illumination without any changes to the rest of our architecture. Again the introduction of general interfaces allows for this kind of flexibility. For example, Shader objects request illumination information from the Lighting subsystem using a very general interface. Depending on the implementation of the Lighting object, different algorithms can be used to fulfil this request.

In contrast, many other rendering architectures use active objects in their scene description, especially for shaders, e.g. [21, 8]. In ray tracing based architectures the shaders actively send out rays to sample incident illumination, while in finite element systems they actively distribute light energy to related patches.

Both of these approaches are in essence a kind of functional or algorithmic design because they embed a functional description of *how* to compute some value into the software architecture. In contrast, our interface to obtain illumination for a Shader object request this information from the Lighting object in general terms. This request also indicates how important illumination from different directions is to a Shader [19, 18].

Based on this description of *what* information is important to a Shader, a particular implementation of the Lighting object can then decide *how* this illumination is computed. Using this design approach eliminates many of the problems that appeared in other systems, e.g. the question, whether the LightSource or the Shader class is responsible for computing illumination [8, 6, 10, 5]

# 4 Separation of Geometry and Attributes

Attributes in our context are objects that describe certain properties of the scene, but which are not bound to a particular geometric primitive (e.g. like the radius of the sphere). An important aspect that differentiates the Vision architecture for other rendering systems is the complete separation of geometric primitives and their attributes.

Attributes neither have any information about the geometric primitives they apply to, nor have geometric primitives information about the attributes which apply to them.

In Vision an attribute is described by its name, its type, and a value, in contrast to traditional systems, which usually do not differentiate between the name and the type of an attribute. The association between attributes and primitives is performed through the scene graph described in more detail in Section 4.3. The scene graph is a *directed acyclic graph* (DAG), where the primitives are the leaves and interior nodes are container objects, which manage their subgraph and associate attributes with it.

The separation of primitives and their attributes is the consequent application of object-oriented design to image synthesis. In the real world, the shape of an object, its position, and its optical attributes are completely independent aspects. The same shape can be made of different materials and can be placed in different locations, without any need for the shape to "know" about its configuration. This fact suggests a separation of these concepts also in the corresponding software model.

In the following sections we discuss some of the implications and a few implementation aspects of this design approach.

## 4.1 Geometric Transformations

In the Vision architecture all geometric primitives are defined in respect to their own local (modelling) coordinate system and all interface requests are assumed to be relative to this system. The arrangement of primitives in a scene and the handling of transformations is not specified by the geometry subsystem, but is described at a higher level in the SceneGraph subsystem (see Section 4.3).

Especially, objects do not know where they are located in world space. This is necessary in order to allow for objects that are multiply instantiated in a scene. It also allows for applying other than the normal matrix transformations to an object, such as non-linear or free-form deformations. Because all requests are transformed into the coordinate space of the object before being sent to the object, there is no need for having the object to deal with the special problems of these transformations.

It is interesting to note that many other rendering systems use a similar technique implicitly: Geometric primitives, e.g. a torus, can best be described in a canonical coordinate system. Thus, any operation on the object is transformed into this canonical coordinate system and the results are transformed back. For example, for ray intersection calculations the ray is transformed into torus space, the intersections are calculated, and the intersection points are finally transformed back.

Instead of placing this transformation within each object, it can be incorporated into the scene graph by associating a transformation attribute to a subgraph of the scene. The individual objects need not be aware of these transformations and can perform all its operations in its intrinsic coordinate system. This requires that the architecture is able to transform any operation parameter and the result into the objects coordinate system and back. This makes the scene management a bit more complicated, but also more consistent and uniform. The responsibility for handling the transformation is moved from each object to the central scene management. Thus, it simplifies the implementation of geometric primitives and allows for optimizing the code at a single location.

Similar to the approach suggested in [13] we use Container objects, which are also derived from the GeoObject class, to build a hierarchical scene description. A Container object may contain other geometric objects and forwards requests through its interface to them. In that sense a Container object represents a compound geometric object. In particular, clients of a geometric object cannot distinguish between a Container object and a simple primitive through the usual interface methods.

## 4.2 Optical Attributes

Similar to the separation of transformation attributes from the primitives, we also separate optical and other rendering attributes from the primitives. For optical attributes this separation is also motivated by the mathematical structure of the operator describing the interaction of light with surfaces, which can be split into a purely geometric and a purely optical operator [18, 15].

In the Vision architecture LightSourceShader and Shader objects are simply attributes that are associated with geometric primitives through the scene graph subsystem. Due to the very general interfaces of these subsystems the same attribute object can apply to any of the surface primitives. This is possible by having a common class SurfaceInfo, which describes the geometric properties at a single point on a surface. These properties include the location, parametric coordinates, tangents, and normal vectors.

## 4.3 Scene Graph

The SceneGraph subsystem maintains this association of rendering attributes with the geometric primitives of the scene. Two separate issues arise when rendering attributes are independent of the geometric description: How are the attributes associated with the primitive they apply to and when is this association resolved?

There are two general approaches to associate attributes with the primitives in the scene.

**Direct Association**  With direct association, a particular attribute is associated with a subgraph of the scene by directly storing references with each primitive in the subgraph, i.e. each object carries a list of all its attributes. This approach is used in many rendering systems, e.g. [21, 2].

In this approach the renderer looses much of the coherence information of a hierarchical scene description. Thus, we end up rendering 1000 transformed triangles instead of a single transformed chair made of many triangles. This coherence information can be very important for optimized rendering of animations.

**Hierarchical Association**  Using a hierarchy allows for a much more flexible association of attributes with primitives. In a hierarchical scene description attributes can be associated with a subset of the primitives by assigning them to an internal node of the graph (a part). The attribute then applies to all primitive in the subgraph of this node, unless overridden by another attribute further down the graph.

In Vision an algorithm working on a particular object in the scene requests an attribute from the DAG by supplying its name and type. Because the scene object corresponds to a unique path through the DAG the particular attribute applying to the object can easily be located.

The SGI Inventor toolkit [20] applies attributes to all objects that follow in a depth first traversal of the DAG, unless this behaviour is explicitly isolated by special "Separator" nodes in the graph. As a result, the association of attributes with an object also depends on the order of the objects in the graph. This is not the case in Vision which simplifies many operations.

### 4.3.1 Using AttributeSlots for Remapping Attributes

For multiple instantiations of scene objects we still face the problem of assigning attributes to selected parts of a multiply instantiated subgraph. For example, we may want to place multiple copies of the same chair in a scene where only the cover of each chair should have a different "Shader" attribute. Because attributes are overridden by the same attribute further down in a subgraph this kind of change is not possible with the approach described above.

In our approach we view each subgraph of the scene description as an encapsulated object with an implicit set of methods to supply attributes to it. By associating an attribute to the root of this subgraph (or above in the DAG) we essentially call the objects method to set this attribute. In the traditional hierarchical attribute scheme the subgraph can either use the supplied attribute or it can override the assignment. However, this scheme cannot differentiate between the same type of attribute at different primitives in a subgraph, e.g. colouring one primitive red and another blue. In a sense, the object only offers a single method for setting attributes of this type.

This problem can be solved by using AttributeSlots in addition to standard attributes. An AttributeSlot basically contains a default attribute value and a new attribute name. If a matching AttributeSlots is found during the bottom-up search for an attribute value, the new name is used further up in the graph. An empty new name in an AttributeSlot terminates the search for new values. The use of AttributeSlot objects is somewhat similar to the concept of dynamic binding with method renaming as present in the object-oriented language Eiffel.

Let us again consider the chair example from above: We model the chair with an AttributeSlot containing a new name "Covering" assigned to the "Shader" attribute of the geometry for the covering. The object now implicitly offers two methods to change attributes of geometry, "Covering" and "Shader", both taking a Shader object as a value. Now, the shader attribute of the covering geometry can be changed from outside the subgraph by placing a corresponding attribute with the name "Covering" at a higher level in the DAG. This renaming of attributes can also be applied recursively.

This scheme can be kept efficient, because the delayed binding of an attribute is only necessary for attributes values where AttributeSlot objects have been used. No overhead is introduced for standard attributes.

We should also note that this scheme cannot be modelled with other object-oriented attribute schemes as presented in [25, 2]. However, this scheme does not solve the problem of changing member variables of multiply instantiated objects. However, in our scheme such a change would violate the encapsulation of the subgraph objects, because a non-public member variable of the part is being changed.

### 4.3.2 Application of Attributes

In the Vision rendering architecture, attributes are kept in the DAG during rendering and they apply to operations on objects and not to the object itself. An example is the Shader attribute from the scene graph, which is used by all Intersection objects that are generated as the result of ray intersection operations on objects.

An alternative that requires less computations during rendering is to apply attributes to the primitives before rendering. However, this approach can introduces problems. An example for the kind of problem is a rotation of the texture space for a sphere subdivided into quadrilaterals along latitude and longitude. Applying the texture transformation to the texture coordinates at the vertices of the quadrilaterals would result in severe mapping artefacts near the poles of the sphere due to bilinear interpolation across the quadrilateral. In many cases, this kind of problems requires storing the attribute within the primitive and applying it to the invoked operations during rendering, anyway.

Our approach of explicitly applying attributes to operations and their results during rendering by the DAG has the advantage of offering the ability to optimize this code at one place in the DAG instead of within each primitive. Moreover, greater effort can probably be justified for a central optimization. At a first sight, applying the attributes during rendering might seem very expensive, but it can be made efficient. In the next section, we discuss ways to efficiently implement this strategy in the Vision architecture.

### 4.4 Scene Graph Traversal

An important consideration for our design is the efficient traversal of the scene graph. The scene graph in the Vision architecture is the central data base to which all other algorithms have access. We have chosen to loosely associate attributes with parts, which requires additional work during traversal, because the set of attributes that apply to a primitive must be identified. The traversal of the scene graph is a very frequent operation during rendering (e.g. for ray tracing) and it must be made as efficient as possible.

However, the situation is not as bad as it first seems, because attributes are not normally required during the traversal of the scene graph. They must only be available once a particular place in the graph has been found, e.g. an object that intersects a given ray. Thus, attributes can mostly be ignored during normal traversal operations.

To speed up the traversal process several optimizations have been made. First of all, a separate class TraversalContext has been introduced which stores whatever information is required to efficiently access data that is accumulated during traversal, i.e. transformations and other attributes. Because most information in the scene graph need not be processes immediately during the traversal, it is sufficient to only maintain the necessary information in order to derive the required data when it is needed. One example is the intersection traversal operation which is a frequent operation for many rendering algorithms (e.g. for visibility testing, etc.).

The TraversalContext object maintains the stack of transformations which is pushed and popped as the scene graph is traversed. For the intersection traversal the accumulated

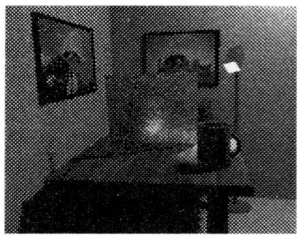

Fig. 2: Three sample images generated with the Vision rendering architecture. The images show a glossy-reflection in the metal plate calculated with path-tracing (left), sharp shadows using multiwavelet radiosity with shadow masks (centre), and volume integrated rendering (right).

transformation is not immediately computed, because matrix multiplications are very expensive, if they are performed for each step through the graph. All that is required for the calculation of intersections is the ray, which must be transformed into the proper coordinate systems. Thus, we only compute the transformed ray instead of the complete matrix multiplication. The full accumulated transformation is only computed when e.g. an intersection is found.

## 5 Conclusion

In this paper we have discussed several object-oriented design strategies for implementing a physically-based image synthesis architecture. We discussed a solution to the problem of computing the global illumination in a scene. In contrast to other papers, e.g. [5], we demonstrated that no violation of object-oriented principles occurs using after introducing a new Lighting class and suitably general interfaces between subsystems.

We also discussed the use of attributes in an object-oriented rendering system. For the idea of object-oriented design we motivated the strict separation of geometric primitives from transformation, optical or other attributes. We also described how this separation can be implemented uniformly for a rendering architecture and discussed implementation issues.

The presented object-oriented design approaches has been successfully used for the design and the implementation of the Vision rendering architecture [19, 18]. This physically-based rendering system implements state-of-the-art rendering techniques (local and ray traced illumination, path tracing, bidirectional estimators, backward ray tracing, irradiance caching, progressive, hierarchical, and wavelet radiosity, wavelet radiance, etc.) in a common framework and allows for switching between different implementations of a particular subsystem without changes to the rest of the architecture. Example images are shown in Figure 2 and in colour in Figure 3 (see Appendix).

# References

[1] James Arvo and David Kirk. Particle transport and image synthesis. *Computer Graphics (SIGGRAPH '90 Proceedings)*, 24(4):63–66, August 1990.

[2] Ekkehard Beier. Object-oriented design of graphical attributes. In *Fourth Eurographics Workshop on Object-Oriented Graphics*, pages 41–50. Sintra, May 1994.

[3] Grady Booch. *Object-Oriented Analysis and Design with Applications*. Benjamin/Cummings Publishing, 2. edition, 1994.

[4] Michael Cohen, Shenchang E. Chen, John R. Wallace, and Donald P. Greenberg. A progressive refinement approach to fast radiosity image generation. *Computer Graphics (SIGGRAPH '88 Proceedings)*, 22(4):75–84, August 1988.

[5] Parris K. Egbert and Travis L. Hilton. Mixed paradigm graphics. In *Fourth EUROGRAPHICS Workshop on Object-Oriented Graphics*, Sintra, May 1994.

[6] Dieter W. Fellner. Extensible image synthesis. In *Fourth EUROGRAPHICS Workshop on Object-Oriented Graphics*, Sintra, May 1994.

[7] B. N. Freeman-Benson and A. Boring. Integrating constraints with object-oriented programming. In O. L. Madsen, editor, *Proceedings ECOOP'92 – European Conference on Object-Oriented Programming*, pages 268–286, Utrecht, 1992.

[8] Andrew Glassner. Spectrum: An architecture for image synthesis, research, education, and practice. In Paul S. Strauss, editor, *Developing Large-scale Graphics Software Toolkits*, (SIGGRAPH '93 Course Notes 3), pages 1.1–1.44. SIGGRAPH, August 1993.

[9] Steven J. Gortler, Peter Schröder, Michael Cohen, and Pat M. Hanrahan. Wavelet radiosity. *Computer Graphics (SIGGRAPH '93 Proceedings)*, 27:221–230, August 1993.

[10] Alwin Gröne. RayVis – a visualization system based on object-orientation. In *Fourth EUROGRAPHICS Workshop on Object-Oriented Graphics*, Sintra, May 1994.

[11] James T. Kajiya. The rendering equation. *Computer Graphics (SIGGRAPH '86 Proceedings)*, 20(4):143–150, August 1986.

[12] Malvin H. Kalos and Paula A. Whitlock. *Monte Carlo Methods*. John Wiley & Sons, 1986.

[13] David Kirk and James Arvo. The ray tracing kernel. In *Proceedings of Ausgraph*, pages 75–82, July 1988.

[14] S. N. Pattanaik. *Computational Methods for Global Illumination and Visualization of Complex 3D Environments*. PhD thesis, Birla Institute of Technology & Science, Pilani, India, February 1993.

[15] Peter Schröder. *Wavelet Algorithms for Illumination Computations*. PhD thesis, Princeton University, November 1994.

[16] Peter Shirley. *Physically Based Lighting Calculations for Computer Graphics*. PhD thesis, Dept. of Computer Science, U. of Illinois, Urbana-Champaign, November 1990.

[17] Peter Shirley and Kelvin Sung. A ray tracing framework for global illumination systems. In *Proceedings Graphics Interface '91*, pages 117–128, Calgary, June 1991.

[18] Philipp Slusallek. *Vision – An Architecture for Physically Based Rendering*. PhD thesis, University of Erlangen, IMMD IX, Computer Graphics Group, April 1995.

[19] Philipp Slusallek and Hans-Peter Seidel. Vision: An architecture for global illumination calculations. *IEEE Transactions on Visualization and Computer Graphics*, 1(1):77–96, March 1995.

[20] Paul S. Strauss and Rikk Carey. An object-oriented 3D graphics toolkit. *Computer Graphics (SIGGRAPH '92 Proceedings)*, 26(2):341–349, July 1992.

[21] Ben Trumbore, Wayne Lytle, and Donald P. Greenberg. A testbed for image synthesis. In Paul S. Strauss and Ben Trumbore, editors, *Developing Large-Scale Graphics Software Toolkits (SIGGRAPH '93 Course Notes 3)*, pages 4.7–4.17, Anaheim, August 1993.

[22] Remco C. Veltkamp and Edwin Blake. Event-based.constraints: Coordinate.satisfaction →

object.solution. In *Fourth EUROGRAPHICS Workshop on Object-Oriented Graphics (Part. Edition)*, pages 251–261, Sintra, Portugal, May 1994.

[23] Rebecca Wirfs-Brock and Ralf Johnson. Surveying current research in object-oriented design. *Communications of the ACM*, 33(9):104–123, September 1990.

[24] Rebecca Wirfs-Brock and Brian Wilkerson. Object-oriented design: A responsibility-driven approach. In *OOPSLA 89 Conference Proceedings*, pages 71–75, New Orleans, 1989.

[25] P. Wisskirchen. GEO++ – a system for both modelling and display. In *EUROGRAPHICS '89 Proceedings*. Hamburg, September 1989.

**Editors' Note: see Appendix, p. 169 for coloured figure of this paper**

# Part II: Constraints

# Supporting Interactive Animation Using Multi-way Constraints

Jean-Francis Balaguer and Enrico Gobbetti

CRS4
Center for Advanced Studies, Research and Development in Sardinia
Scientific Visualization Group
Via Sauro 10
09123 Cagliari, Italy
E-mail: balaguer@crs4.it, gobbetti@crs4.it

**Abstract** The animation subsystem of an interactive environment for the visual construction of 3D animations has been modelled on top of an object-oriented constraint imperative architecture. There is no intrinsic difference between user-interface and application objects. Multi-way dataflow constraints provide the necessary tight coupling among components. This makes it possible to compose animated and interactive behaviours seamlessly. Indirect paths allow an effective use of the constraint model in the context of dynamic applications. Most of the behaviours of the modelling and animation components in a declarative way.

The integration of all the system's components allows novel interactive solutions to modelling and animation problems. This performance-based approach complements standard key-framing systems by providing the ability to create animations with straight-ahead actions.

The system demonstrates that, although they are limited to expressing acyclic conflict-free graphs, multi-way dataflow constraints are general enough to model a large variety of behaviours while remaining efficient enough to ensure the responsiveness of large interactive 3D graphics applications.

## 1 Introduction

Modern 3D graphics systems allow a rapidly growing user community to create and animate increasingly sophisticated worlds. Despite their inherent three-dimensionality, these systems are still largely controlled by 2D WIMP (Window, Icon, Menu, Pointing device) user-interfaces. The inadequacy of user-interfaces based on 2D input devices and mindsets becomes particularly evident in the realm of interactive 3D animation. In this case, the low-bandwidth communication between user-interface and application and the restrictions in interactive 3D motion specification capabilities make it very difficult to define animations with straight-ahead actions. This inability to interactively specify the animation timing is a major obstacle in all cases where the spontaneity of the animated object's behaviour is important [1][9].

To explore the enormous potential of 3D interactive techniques for providing solutions to modelling and animation problems, we have developed *Virtual Studio*, an integrated 3D animation environment where all interaction is done in three dimensions and where multi-track animations are defined by recording users' manipulations on

3D models. This way, we bring the expressiveness of real-time motion capture systems into a general-purpose multi-track system running on a graphics workstation. 3D devices allow the specification of complex 3D motion, while virtual tools are visible mediators that provide interaction metaphors to control application objects. Effective editing of recorded manipulations is made possible by compacting a continuous parameter evolution with an incremental data-reduction algorithm, able to compute spline representations that preserve both geometry and timing.

In this paper, we concentrate on how we modelled the animation subsystem of *Virtual Studio*. First, we present the object model and describe the class hierarchy of the animation subsystem. Then we show how the animation behaviour is obtained using hierarchical data-flow constraints. Other aspects of *Virtual Studio* are presented elsewhere: [13][14] presents the underlying graphics architecture (named *VB2*), [1][2][15] provides a general overview of the animation system, and [1][3] detail the data reduction algorithm.

# 2 Object Model

## 2.1 Primitive Elements

In *Virtual Studio*, there is no intrinsic difference between user interface and application objects. The tight integration between all the components of an animated environment (i.e. interaction, application, and animation objects) is obtained by the means of a constraint-imperative object-oriented (OOCIP) architecture [11]. In our architecture, the state of the system, the long-lived relations between state components, and the sequencing relations between states are represented by different primitive elements: *active variables*, *hierarchical constraints*, and *daemons*.

**Active variables and information modules.** An *active variable* maintains its value and keeps track of state changes by recording its value every time it is modified. The history of the values of each variable is limited by the user (by default, each active variable maintains only one value). All *VB2* objects are instances of classes in which dynamically changing information is defined with active variables related through hierarchical constraints. Grouping active variables and constraints in classes permits the definition of *information modules* that provide levels of abstraction that can be composed to build more sophisticated behaviour.

**Hierarchical constraints.** The bi-directional information exchange between components required to integrate animated and interactive behaviours [6][12][14][15] is obtained with *hierarchical multi-way constraints* [5] maintaining long-lived relations between active variables. To support local propagation, constraint objects are composed of a declarative part defining the type of relation that has to be maintained and the set of constrained variables, as well as of an imperative part, the list of possible methods that could be selected by the constraint solver to maintain the constraint.

A *priority level* is associated with each constraint to define the order in which constraints need to be satisfied in case of conflicts [5]. This way, both required and preferred constraints can be defined for the same active variable. Constraint methods can be general side-effect free procedures that ensure the satisfaction of the constraint, after their execution, by computing some of the constrained variables as a function of the others. Constraints are maintained using an efficient local propagation algorithm based on *Skyblue* [13][14][19], a domain-independent solver able to maintain a hierarchy of multi-way, multi-output dataflow constraints.

The main drawback of such a local propagation algorithm is the limitation to acyclic constraint graphs. However, as noted by Sannella et al. [21], cyclic constraint networks are seldom encountered in the construction of user interfaces, and limiting the constraint solver to graphs without cycles gives enough efficiency and flexibility to create highly responsive complex interactive systems. In *VB2*, introducing at runtime a constraint that would create a cyclic graph causes an exception that can be handled to remove the offending constraints[1]. The state manager behaviour and the constraint solving techniques are detailed in [13][14].

**Daemons.** *Daemons* are the imperative portion of *VB2*. Daemons register themselves with a set of active variables and are activated each time their value changes. They are executed in order of their activation time, which corresponds to breadth-first traversal of the dependency graph. The action taken by a daemon can be a procedure of any complexity that may create new objects, perform input/output operations, change active variables' values, manipulate the constraint graph, or activate and deactivate other daemons. The execution of a daemon's action is sequential and each manipulation of the constraint graph (assignment, assertion and retraction of a constraint) advances the state manager time for recording the variable's history. State manager time and animation time are kept separate: state manager time always goes forward and is used to keep track of the successive states of the system; animation time can instead be controlled by the user, to move backwards and forwards in a sequence, and is bound to real-time during animation recording and playback.

**Variable paths.** In *VB2*, daemons and constraints locate their variables through *indirect paths*. An indirect path is an object able to compute the location of a variable as well as the list of the intermediary variables that were used to compute this variable. Active variables are viewed in this context as self-referencing indirect paths using no intermediary variables. When a path is not capable of locating the variable, it is said to be *broken*. A simple example of indirect path is the *symbolic path*, which corresponds to Garnet's pointer variable [23] (an example is *parent_global_transf := Current/"parent"/"global_transf"*, where *"/"* indicates indirection, and quoted names correspond to the names of active variables in constraint modules). As stated by Vander Zanden et al. [23], the use of indirect paths allows constraints to model a wide array of dynamic application behaviours, and promotes a simpler, more effective style of programming than conventional constraints. Indirect paths are implemented in *VB2* by deactivating and reactivating constraints and daemons as soon as an intermediary variable used for computing one of their paths is modified [13], as in the user interface toolkit *Multi-Garnet* [20]. Only daemons and constraints that do not have any broken path are successfully activated. The others remain on wait until active variable modifications allow their paths to locate all the variables.

*VB2* and *Virtual Studio* are implemented in the object-oriented language *Eiffel* [17].

---

[1] *VB2*'s current constraint solver [13][19] is unable to find acyclic solutions of potentially cyclic constraint graphs. An algorithm that removes this limitation is presented in [22].

40

All the primitive elements of *VB2* are modelled using abstract classes from which all the other components of the systems are derived. The class C_MODULE represents a *VB2* core object, composed of variables, constraints, and daemons. Variables are represented as instances of C_VARIABLE, daemons as instances of DAEMON, and constraints of CONSTRAINT. Selective export rules are used to solve one of the problems of the integration at the library level of constraints with an object oriented framework [4][11]. In particular, only constraint methods (instances of descendants of class C_METHOD) have the right to assign new values to active variables, and assertions control that these assignments are done exclusively during constraint propagation.

## 2.2 Modelling Subsystem

The central component of *Virtual Studio*'s modelling subsystem is the NODE_3D class, whose instances, related in a hierarchical fashion, represent the transformation hierarchy. Position, orientation, shearing and scaling of the reference frame are packaged in TRANSFORM_3D objects. Degrees of freedom can be attached to a node in order to define additional constrained motion, as in articulated structures. Instances of MATERIAL and TEXTURE are used to define the behaviour of physical objects with respect to light. Placing instances of MATERIAL and TEXTURE in a node allows instance inheritance through the hierarchy. Instances of LIGHT represents light sources whose colour and intensity are defined by instances of MATERIAL and TEXTURE. An instance of CAMERA represents a camera viewing the scene. It has information about its viewing frustum and a possibly stereoscopic projection. Instances of SHAPE encapsulate the concept of physical objects having a geometry, material and texture in the Cartesian space. See [13] for more details on the class hierarchy of the modelling and rendering clusters. Figure 1 shows a simplified object-relation diagram of the modelling subsystem as well as the design notation.

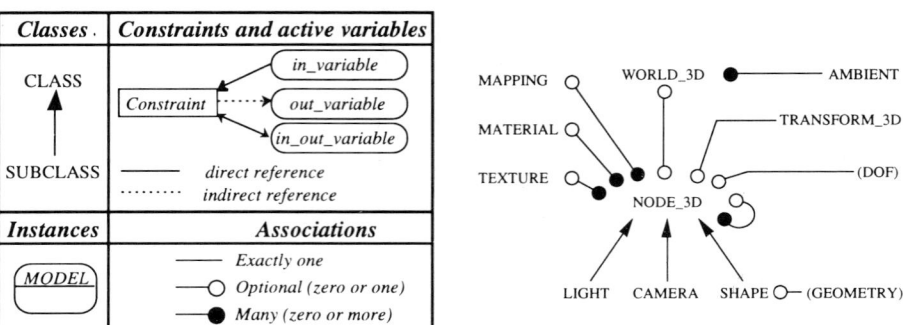

Fig. 1: Design notation and simplified modelling hierarchy.

## 2.3 Animation Subsystem

The animation is viewed as a time interval hierarchy where each level is represented by an instance of subclasses of the TIME_INTERVAL class. Its root is an instance of the ANIM_MANAGER class representing the overall animation. This object is responsible for maintaining the animation time (represented as active variables), which can be controlled by the user to access different parts of a sequence, and is bound to real-time during animation playback. Animation time, as opposed to the state manager time, is continuous, and frames in the animation are sampled when needed. An instance of ANIM_MANAGER is composed by a set of CONTROLLER instances. Controllers are objects allowing the animation of the parameters of a *Virtual Studio*'s graphical object. They are composed of a set of instances of TRACK, one for each animated parameters. The generic class VALUE_INTERVAL defines the concept of

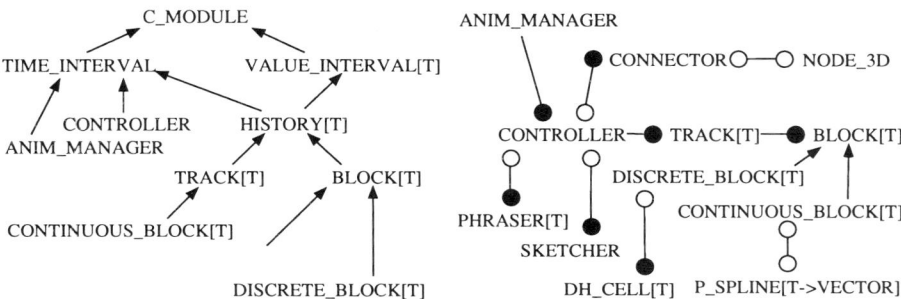

Fig. 2: Class hierarchy and object-relation diagram of the animation subsystem.

interval of values. Through multiple inheritance, the behaviours of TIME_INTERVAL and VALUE_INTERVAL are composed to define the HISTORY class, where each value of the value interval is put in correspondence with a time in the time interval. The subclass TRACK represents a track of values as a function of animation time, and is defined as a list of instances of subclasses of the BLOCK class. The subclass CONTINUOUS_BLOCK defines a history of continuous values, represented using a parametric B-spline curve [10] (instances of P_SPLINE). The subclass DISCRETE_BLOCK defines a history of discrete values represented as the successive value changes in time. Discrete history values can be of any type, from atomic types to aggregate objects. Finally, the subclass CONSTANT_BLOCK defines a history with a constant value over the time interval. The controller uses SKETCHER and PHRASER objects to handle continuous tracks. SKETCHER objects apply an incremental data reduction algorithm [1][3] to convert a series of sampled values of a variable to a B-spline representation that is then stored in instances of CONTINUOUS_BLOCK. PHRASER objects are used to blend animations defined in adjacent blocks using Hermite spline segments that join the blocks with $C^1$ continuity [1][10]. The class hierarchy and the relation between instances of the animation subsystem are presented in Figure 2.

## 2.4 Controller-Model Protocol

Animation recording and playback is obtained by binding controllers to models. When *binding* a model to a controller, the controller must first determine if it can animate the given model, identifying on the model the set of public active variables requested to

42

activate its binding constraints. Once the binding constraints are activated, the model is ready to be animated. The binding constraints being generally bi-directional, the controller is always informed of model's information changes even if it is modified by other objects, and conversely, during animation playback, the state of the model is modified to reflect the tracks' state changes. *Unbinding* a model from a controller detaches it from the object it animates. The effect is to deactivate the binding constraints in order to suppress dependencies between controller's and model's active variables. Once the model is unbound, it does not participate to the animation and its state remains unchanged during playback. When the user manipulates the model, the constraint network is oriented from the model to the tracks, while during animation playback it is oriented in the opposite direction (from the tracks to the model). This behaviour is obtained by associating to interaction constraints a priority higher than that of playback constraints.

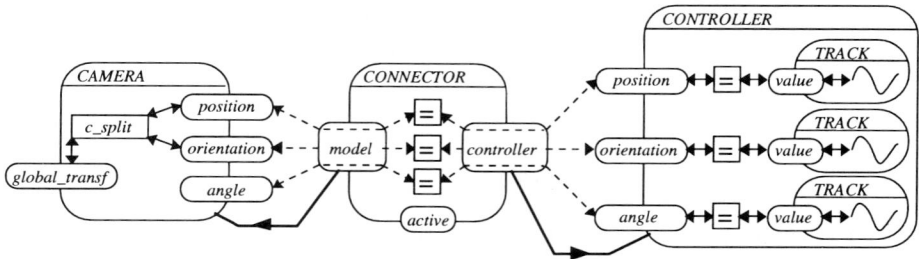

Fig. 3: Animating a model is obtained by binding a controller.

Indirect constraints allow to define a controller's binding mechanism entirely in a declarative way. In Figure 3, the connector object defines the binding with equality constraints between the camera's and the controller's state variables. These variables are located with indirect paths that use the connector's ports as intermediary variables. Second-order control is used inside the connector to ensure that all binding constraints are bound or unbound simultaneously [13].

## 3 Animation

### 3.1 Maintaining the Temporal Coherence

All objects involved in the definition of the temporal subdivision of the animation are instances of subclasses of the abstract class TIME_INTERVAL, which defines the behaviours used to maintain a time interval. The *start_time* and *end_time* active variables of TIME_INTERVAL instances store the lower and upper limits of the interval, expressed in absolute animation time. The *time* and *local_time* active variables stores the current time value expressed, respectively, in absolute animation time and track local time.

Daemons depending on the *start_time* and *end_time* variables of each time interval object, are responsible for the propagation of timing modifications between the levels of the hierarchy, so as to permanently maintain the temporal coherence between the

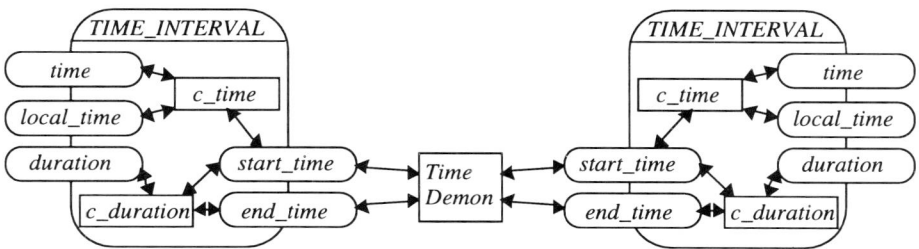

Fig. 4: Simplified constraint network for instances of TIME_INTERVAL.

hierarchy levels. That way, the animation timing can be manipulated globally or locally. For example, changing the duration of a single track will propagate up in the hierarchy so as to modify the total duration of the animation. Conversely, changing the duration of the overall animation will propagate down in the hierarchy and apply a scale factor to subdividing intervals. Modifying an intermediate level will propagate down to scale its subdividing intervals and up to update the total duration of the animation. Figure 4 shows the constraint network formed by two levels of the time interval hierarchy.

Since the temporal coherence of the time interval hierarchy is being permanently maintained, it is possible to declaratively specify synchronization between tracks by introducing constraints between their timing variables. When tracks are made visible, the start and end time variables can be manipulated through the associated binders. Figure 7 (see colour plates) shows an animated camera tool together with the camera position track. Synchronization between the evolution of different parameters may be obtained by interactively connecting together time binders of the associated tracks. In the figure, the start binder is represented by the 3D widget on the left, which has a value of 0.6, while the end binder is on the right and has a value of 4.0. Start and end times can be interactively controlled by selecting one of these widgets with the 3D cursor and dragging a line to a time binder of the object with which we want to synchronize the animation. Internally, this operation enforces an equality constraint between the active variables controlled by the binders.

### 3.2 Playing the Animation

One of the basic features of an interactive animation system is to provide real-time interactive animation playback. This is obtained by evaluating all animation tracks at the desired time, updating the scene's state and rendering the frame. The following frame time is computed by taking into account the time needed to generate the previous frame in the animation. Animation can thus be played in real-time and synchronized with external data sources. This is possible because the animation time is continuous and frames appear only as a result of sampling operations. Animation playback is obtained by having the values of the animation time control the sampling time of each of the tracks in the system. The beginning and end of the animation playback are indicated by modifying the value of a Boolean variable in the animation manager. This triggers the activation or deactivation of a constraint between the system's time and the animation

44

manager's time. Once the constraint is activated, time changes propagate through the time interval hierarchy triggering the tracks' evaluation and the models' update (see Figure 5).

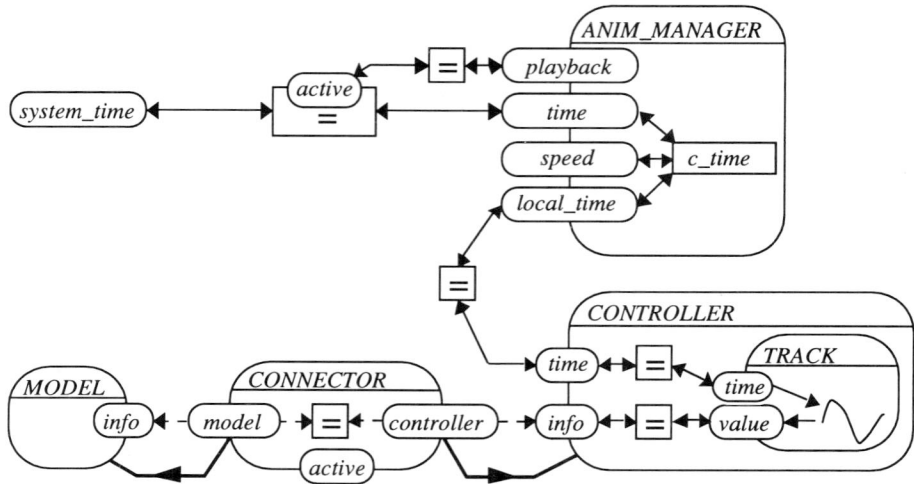

Fig. 5: Time propagation during animation playback triggers model updates.

Evaluating a continuous parameter track involves determining which block is active at the current time and asking its value. If the current time falls into the transition period between two successive blocks, then the value is computed by a PHRASER object whose behaviour is to blend the value of successive blocks in order to ensure a smooth transition. Discrete tracks are defined by the successive transitory values together with the times at which the value change events occur. The value of the track is the value of the event coming before the time at which the track is evaluated. To allow track evaluation at any time, evaluation requests at times before the track's start time or after the track's end time return the value at, respectively, start and end time.

### 3.3 Recording the Animation

In *Virtual Studio*, animation is specified with a performance-based approach by recording the effects over time of the user's manipulation on the models. A 3D cursor, controlled by a *Spaceball*, is used to select and manipulate objects of the synthetic world. Direct manipulation and virtual tools are the two techniques used to input information. Both techniques involve using mediator objects that transform cursor's movements into modifications of manipulated objects.

Virtual tools are visible first class objects that lie in the same 3D space as application objects and offer the interaction metaphor to control them. Their visual appearance is determined by a modelling hierarchy, while their behaviour is controlled by an internal constraint network [14]. As in the real world, the user configures its workspace by selecting tools, positioning and orienting them in space, and binding them to application objects. At the moment of binding, the tool's and the application object's constraint networks become connected, so as to ensure information propagation. When bound, the tool changes its visual appearance to a shape that provides information about its behaviour and offers semantic feedback. Multiple tools can be active simultaneously in the same 3D environment in order to control all its aspects. The environment's consistency is continuously ensured by the underlying constraint solver. The bi-directionality of the relationships between user-interface and application objects makes it possible to use virtual tools to interact with a dynamic environment, opening the door to the integration of animation and interaction techniques.

During manipulation, the internal constraint networks of the user-interface mediator object are connected to the 3D cursor and to the manipulated model with binding constraints. If the manipulated object can be animated, binding constraints are also in place to connect the manipulated model to its controller. The user becomes thus the source of a flow of information that propagates through the internal constraint networks of the user-interface mediator object, of the manipulated object and of the animation controller (see Figure 6).

In order to be able to record the evolution over time of the model's information during manipulation, each track owns a recording daemon whose task is to store the variations of the monitored variable and to update the track at the end of the manipulation. For continuous tracks, the data reduction algorithm is applied to the incoming data and the approximation spline is inserted in the track. Discrete tracks are built from the successive transitory value changes triggered by the user's manipulations. Multiple recording daemons may be active simultaneously so as to record the variations of all variables influenced by the manipulation. That way, it is possible to interact with the animated object at the task level [16], as the 3D motion described by the 3D cursor can be interpreted as a high-level goal allowing the simultaneous and coordinated control of several parameters as, for example, when guiding a walking articulated figure.

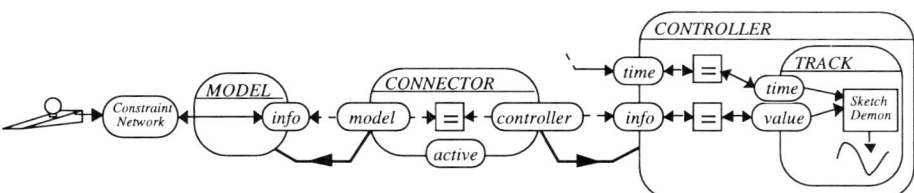

Fig. 6: While recording, device sensor values are connected to tracks' variables.

Since interaction constraints have a higher priority than the binding constraints of the controllers, recording can occur during animation playback. For a given model, the tracks that are not influenced by the interaction participate in the animation playback, while the variations of the variables being modified by the interaction are recorded. The recording daemons are able to determine when to record the modifications of the variable they monitor by analysing the local orientation of the constraint network that binds the controller to the model: an incoming constraint network means that the variable is modified due to the user's manipulation, and not by animation playback. This behaviour is obtained in a declarative way by exploiting the ability of the constraint solver to deal with hierarchies of dataflow constraints. It allows the system to promote the use of a layered approach to animation specification, where the user starts by recording some part of the animation, and later defines additional pieces that are automatically synchronized with the rest of the animation by manipulating the models during animation playback.

### 3.4 Example

The example scene (see Figure 8 — colour plate) is composed of a character, a light and a camera. An appropriate virtual tool and a controller object has been connected to each scene element to provide support for manipulation and animation. A tool encapsulating a walking engine has been bound to the character to provide the model with a walking behaviour. During manipulation or animation, the tool is responsible to generate the walking cycle animation according to the translation speed. Lookat constraints make the camera and the light always point towards the character head. During animation playback, the camera and the light positions are determined by their recorded paths, while their orientations are determined by the lookat constraints. By connecting together the start and end time binders of the character's and light's tracks, we introduced synchronization constraints so that both motions perform in parallel. The camera motion has been made to start after the character's motion by interactively connecting the camera's start time binder with the character's end time binder.

The environment presented in Figure 8 (see colour plates) is composed of 5632 constraints and 13659 active variables. The scene's graphical representation contains 3000 polygons illuminated by a spot light (the animated light source) and a directional light (a light attached to the user's viewpoint). The redraw rate was 10 frames per second on a *Silicon Graphics Crimson VGX*. Despite the complexity of the constraint network, rendering speed was largely the limiting factor, since 80% of the application time was spent in rendering operations.

# 4 Conclusion

In this paper, we have shown how the animation subsystem of *Virtual Studio* has been modelled on top of the OOCIP *VB2* architecture. In *VB2*, there is no intrinsic difference between user-interface and application objects. Multi-way dataflow constraints provide the necessary tight coupling among components that makes it possible to seamlessly compose animated and interactive behaviours.

Indirect paths allow an effective use of the constraint model in the context of dynamic applications. The ability of the underlying constraint solver to deal with hierarchies of multi-way, multi-output dataflow constraints, together with the ability of the state manager to handle indirect constraints, are exploited to define most of the behaviours of the modelling and animation components in a declarative way. The ease of integration between all system's components opens the door to novel interactive solution to modelling and animation problems. By recording the effects of the user's manipulations on the models, all the expressive power of the 3D user interface is exploited when defining animations.

This performance-based approach complements standard key-framing systems by providing the ability to create animations with straight-ahead actions. At the end of the recording session, animation tracks are automatically updated to integrate the new piece of animation. Animation components can be easily synchronized using constrained manipulation during playback.

Our system demonstrates that, although they are limited to expressing acyclic conflict-free graphs, multi-way dataflow constraints are general enough to model a large variety of behaviours, while remaining efficient enough to ensure the responsiveness of large interactive 3D graphics applications. In the graphics community, these techniques have until recently been largely confined to 2D applications [7][18]. To our knowledge, *VB2* and *TBAG* [8] are the first 3D graphics systems that uniformly use multi-way constraint networks to model large animated environments.

# Acknowledgements

The authors would like to thank Ronan Boulic for providing the walking engine software, and the workshop reviewers for their helpful comments and suggestions.

This research was conducted while the authors were at the Swiss Federal Institute of Technology in Lausanne.

# References

[1] Balaguer JF (1993) *Virtual Studio*. PhD Thesis, EPFL, Switzerland.

[2] Balaguer JF, Gobbetti E (1995) Animating Spaceland. *IEEE Computer* 28(7).

[3] Balaguer JF, Gobbetti E (1995) Sketching 3D Animations. *Proc. EUROGRAPHICS*: 241-258.

[4] Blake E, Hoole Q (1992) Expressing Relationships between Objects: Problems and Solutions. *Proc. Third EUROGRAPHICS Workshop on Object-Oriented Graphics*: 159-162.

[5] Borning A, Freeman-Benson B, Wilson M (1992) Constraint Hierarchies. *Lisp and Symbolic Computation* 5(3): 221-268.

[6] Conner DB, Snibbe SS, Herndon KP, Robbins DC, Zeleznik RC, Van Dam A (1992) Three-Dimensional Widgets. *Proc. SIGGRAPH Symposium on Interactive 3D Graphics*: 183-188.

[7] Duisberg R (1986) *Temporal Constraints in the Animus System*. PhD Thesis, TR-86-09-01, Computer Science Department, University of Washington.

[8] Elliott C, Schechter G, Yeung R, Abi-Ezzi S (1994) TBAG: A High Level Framework for Interactive, Animated 3D Graphics Applications. *Proc. SIGGRAPH*: 421-434.

[9] Elson M (1993) *Character Motion Systems*. SIGGRAPH Course Notes 1.

[10] Farin G (1990) *Curves and Surfaces for Computer Aided Geometric Design*. Academic Press.

[11] Freeman Benson B (1990) Mixing Objects, Constraints, and Imperative Programming. *Proc. ECOOP/OOPSLA*: 77-87.

[12] Gleicher M (1993) A Graphics Toolkit Based on Differential Constraints. *Proc. UIST*: 109-120.

[13] Gobbetti E (1993) *Virtuality Builder II*. PhD Thesis, EPFL, Switzerland.

[14] Gobbetti E, Balaguer JF (1993) VB2: A Framework for Interaction in Synthetic Worlds. *Proc. UIST*: 167-178.

[15] Gobbetti E, Balaguer JF (1995) An Integrated Environment to Visually Construct 3D Animations. *Proc. SIGGRAPH*: 395-398.

[16] McKenna M, Pieper S, Zeltzer D (1990) Control of a Virtual Actor: The Roach. *Proc. SIGGRAPH Symp. on Interactive 3D Graphics*: 165-174.

[17] Meyer B (1993) *Eiffel: The Language*. Prentice-Hall.

[18] Myers BA, Giuse GA, Dannenberg RB, Vander Zanden B, Kosbie DS, Pervin E, Mickish A, Marchal P (1990) Garnet: Comprehensive Support for Graphical, Highly-Interactive User Interface. *IEEE Computer* 23(11): 71-85.

[19] Sannella M (1994) Skyblue A Multi-Way Local Propagation Constraint Solver for User Interface Construction. *Proc. UIST*: 137-146.

[20] Sannella M, Borning A (1992) *Multi-Garnet: Integrating Multi-way Constraints with Garnet*. TR-92-07-01, Dept. of Computer Science, University of Washington.

[21] Sannella M, Maloney J, Freeman Benson B, Borning A (1992) Multi-way versus One-way Constraints in user-Interface Construction. *Software Practice and Experience* 23(5): 529-566.

[22] Vander Zanden B (1995) *An Incremental Algorithm for Satisfying Hierarchies of Multi-Way, dataflow Constraints*. Technical Report, University of Tennessee, Knoxville.

[23] Vander Zanden B, Myers BA, Giuse D, Szeleky P (1991) The Importance of Pointer Variables in Constraint Models. *Proc. UIST*: 155-164.

**Editors' Note: see Appendix, p. 170 for coloured figures of this paper**

# Information Hiding and the Complexity of Constraint Satisfaction

Remco C. Veltkamp

Utrecht University, Department of Computing Science
Padualaan 14, 3584 CH Utrecht, The Netherlands
e-mail: Remco.Veltkamp@cs.ruu.nl

Richard H. M. C. Kelleners

CWI, Department of Interactive Systems
Kruislaan 413, 1098 SJ Amsterdam, The Netherlands
e-mail: richard@cwi.nl
and
Technical University of Eindhoven, Department of Computing Science
Den Dolech 2, 5612 AZ, Eindhoven, The Netherlands

**Abstract** This paper discusses the complexity of constraint satisfaction, and the effect of information hiding. On the one hand, powerful constraint satisfaction is necessarily global, and tends to break information hiding. On the other hand, preserving strict information hiding increases the complexity of constraint satisfaction, or severely limits the power of the constraint solver. Ultimately, under strict information hiding, constraint satisfaction on complex objects cannot be guaranteed.

## 1 Introduction

Graphics systems are typically very large integrated programs that use a wide range of techniques. They may deal with various types of data and allow concurrent interaction with a user and between a large number of agents/actors/active objects. A well founded and appropriate underlying abstraction is needed to deal with the complexity of computer graphics. The aim of any abstraction is to provide a context within which problems can easily be solved, and to provide a formal framework for thinking about the solutions and implementing them. *Object-orientedness* provides such an underlying abstraction to deal with complexity.

The concept of *constraints* is another such abstraction. Constraints specify relations between objects which must be maintained. When a change occurs to one of the constrained objects, all affected objects must be adjusted such that all the constraints remain satisfied. There are two aspects to constraints:

- Description: constraints specify the relation between objects; this is the declarative aspect.

- Satisfaction: in order to solve a set of constraints, methods of constraint satisfaction have to be given; this is the procedural aspect.

Programming with constraints is a form of declarative programming. A declarative program specifies the relations which have to hold in the results of the computation. It specifies what the result of the computation should be, not how to go about the computation. The underlying solving engine takes care of the procedural part, and has to resolve the constraints in order to produce the solution. The principal benefit of declarative approaches is that they shift the burden of deciding how something has to be done from the application programmer to the system environment he is working in.

The use of constraints in managing the complexity of designing interactive graphics systems dates back to the earliest days of interactive graphics (consider Sutherland's Sketchpad from the early sixties [20]), and still receives much attention. It has an intuitive appeal to regard the requirements of a model, interaction, or animation as constraints that have to be maintained. The strength of constraints in computer graphics is the rich set of associations with the modelled reality: reality often behaves like it is driven by constraints.

A concept complementary to abstraction is *encapsulation*. Whereas abstraction focuses on the observable behaviour of an object, encapsulation focuses on the implementation behind that behaviour. Encapsulation is the process of compartmentalizing the elements of an abstraction that constitute its structure and behaviour. It serves to separate the contractual interface of an abstraction and its implementation [2].

Encapsulation could be achieved by physical separation, e.g. residing the data structures and methods of each object on a private processor. Encapsulation is most often achieved through *information hiding*, i.e. the process of hiding all the secrets of an object that do not contribute to its essential characteristics. Typically, the structure of an object is hidden, as well as the implementation of its methods [2].

The justification for combining objects and constraints derives from the fact that it addresses the problems of complexity in large interactive graphical systems which arises on two fronts. The first is the complexity inherent in specifying the behaviour of animations and interactions with many components or objects. Constraints allow the declarative modelling of the behaviour of such systems. The second front is the complexity due to the fact that we are dealing with large software systems. Sound software engineering principles, such as data encapsulation, are needed to cope with large complex software systems.

Abstraction and encapsulation combine well in the object-oriented paradigm. However, the combination of objects with constraints fits less well: a constraint solver looks at, and sets, the constrained objects' internal data, which conflicts with the data encapsulation concept in the object-oriented paradigm. This paper discusses one aspect of this incompatibility. It appears that most constraint systems in an object-oriented environment infringe the information hiding principle to some extent. It is an interesting question if strict information hiding limits the power of constraint satisfaction and may increase the time complexity to exponential orders. In this paper we consider the effect of information hiding on the time complexity of constraint satisfaction.

# 2 Constraint satisfaction

Formally, a constraint satisfaction problem (CSP) can be specified by a finite set of variables $v_1, \ldots, v_n$, a domain $D_i$ of possible values for each $v_i$, and a set of constraints $C_1, \ldots, C_m$. Solving a CSP is finding a valuation $(s_1, \ldots, s_n) \in D_1 \times \ldots \times D_n$ of the variables for which all constraints are satisfied. A domain can be explicit, e.g. a finite enumeration of values, or implicit, e.g. $\mathbb{N}$ for an integer variable. In the latter case the constraint solver must have knowledge about the domain of variables in order to generate correct values. For instance, it may not generate real values for an integer variable.

Possible variants of the CSP are: find a single solution (valuation), find all solutions, find a best solution, find the number of solutions, determine satisfiability (whether or not a solution exists). The satisfiability variant is the simplest one (indeed, it follows from all the others), and even this one is in NP: it is in the class of Nondeterministic Polynomial-bounded problems, i.e. it can be solved by a nondeterministic algorithm in polynomial time, but there is no deterministic algorithm known to solve the problem in polynomial time. It is even NP-complete, i.e. if there were a polynomial-bounded algorithm to solve the problem, then there would be a polynomial-bounded algorithm for each problem in NP. This can be deduced from the fact that the satisfiability variant can be converted in polynomial time into the CNF-satisfiability problem, which is NP-complete [1]. The CNF-satisfiability problem is to determine if there is a truth assignment (a way to assign the values true and false) for the variables in a logical expression in conjunctive normal form (CNF) such that the value of the expression is true. A logical expression in conjunctive normal form is a sequence of clauses separated by conjunctions ($\wedge$), where a clause is a sequence of variables and negations of variables separated by disjunctions ($\vee$).

Because the general CSP is a hard problem, satisfaction algorithms are often slow. One way to speed up satisfaction is to perform computations in parallel. For example, [14] performs massively parallel computations by means of chemical reactions on DNA strands. One can also confine the domain of the constraints and the variables and exploit some of the specific knowledge of the domain. The time complexity of such specialized constraint satisfaction depends on both the domain and the kind of constraints. Symbolic solution of the algebraic expressions describing geometric constraints is known to be NP-hard; tree structured constraint networks can be solved in linear time; linear constraints over real numbers are solvable in polynomial time; a single polynomial constraint of degree higher than four does not even have an analytical solution; and the complexity of solving polynomials on integers of degree higher than two is still unknown.

There are basically two different models that constraint solvers can use for determining solutions (values for variables) to the constraints: the alternation and the refinement model. In the alternation (also called perturbation) model, each variable $v_i$ gets assigned a single value $s_i$. If a variable's value does not satisfy the constraints on it, the constraint solver tries alternative values from its domain (possibly eliminating the incorrect value from the domain). Satisfaction is completed if each variable has a solution such that all constraints hold. After satisfaction, the current domain of each variable can still contain values that do not satisfy constraints. In the refinement model, each variable $v_i$ gets assigned a subset $S_i$ of its domain $D_i$. If a value $s_i$ in the proposed solution $S_i$

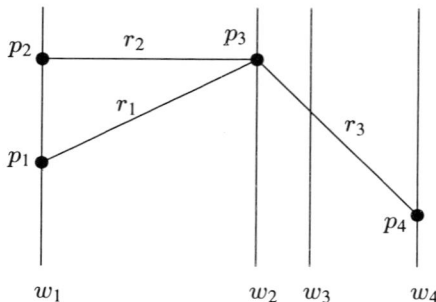

Fig. 1: Example of the Linkage Positioning problem.

does not satisfy the constraints on $v_i$, then the constraint solver eliminates that value. Satisfaction is completed when the solution set of each variable satisfies the constraints on that variable. After satisfaction, not every valuation $(s_1, \ldots, s_n) \in (S_1, \ldots, S_n)$ needs to satisfy all constraints, but for every $s_i \in S_i$, values $s_j \in S_j, j \neq i$ can be found that satisfy all constraints.

Many constraint solvers in computer graphics use the alternation model with continuous domains of the variables. Many algorithms in artificial intelligence use the alternation model with discrete domains. In constraint logic programming the refinement model with continuous domains is mostly used. The two approaches can also be combined.

## 3 The Linkage Positioning Problem

In this paper we use the following running example. Let $R = \{r_1, \ldots, r_m\}$ be a set of $m$ rods. The set of endpoints of these rods is $P = \{p_1, \ldots, p_n\}$, a set of $n$ points $p_i = (x_i, y_i)$ in $\mathbb{R}^2$. Each rod $r_i$ has a fixed length $d_i$. The rods $r_i$ are alternatively denoted as its pair of endpoints: $r_i = (p_{i_1}, p_{i_2})$, $i_1, i_2 \in \{1, \ldots, n\}$. The length of rod $(p_{i_1}, p_{i_2})$ is alternatively denoted as $d_{i_1 i_2}$. The rods form a single linkage structure, $\ell$; if two rods are joined, then they share an endpoint. Let $W = \{w_1, \ldots, w_k\}$ be a set of $k$ vertical walls (in $\mathbb{R}^2$); each $w_i$ is represented by its x-coordinate. The rods must be positioned on the walls in such a way that the endpoints of each rod lie on different walls. See Figure 1 for an example.

This Linkage Positioning problem can be modelled as a constraint problem in various ways.

### Constraint Problem 1 (CP-1)

The set of constraint variables is $V = \{p_1, \ldots, p_n\}$. The domain of each variable $(x_i, y_i)$ is $W \times \mathbb{R}$. The constraints are a set of $m$ binary constraints that fix the length between two points that belong to the same rod and prohibit these points to lie on one wall.

**Constraint Problem 2 (CP-2)**

The set of constraint variables is $V = \{r_1, \ldots, r_m\}$. Each variable is responsible for maintaining its internal integrity, i.e. it retains a fixed length. The domain of each variable $r_i = (p_{i_1}, p_{i_2})$ is $(W \times \mathbb{R})^2$. The constraints are a set of $m$ unary constraints that prevent each rod from being vertical, and $q$ binary constraints to specify incident rods. The $q$ binary constraints construct the linkage, and the value of $q$ depends on the structure of the linkage, but is at least $m - 1$. If the maximal number of rods incident to a point is constant (independent of $n$ or $m$) then $q = \mathcal{O}(n)$. If a constant number of points are incident to $\mathcal{O}(n)$ points then $q = \mathcal{O}(n^2)$. If $\mathcal{O}(n)$ vertices are incident to $\mathcal{O}(n)$ points then $q = \mathcal{O}(n^3)$.

**Constraint Problem 3 (CP-3)**

The constraint variable is the whole linkage $\ell$. The domain of this variable is $(W \times \mathbb{R})^n$. The linkage should maintain the fixed lengths of the rods, and the incidence relations between the rods. As in CP-2, there are $m$ unary constraints to prevent each rod from being vertical. These are unary constraints on the single linkage variable.

Typically, the internal variables of the objects are the points, and they attain a value from $W \times \mathbb{R}$, or they are unspecified, i.e. have no value yet. Instead of restricting the domain of the $x_i$'s to $W$ in each of the three constraint problems above, we could let the domain be $\mathbb{R}$, and add extra unary constraints to place the points on the wall.

The Linkage Positioning Problem illustrates different types of constraints (unary, binary) and different types of domains (discrete, continuous). It is suitable to demonstrate both the alternation and the refinement models of constraint satisfaction.

The Linkage Positioning Problem is equivalent to a famous problem in computability and complexity theory: $(k\text{-})$Graph Colouring. The problem there is to assign a colour from a given set of $k$ colours to each vertex of the graph, such that vertices connected by an edge have different colours. The set of vertices corresponds to $P$ from the Linkage Problem, the set of edges to $R$, and the set of colours to $W$. The condition of 'different colours' corresponds to 'different walls, plus fixed distance'; both conditions take constant time to check. Just like general constraint satisfaction, $k$-Graph Colouring is known to be NP-complete [1]. Determining if a graph is 2-colourable is easy (polynomial). Determining if it is 3-colourable is NP-complete. It is still NP-complete if the graphs are planar and the maximal degree is four. If the maximal degree is at most two, the $k$-colouring problem is easy. Colouring bipartite graphs (e.g. trees) is also easy.

# 4 Constraints vs information hiding

Consider the following constraints on rods $r_1$, $r_2$, $r_3$:

$$r_1.p_1 = r_2.p_1, \quad r_2.p_2 = r_3.p_1$$
$$r_1.p_1.x \neq r_1.p_2.x, \quad r_2.p_1.x \neq r_2.p_2.x, \quad r_3.p_1.x \neq r_3.p_2.x$$

A possible solution is the following (for some $y$):

$$r_1.p_1 = (w_1, y), \quad r_1.p_2 = (w_2, \; y + \sqrt{(r_1.\text{length})^2 - (w_2 - w_1)^2})$$
$$r_2.p_1 = (w_1, y), \quad r_2.p_2 = (w_2, \; y - \sqrt{(r_2.\text{length})^2 - (w_2 - w_1)^2})$$
$$r_3.p_1 = (w_2, \; y - \sqrt{(r_2.\text{length})^2 - (w_2 - w_1)^2})$$
$$r_3.p_2 = (w_1, \; r_3.p_1.y + \sqrt{(r_3.\text{length})^2 - (w_1 - w_2)^2})$$

Information hiding is first violated by the constraint expressions, and then by expressing the solution. To avoid this problem, approaches based on message passing have been proposed. In [12], the methods of an object that may violate constraints are guarded by so-called propagators. The propagators send messages to other objects to maintain the constraints. This technique is similar to the pre- and postcondition facilities in Go [5]. It is limited to constraint maintenance (i.e. truth maintenance, as opposed to starting with an inconsistent situation that is then resolved), and not further considered in this paper.

A more powerful technique is presented in [23]. There, the constraint solver produces a set of programs that solve constraints which are stated in the form of equations. It translates a declarative constraint equation into procedural solutions in terms of messages back to objects.

The problem is the local character of the solution. More powerful solutions are necessarily global in nature. The danger is that all objects need methods to get and set their internal data. This however, allows every other object to get and set these values, which is clearly against the object-oriented philosophy.

One way to restrict this, is to have an object allow value setting only when its internal constraints remain satisfied (see [18]). A constraint could be made internal by constructing a 'container object', which contains the constraint and the operand objects, but this does not solve the basic problem. In particular, the state of active objects cannot be changed without their explicit cooperation. (Active objects, or actors, conceptually have their own processor and behave autonomously, which is typical in animation and simulation.) Another approach is to limit access to private data to constraint-objects or the constraint solver-objects only. For example C++ provides the 'friend' declaration to grant functions access to the private part of objects. This is also comparable to the approach taken by [4], where special variables (slots) are accessible by constraints only. One can argue that encapsulation is still violated (and specifically that the C++ friend construct could be easily misused).

This raises the question how strict information hiding affects (the complexity of) constraint satisfaction. In the following sections we will review a number of constraint satisfaction methods, determine their time complexities, and illustrate that with the particular time complexities for the instances of the Linkage Positioning Problem.

# 5 Backtracking

The first constraint satisfaction algorithm we consider is backtracking. The basic operation is to pick one variable at a time and assign a value from the domain to it. If the assignment violates some constraints, another value, when available, is chosen. If all variables are assigned a value, the problem is solved. If at any stage no value can be found for a particular variable without violating any constraints, the variable which was last picked is revised and an alternative value, when available, is assigned to that variable. This carries on until either a solution is found or all combinations of values have been tried and have failed.

Below, the backtrack algorithm is given in pseudocode (see [21]).

```
BT (V, C)
{ if (V=={}) return TRUE;
  v = V.select();
  do
  { s = v.domain().select();
    v.assign(s);
    v.domain().remove(s);
    if (v violates no constraints in C)
    { success = BT(V - {v}, C);
      if (success) return TRUE;
    }
  } while (v.domain() ≠ {})
  return FALSE;            // no solution found:  backtracking
}
```

This recursive algorithm is called with a set of unassigned variables V and the set of constraints C. Each time BT is called, it picks a value from the domain of the current variable, assigns this to the variable, and removes the value from its domain. Then is tested if the current assignment together with all previous assignments violate any constraints in C. If this is the case, another value from the variable's domain is chosen. If the domain runs empty, no solution can be found for this particular variable and backtracking is performed.

Backtracking is applicable in the alternation model of satisfaction with discrete domains. If there are $b$ variables and the maximum initial domain size for a variable is $a$, there are at most $a^b$ candidate solutions. Every candidate solution can be checked against all constraints in C. If the number of constraints is $e$, then the complexity of the algorithm is $\mathcal{O}(ea^b)$.

## 5.1 Linkage Positioning Problem

The backtracking algorithm assumes the domains of a variable to be discrete and finite. In Constraint Problem 1 (CP-1) of the Linkage Positioning Problem, the domain of each variable is $p_i (= (x_i, y_i))$ is $W \times \mathbb{R}$. In order to be able to apply the backtracking algorithm, we have to restrict the domain to $W$ only. The y-coordinate of a point is continuous, and its value is not known at the time a value is picked for the x-coordinate. Therefore, we change the binary constraint $d(p_{i_1}, p_{i_2}) = d_{i_1 i_2}$ into $|x_{i_1} - x_{i_2}| < d_{i_1 i_2}$, with $i_1, i_2 \in \{1, \ldots, n\}$. This forces connected points to lie on walls whose distance is smaller than the fixed distance between $p_{i_1}$ and $p_{i_2}$. If there are no cycles in the linkage structure, the y-coordinates are of no significance: if the x-coordinates have values which do not violate the constraints, proper values can always be found for the y-coordinates in time linear in the number of variables. The complexity is in that case $\mathcal{O}(mk^n)$.

In CP-2, the set of constraint variables is $V = \{r_1, \ldots, r_m\}$. The domain of each variable $r_i = (p_{i_1}, p_{i_2})$ is $(W \times \mathbb{R})^2$. The unary constraints must be extended with $\|x_{i_1}, x_{i_2}\| < d_{i_1 i_2}$, to assure that the rod objects can always retain their fixed length. In order to be able to apply the backtracking algorithm, we restrict the domain to $W^2$ only, which has size $k^2$. The time complexity changes accordingly. In the case the linkage structure contains no cycles, there are $k^{2m}$ candidate solutions. For every candidate solution, all constraints will be checked. The number of constraints is $m + q$, so the complexity of the algorithm is $\mathcal{O}((m + q)k^{2m})$.

In the case of CP-3, the single variable is a complete linkage. An assignment to this variable is a tuple of $n$ walls. The size of its domain equals $k^n$, which is also the number of candidate solutions to the problem. For every candidate solution, all constraints have to be checked. The number of constraints is $m$, so the complexity of the algorithm is $\mathcal{O}(mk^n)$, which is the same as for CP-1.

# 6 Node and arc consistency

Node and arc consistency applies to the refinement model of satisfaction. We call a constraint satisfaction problem *node-consistent* if and only if for all variables, all values in its domain satisfy the unary constraints on that variable (cf. [15]).

The following algorithm achieves node-consistency for discrete domains:

```
NC (V, C)
{ for (each v in V)
  { for (each value s in v.domain() )
    { if (unary constraints from C on v are violated)
      remove s from v.domain();
} } }
```

If the size of each domain is at most $a$ and the total number of unary constraints is $e$, then the time complexity of this algorithm is $\mathcal{O}(ae)$. The algorithm is easily adapted for continuous domains. The time complexity then is $\mathcal{O}(Re)$, with $R$ the time needed to check a single constraint.

We call a constraint satisfaction problem *arc-consistent* if and only if for all values in the domain of each variable $v$, and for all constraints $c$ on $v$, we can find a value in the domain of the other variables of $c$ that satisfy the constraint.

The following algorithm for achieving arc-consistency assumes that the constraints are unary or binary, and have discrete domains. For each binary constraint c on variables $v_1$ and $v_2$, the domains of the variables are examined separately by the method revise. When the domain is examined, all values are deleted which do not satisfy the constraint. If any value is removed, the other constraints on the variable must be reconsidered.

First the method revise of constraint c:

```
c::revise(v₁,v₂)
{ changed = FALSE;
  for (each s₁ in v₁.domain())
  { delete = TRUE;
    for (each s₂ in v₂.domain())
    { if (check(s₁,s₂))
      { delete = FALSE;
        break;
    } }
    if (delete)
    { v₁.domain().remove(s₁);
      changed = TRUE;
  } }
  return changed;
}
```

The following simple algorithm for arc-consistency is called AC-3, after [15]:

```
AC-3 (V, C)
{ NC (V, C);
  while ( NOT C.empty())
  do
  { C.select(c₁, v₁, v₂);
    C.remove(c₁, v₁, v₂);
    if (c₁.revise(v₁,v₂))
       for (each (c₂,v₂,v₃) ≠ (c₁, v₁, v₂))
          C.add(c₂,v₂,v₃);
} }
```

Its time complexity is $\mathcal{O}(ea^3)$, with $a$ the maximum domain size and $e$ the number of binary constraints, which is linear in the number of constraints. If the constraint graph is planar, then the time complexity is also linear in the number of variables [16]. A less simple but optimal algorithm, AC-4, is presented in [17]. It has time complexity $\mathcal{O}(ea^2)$.

The algorithm is easily adapted for continuous domains, but termination of the algorithm then is not assured. The time complexity becomes $\mathcal{O}(\lambda Re)$, with $\lambda$ the number of loops taken in the algorithm, and $R$ the time necessary to revise a constraint.

Achieving node and arc-consistency does not solve the constraint satisfaction problem. These algorithms are used to reduce the search space of the problem. E.g., when there are no cycles in the constraint graph, achieving node and arc-consistency implies that the graph is backtrack-free, i.e. a solution can be found without backtracking [8]. In a backtrack-free graph, a solution is found in time linear in the number of nodes [6]. When there are cycles in the graph, additional algorithms have to be used to reduce the problem, such as the recognition of certain patterns (e.g. k-trees).

### 6.1 Linkage Positioning Problem

In CP-1, there are no unary constraints on the variables, thus, by definition it is node-consistent. Node-consistency for CP-2 is achieved by removing all wall-tuples from the domain of a rod $r_i$ on which the segment cannot lie. These are the wall-tuples whose distance is larger than the rod length and the tuples which contain two the same walls. In CP-2 the domain size is $k^2$ and the number of unary constraints is $m$. This results is a time complexity of $\mathcal{O}(mk^2)$ The domain size in CP-3 equals $k^n$, and the number of unary constraints is $m$. This results is a time complexity of $\mathcal{O}(mk^n)$ for NC.

In CP-1, arc-consistency means that if we assign to a point $p_i$ an arbitrary wall from its domain, then all other points to which it is adjacent, can be placed on walls so that the constraints still hold. The domain size in CP-1 is $k$, the number of constraints $m$, thus the complexity for AC-3 is $\mathcal{O}(mk^3)$. If we assume that there are no cycles in the linkage, finding an actual solution takes an additional $\mathcal{O}(n) = \mathcal{O}(m)$ amount of time.

In the case of CP-2, arc-consistency means that once a rod is placed on two walls, all adjacent rods can also be placed. The difference with CP-1 is that the domain size has increased to $k^2$ and the number of constraints has become $(m+q)$. The complexity of algorithm AC-3 is now $\mathcal{O}((m+q)(k^2)^3)$. Again, if there are no cycles in the linkage, an actual solution can be found in $\mathcal{O}(n) = \mathcal{O}(m)$ additional time.

Since CP-3 only contains one variable which is the complete linkage, there are no binary constraints. So, if it is node-consistent, it is also arc-consistent.

# 7 Local propagation

Propagation of known states, or just local propagation, can be performed when there are parts in the network whose states are completely known (have no degrees of freedom). The satisfaction system looks for one-step deductions that will allow the states of other parts to be known. This is repeated until all constraints are satisfied or no more known states can be propagated. If not all constraints can be satisfied, the remaining constraints must be resolved by, for example, numerical relaxation (see next section). Most constraint satisfaction systems use some form of local propagation. For an arbitrary constraint graph, we can use the following local propagation algorithm:

```
LP (v₁)
{ for (each constraint c₁ on v₁)
     fifo.push(c₁,v₁);
  while(NOT fifo.empty())
  { fifo.pop(c₁,v₁);
    changed = c₁.revise(v₁);
    for (each v₂ in changed)
       for (each c₂ ≠c₁ on v₂)           // effectively
          fifo.push(c₂,v₂);              // LP (v₂)
} }
```

Algorithm LP is invoked with the variable that triggers the propagation. The constraints on the variables are pushed onto a first-in-first-out queue. In the while-loop every constraint in this queue is revised by possibly changing the variables subject to the constraint other than the variable that triggered the constraint. All other variables that have been modified are put in the set changed. These variables and the constraints on them are put into the queue. Because constraints on changed variables are placed in a first-in-first-out queue (as opposed to an unordered set), they are guaranteed to be revised later on, whether the propagation is finite or infinite. This is called fair propagation [9].

If there are no cycles in the constraint graph, LP solves each constraint exactly once, and so the time complexity is linear in the number of constraints. Let $R$ be the time needed to revise a constraint. The time complexity for LP is then $\mathcal{O}(Re)$. The time $R$ depends on the problem. For discrete domains of size $a$, $R$ is typically $\mathcal{O}(a)$ in the alternation model, and $\mathcal{O}(a^2)$ in the refinement model. If there are cycles in the constraint graph, there is in general no way to determine the complexity of the algorithm except for the refinement model on discrete domains. E.g. for binary constraints, it becomes $\mathcal{O}(ea^3)$, equal to the time complexity of AC-3. For the other cases, let $\lambda$ be the number of loops done by the algorithm. The time complexity is then $\mathcal{O}(\lambda Re)$.

In the case that the constraint graph contains no cycles, the variables of a solved constraint are not changed by the same constraint again during further propagation. However, if that value prevents other variables to satisfy constraints, no solution is found, since backtracking is not possible. This problem could be circumvented by allowing a constraint to change the value of the variable it was triggered from.

Prior to performing local propagation one can perform an analysis to plan the best order to propagate constraints [19]. It is sometimes efficient to plan how to solve constraints before actually doing it. For example if one drags an graphics object which is constrained and must remain constrained, the planning can be done at the beginning of the drag operation, and the execution can be done in real time.

## 7.1 Linkage Positioning Problem

In CP-1, the constraint variables are the $n$ points. These are connected to each other by $m$ binary constraints. The number of walls, which is also the size of the domain for a point, is $k$. If we apply LP to CP-1, the time complexity is $\mathcal{O}(km)$, assuming that there are no cycles. However, as is pointed out above, it cannot always find a solution. In constraint problem CP-2, the variables are the $m$ rods. The domain size has increased to $k^2$, because every rod contains two points. The total number of constraints are the $m$ unary constraints and the $q$ binary constraints. The complexity for LP is then $\mathcal{O}(k^2(q+m))$. In CP-3, the constraint variable is the complete linkage, consisting of $n$ points and $m$ rods. Consequently, the domain size has increased to $k^n$, the number of unary constraints is $m$. The resulting complexity is $\mathcal{O}(k^n m)$.

# 8 Relaxation

Relaxation is an iterative numerical approximation technique that is often used in cases where local propagation fails, such as cycles in the constraint graph. Relaxation can only be used on variables with continuous numeric values. It makes an initial guess at the values of the unknown variables, and then estimates the error that would be caused by assigning these values to the variables. New guesses are then made, and new error estimates calculated. This process repeats until the error is minimized. The number of iterations can also be limited by a constant in case the error doesn't converge fast enough.

An algorithm for relaxation is given below:

```
RX (V, C)
{ times = 0;
  do
  { error = 0;
    times = times + 1;
    for (each v in V)
    { v.guess(C);
      error = max{error,v.error(C)};
    }
  } while (error > ε AND times < λ)
}
```

The algorithm RX applies to all the variables in the set V, subject to the constraints in the set C. The local variables of the algorithm, `times` and `error`, denote the number of iterations that have elapsed and the maximum error estimate, respectively. The variable `error` could also be a vector containing the error terms for all variables. In the while-loop, first initial values are guessed for the variables. Then the error is determined by testing the values of the variables against the constraints. The while-loop is repeated until the error term is smaller than a certain value $\epsilon$ or the maximum number of iterations $\lambda$, is reached.

Let again $b$ be the number of variables and $e$ the number of constraints. If we assume that a variable value can be guessed, and its error estimated, in time linear in the number of constraints on the variable, the complexity for guessing and error estimation of all variables is $\mathcal{O}(be)$. Since the number of iterations is at most $\lambda$, the time complexity of RX is $\mathcal{O}(\lambda be)$.

Although the relaxation algorithm is linear in the number of variables and constraints, in practice it can be slow because expensive floating point calculations have to be performed to guess values or estimate errors. In combination with local propagation however, relaxation can often be speeded up.

## 8.1 Linkage Positioning Problem

In order to be able to use the relaxation algorithm on the Linkage Positioning Problem, we allow the x-coordinates of the variables to be continuous and infinite. This means that the domain for points is $\mathbb{R}^2$.

For CP-1, the set of $m$ binary constraints is now extended with $n$ unary constraints, which state that the points must reside on walls. Error estimation is done by calculating distances between points and distances between points and walls. There are $n$ variables and $m+n$ constraints, so the complexity for RX is $\mathcal{O}(n(m+n)\lambda)$. For CP-2, the number of variables is $m$ and the number of constraints is increased by $n$ unary constraints to constrain the endpoints of a rod to lie on walls. The total number of constraints is thus $n+q+m$. The complexity for RX is then $\mathcal{O}(m(q+m+n)\lambda)$. For CP-3, the number of constraints increases to $n+m$, resulting in a complexity of $\mathcal{O}((m+n)\lambda)$.

# 9 Equate and OOCS

Equate [23] is a constraint satisfaction system that uses *term rewriting* as a guide to find solutions. Constraints are specified as equations. Rewrite rules convert equations into equivalent sets of equations that can more easily be solved. This repeats recursively (zero or more times) until equations are simple enough to be rewritten to a set of instructions (messages to an object). The *rewrite rules* which rewrite the equations are provided by the classes and are similar to the program clauses of logic programs. Several rules may apply to rewrite an equation.

The partial solutions for every constraint have to be combined in order to provide a solution program for the whole constraint problem. Equate uses so-called *read-sets* and *write-sets* to determine which instructions interfere with the accomplishments of others. These sets contain the (internal) variables of objects that will be read or written to during the execution of the instruction. For example, when an instruction $A$ writes to a variable which is read by another instruction $B$, instruction $A$ can undo some of the achievements of $B$ and is therefore executed first. If no proper order can be found, Equate finds no solution. In this way, a set of solution programs is generated, which is offered to the application. The application must choose a solution program from that set to execute in order to satisfy the constraints.

Another system, which is quite similar to Equate, is the Object-Oriented Constraint System, OOCS [10]. The main difference between these systems is that OOCS does not use term rewriting. Instead, an object supplies a set of *solution program segments* for each constraint that has been imposed upon it. The object guarantees that execution of any of these segments will leave the object in a state which satisfies the constraint. OOCS then solves a set of constraints by determining which program segment steps interfere with each other. This is achieved in the same way as in Equate by using read-sets and write-sets. By arranging the solution steps using these sets, the OOCS solver is able to decide which are feasible solutions.

Constraint solving with Equate takes the following four steps: (i) rewrite all the constraints, (ii) order the partial solutions into solution programs, (iii) make a selection out of the set of solution programs, (iv) execute a program. does not perform the first step. The last two have to be executed by the application program.

Let $e$ be the number of constraints (initial equations), and $s$ the maximum number of rules to rewrite an equation. Let $t$ be the maximum number of *terms* (instructions) in the body of a rewrite rule, and $r$ the maximum number of rewrite iterations. The number of rewrite steps is then $\mathcal{O}(e \sum_{i=1}^{r} s^i t^{i-1}) = \mathcal{O}(es^r t^{r-1})$. The total number of different solution programs (sets of instructions) is $\mathcal{O}(e \sum_{i=1}^{r} (st)^i) = \mathcal{O}(e(st)^r)$, each solution consisting of $\mathcal{O}(et^r)$ terms.

Very little has been written about the complexity of term rewriting. An approach to determine the complexity of term rewriting systems is given in [3], where a notion of the complexity is given by means of the cost of terms. In [13] is mentioned that if the set of terms is strictly left-sequential, there is a fast algorithm which can find a rule in the rule-base in time linear in the length of the expression to be rewritten (the head of the rule). Assuming that this length is bounded by a low constant number, rewriting a single equation takes constant time. The time for rewriting all constraints is then $\mathcal{O}(es^r t^{r-1})$.

In each solution program, the read and write sets of each of the $\mathcal{O}(et^r)$ instructions have to be checked against the read and write sets of all the other instructions in the solution program, requiring $\mathcal{O}(e^2 t^{2r})$ checks. This must be done for all the $\mathcal{O}(e(st)^r)$ solution programs, giving a total of $\mathcal{O}(e^3 s^r t^{3r})$ checks.

The actual satisfaction of the constraints is done by selecting one of the solution programs and executing the $\mathcal{O}(et^r)$ instructions (method calls).

The total complexity of satisfaction is the sum of complexities of the separate steps. It is dominated by the checking of the read and write sets, i.e. $\mathcal{O}(e^3 s^r t^{3r})$. Assuming that $r$, $s$, and $t$ are small, relative to the number of constraints $e$, and bounded above by a constant, the time complexity is cubic in the number of constraints: $\mathcal{O}(e^3)$.

## 9.1 Linkage Positioning Problem

We shall use Equate here to exemplify how the Linkage Positioning Problem can be solved using this strategy. The line of reasoning for OOCS remains the same. In order to use Equate, classes, constraint equations, and rewrite rules must be defined. The purpose of Equate is to generate a solution in the form of a sequence of method calls that satisfy constraints, rather than to generate and test individual values from the variables' domains.

In CP-1, the objects involved are points, their domain is the set of walls. It is the responsibility of the points to attain values in the domain. A typical rewrite rule could be:

```
d(point₁, point₂)=exp
          ⟵   fail_unless point₁.wall(exp) ≠ NIL;
              point₂.move_to(point₁.wall(exp))
```

where $point_1$.wall($exp$) returns a position on a wall other than its current wall, at distance $exp$. In CP-1, the number of constraints is $m$, so the time complexity becomes $\mathcal{O}(e^3) = \mathcal{O}(m^3)$.

In CP-2 the objects are the rods. Considering the working of Equate, we choose to combine the unary and binary constraints. For example, a typical rewrite rule could be:

```
incident(rod₁, rod₂)=TRUE
          ⟵   fail_unless unary_constraint(rod₁)=TRUE;
              rod₁.rotate(rod₂)
```

where unary_constraint needs further rewriting and $rod_1$.rotate($rod_2$) rotates $rod_1$ to be incident with $rod_2$. The number of constraints is now $q$. The time complexity $\mathcal{O}(e^3)$ thus becomes $\mathcal{O}(q^3)$.

In CP-3 there is only a single variable, the linkage structure. A typical method of this object is to rotate one part of the linkage around a hinge vertex, leaving the other part fixed. The object is responsible for maintaining internal constraints on those points that have a value. As in CP-1, the number of constraints is $m$, resulting in $\mathcal{O}(m^3)$ time complexity.

Equate need not always find a solution. Checking the read and write sets can be overly restrictive and may abort valid solutions. Another reason is that run time checks may fail. In CP-1 for example, in order to satisfy the distance constraint, Equate moves a point to only one of the possible solutions. This assignment satisfies the current constraint, but it is possible that it obstructs other variables to satisfy their constraints. Equate then succeeds in producing a solution program, but if the application executes the program, it fails, i.e. one of the fail_unless statements evaluates to false and the program aborts.

## 10 Discussion

Below, an overview is given of the complexities we have discussed for the different constraint solving techniques. We discriminate between the alternation and the refinement model of solving, and between discrete and continuous domains. As usual, $a$ is the size of a discrete domain, $b$ is the number of variables, $e$ the number of constraints. $R$ is the time needed to solve a single constraint, and $\lambda$ the number of loops or iterations made by the algorithms:

|            | discrete |         | continuous   |            |
| ---------- | -------- | ------- | ------------ | ---------- |
|            | alt      | ref     | alt          | ref        |
| BT         | $ea^b$   |         |              |            |
| NC         |          | $ae$    |              | $Re$       |
| AC-3       |          | $a^3e$  |              | $\lambda Re$ |
| LP         | $\lambda ae$ | $a^3e$ | $\lambda Re$ | $\lambda Re$ |
| RX         |          |         | $\lambda be$ |            |
| Equate/OOCS | $e^3$   |         | $e^3$        |            |

Naturally, all complexities are at least linear in the number of constraints $e$. It is immediately clear why local propagation LP is such a widely used constraint solving method. It is applicable in a wide variety of applications and linear in the number of constraints, if $R$ is independent of $e$. Note however that LP need not always find a solution, which is why it is often preceded by a planning stage.

We have seen in the examples CP-1, CP-2, and CP-3 that the way an application is modelled can largely influence the time complexity of constraint satisfaction. Particularly the number of constraints and the size of domains can vary. By encapsulating more variables into objects (like the vertices in the rods), constraints may move into the objects (like the fixed distances of the rods). On the other hand, new constraints may be needed to describe the relations among the objects (like the incidence constraints between the rods). Furthermore, if the domains of the object variables are discrete, the complexity of the solving algorithm is increased when the domains are enlarged.

## 11 Conclusions

In the alternation model of satisfaction, many algorithms do hard solution assignments to the objects (possibly in combination with domain refinement). E.g., the backtracking algorithm BT by means of v.assign(s), and the arc consistency algorithm AC-3 through c.revise(). The complexities above are valid on the assumption that the objects accept the assignment. However, to maintain any form of information hiding, the assignment should be done through message passing, encapsulating the internal implementation of the objects (as Equate and OOCS do).

Equate and OOCS obey information hiding to some extend: neither the constraints nor the procedural solutions refer directly to an object's implementation. Actually, neither the solver nor the object determines a solution alone. The objects offer possible local solutions, and the solver tries to combine them into a global solution. However, a global solution need not be found, and the complexity is cubic in the number of constraints, which limits the use to small scale applications. Note that in the end the use of read-sets and write-sets in Equate and OOCS, which contain implementation specific knowledge of an object, infringes the concept of information hiding after all. In [10] is put forward that encapsulation is maintained from the application programmer's perspective. The read-sets and write-sets are only available to the constraint solver, thus keeping the benefits of object-oriented programming for the programmer.

If an object has to maintain internal relationships and refuses an assignment, then either the constraints are not satisfied, or the solver has to negotiate with the objects to accept values. In the latter case the time complexity typically becomes exponential in $a$, or worse for continuous domains. Obviously, to avoid a situation that an object can refuse a solution via a message, the methods should be designed so as to obey the internal relationships, or the solver must take into account these relationships. In the first case the satisfaction power of the solver may be limited, in the second case the information hiding principle is broken. Encapsulating the objects and completely hiding them from the constraint solver prevents the solver from doing any global solution. In the case of multiple constraints, this prevents the solver from doing any work at all.

This leads to the following theorem:

**Principal Theorem** Under strict information hiding, constraint satisfaction on objects cannot be guaranteed.

The relaxation algorithms were formulated such that the objects themselves determine a value. However, this also gives them the freedom not to satisfy constraints, which destroys the compelling and declarative nature of constraints. So indeed, under strict information hiding, constraint satisfaction is not guaranteed.

For the refinement model of satisfaction similar problems hold. One may model the domain as a separate object, but conceptually it is the exclusive property of the variable, and in fact a part of it. In that sense, changing the domain of a variable is equivalent to assigning a value.

If the constraint system is part of a programming language, the infringement of information hiding is under control of the constraint solver. From the application programmer's point of view the data encapsulation is still preserved. Indeed, as pointed out by [7], requiring the language's internal constraint system to respect information hiding is similar to requiring an optimizing compiler to respect information hiding, which would make part of its task impossible.

If one is to sacrifice strict information hiding in order to facilitate constraint satisfaction, care should be taken not to allow abuse. In [22] we propose a radical separation of the constraint system and the normal object-oriented framework by means of two orthogonal communication strategies for objects: messages on the one hand, and events and data-flow on the other hand. In this way, the process of constraint management via data-flow networks does not interfere with the communication of the object-oriented world via messages. Because of the global and compelling nature of constraints, this strict separation facilitates the design and debugging of constraints and the constraint system.

## Acknowledgement

The authors are supported by NWO (Dutch Organization for Scientific Research) under Grants SION-612-31-001 and SION-612-322-212, respectively.

## References

[1] Sara Baase. *Computer Algorithms: Introduction to Design and Analysis.* Addison-Wesley, 1978.

[2] Grady Booch. *Object-Oriented Analysis and Design – with applications.* The Benjamin/Cummings Publishing, 1994.

[3] C. Choppy, S. Kaplan, and M. Soria. Complexity analysis of term-rewriting systems. *Theoretical Computer Science*, 67(2/3):261 – 282, 1989.

[4] Eric Cournarie and Michel Beaudouin-Lafon. Alien: a prototype-based constraint system. In Laffra et al. [11], pages 92–110.

[5] Jacques Davy. Go, a graphical and interactive C++ toolkit for application data presentation and editing. In *Proceedings 5th Annual Technical Conference on the X Window System*, 1991.

[6] R. Dechter and J. Pearl. Network-based heuristics for constraint satisfaction problems. *AI*, 34:1–38, 1988.

[7] Bjorn N. Freeman-Benson and Alan Borning. Integrating constraints with an object-oriented language. In O. Lehrmann Madsen, editor, *Proceedings ECOOP'92*, LNCS 615, pages 268–286. Springer-Verlag, 1992.

[8] Eugene C. Freuder. A sufficient condition for backtrack-free search. *Journal of the ACM*, 29(1):24–32, January 1982.

[9] Hans-Werner Güsgen and Joachim Hertzberg. Some fundamental properties of local constraint propagation. *AI*, 36:237–247, 1988.

[10] Quinton Hoole and Edwin Blake. OOCS - constraints in an object oriented environment. In [24], pages 215–230, 1994.

[11] C. Laffra, E. H. Blake, V. de Mey, and X. Pintado, editors. *Object Oriented Programming for Graphics*, Focus on Computer Graphics. Springer, 1995.

[12] Chris Laffra and Jan van den Bos. Propagators and concurrent constraints. *OOPS Messenger*, 2(2):68–72, April 1991.

[13] Wm. Leler. *Constraint Programming Languages.* Addison-Wesley, 1988.

[14] Richard J. Lipton. Dna solution of hard computational problems. *Science*, 268:542–545, April 1995.

[15] A. K. Mackworth. Consistency in networks of relations. *AI*, 8:99–118, 1977.

[16] A. K. Mackworth and E. Freuder. The complexity of some polynomial network consistency algorithms for constraint satisfaction problems. *AI*, 25:65–74, 1985.

[17] R. Mohr and T. C. Henderson. Arc and path consistency revisited. *AI*, 28:225–233, 1986.

[18] John R. Rankin. A graphics object oriented constraint solver. In Laffra et al. [11], pages 71–91.

[19] Michael Sannella. *Constraint Satisfaction and Debugging for Interactive User Interfaces.* PhD thesis, University of Washington, Seattle, Washington, 1994.

[20] Ivan E. Sutherland. Sketchpad: A man-machine graphical communication system. In *Proceedings of the Spring Joint Computer Conference, Detroit, Michigan, May 21-23 1963,* pages 329–345. AFIPS Press, 1963.

[21] Edward Tsang. *Foundations of Constraint Satisfaction.* Academic Press, 1993.

[22] Remco C. Veltkamp and Edwin H. Blake. Event-based.constraints: coordinate.satisfaction –> object.solution. In [24], pages 251–262, 1994.

[23] Michael Wilk. Equate: an object-oriented constraint solver. In *Proceedings OOPSLA'91,* pages 286–298, 1991.

[24] P. Wisskirchen, editor. *Proceedings 4th Eurographics Workshop on Object-Oriented Graphics, Sintra, Portugal, May 1994.*

# Part III: Functional

# Constructive Solid Geometry using Algorithmic Skeletons

John R. Davy, Hossain Deldari and Peter M. Dew

School of Computer Studies
University of Leeds
West Yorkshire, LS2 9JT, UK
E-mail: {davyjr,hd,dew}@scs.leeds.ac.uk

**Abstract** This paper presents a study in the use of parallel algorithmic skeletons to program applications of constructive solid geometry (CSG). The approach is motivated by the frequent use of divide-and-conquer (D&C) methods in this domain, which are amenable to highly parallel implementation. A prototype *Geometric Evaluation Library* (GEL) is presented, with a small set of polymorphic higher-order functions, which capture the fundamental algorithmic structures independently of the underlying geometric domain. An efficient parallel implementation of one of these functions is described. The paper concludes with a discussion of the potential of the algorithmic skeleton paradigm.

## 1 Introduction

Solid modelling is a computationally-intensive technique which can benefit from the exploitation of parallelism. Parallel processing brings substantial performance benefits but creates new programming challenges. Besides writing the code which defines the fundamental computational activity of the applications, the programmer must also consider issues such as decomposition into parallel processes, balancing the load between these processes, communicating between them, and synchronizing their operations. These latter activities, some of which more properly belong to the system level, may occupy a large part of both development time and final code. Moreover, many parallel solutions are heavily dependent on the target machine, so that it has often been difficult to exploit the benefits of previous parallelization when moving to a new platform.

This paper discusses the potential for developing parallel programs for *constructive solid geometry* (CSG) in a way which avoids these problems. Specifically we carry out a case study in the use of *algorithmic skeletons*, enabling applications to be defined in terms of a small number of well-defined constructs which can be mapped onto known parallel implementations. Program development then emphasizes appropriate selection and customization of existing algorithmic components described at a high level of abstraction, leading naturally to faster development times and machine-independent solutions. A similar approach has already been used for special-purpose languages in the domain of image processing [20, 21] and numerical solution of differential equations by multigrid methods [18].

For this paradigm to be successful, two conditions must be satisfied:

- there must be s irable set of skeletons which are adequate to define applications in the domain in question;

- these skeletons must be capable of efficient parallel implementation.

The initial stage of the study addressed the first issue. A prototype *Geometric Evaluation Library* (GEL) was developed in a functional language, to investigate the potential for developing CSG applications by means of a small number of *higher order functions* specific to this application domain. The second stage, still in progress, has begun the process of developing parallel algorithmic skeletons for the key operations in GEL.

A previous paper [7] reported in detail on the development of GEL as an exercise in functional programming. This paper gives a broader view of the algorithmic skeleton paradigm; we briefly summarize GEL, report on progress towards parallelizing CSG skeletons, and evaluate the potential of the paradigm in this field.

## 2 Algorithmic Skeletons

There has recently been considerable interest in the parallel programming world in the use of *algorithmic skeletons* [4, 5, 8]. These are generic patterns of parallel computation which can be parameterized by a small number of sequential functions or procedures (called here *customizing functions*). A complete parallel program can be generated by inserting the customizing functions into a template with an efficient parallel implementation for the generic solution. Thus machine-independent parallel programs can be developed in which all the implementation issues of parallelism are hidden from the programmer.

There is an obvious analogy between skeletons and higher-order functions; indeed much of the existing research in algorithmic skeletons has taken place in the context of higher-order functional languages. This has the benefit that program transformations may be used to derive more efficient implementations. Skeletons can, however, be used within more conventional language paradigms.

Most existing work on skeletons has studied general algorithmic forms, such as pipelines and divide-and-conquer. By contrast, *application-specific languages* exploit skeleton-based computation in a particular application domain. For instance, Apply [20] is a procedurally-based language which capture various aspects of image processing. Here knowledge of the application domain, particularly the underlying data types, enables efficient parallel implementations to be generated from partial sequential descriptions.

In the following section we present initial evidence that CSG computations are also amenable to a skeleton-based application-specific approach. The rest of this paper supports this view, firstly by showing constructs to describe CSG applications in terms of a small number of higher order operations, and secondly through an efficient parallel implementation of one of these key constructs.

# 3 Constructive Solid Geometry (CSG)

Solid modelling systems manipulate descriptions of three-dimensional objects. The distinguishing feature of solid models is *completeness*: a description of a solid contains sufficient information to compute any geometric property of that solid.

Several schemes have been devised for complete representations of solids [17]. One of the most used is CSG, in which solids are represented by a set of *primitive solids* combined using *regularized boolean operations* such as union, intersection and difference. It is common for a small set of *bounded primitives*, such as spheres and cones, to be available to the users of CSG systems. Internally they are often represented as a combination of simpler unbounded primitives called *halfspaces*. These are defined by functions of the form $f(x, y, z) \leq 0$ which partition space into two halves, inside and outside the primitive.

CSG represents a solid as a tree structure with primitives at the leaves and boolean operators at interior nodes. This leads naturally to recursive *divide-and-conquer* (D&C) algorithms, which compute results for primitives, then combine the results using the boolean operators when returning up the tree. Tilove identified this as a generic paradigm for CSG, applying it to *set membership classification* problems [19]. An example used later in this paper is point membership classification (PMC), which determines whether a point is inside, outside or on the boundary of a solid. Classifications are carried out on primitives and results from subtrees are determined using simple rewrite rules: for instance if a point is 'in' two solids it is 'in' their intersection.

## 3.1 Spatial Subdivision

It is common to convert CSG trees into secondary data structures based on *octrees* [15], using a process of *spatial subdivision*. Here the (usually cubical) space containing the solid object is recursively partitioned into eight quasi-disjoint subcells. Associated with each terminal subcell is a localized CSG tree containing only the primitives which intersect the subcell. The depth of subdivision is controlled by the local complexity of the model. For instance, subdivision may stop when the number of primitives in a localized tree falls below some threshold.

The benefits of spatial subdivision are exemplified in ray-tracing [10]. Crude CSG ray-tracing is very expensive, intersecting every ray with every primitive. When ray-tracing a spatially divided model, each ray is tracked through the octree and intersects only the primitives of the localized trees encountered, giving substantial performance improvements.

There are also many algorithms which use spatial subdivision but without explicitly creating a tree: the family of algorithms for computing integral properties of solids [14] is a good example.

Many spatial subdivision algorithms follow a D&C approach. Thus CSG computations lead to D&C algorithms both because of the primary data structure and because of frequently used spatial subdivision techniques. It is these algorithmic structures which we seek to capture and exploit in a generic fashion as skeletons. They are naturally highly parallel, since subtrees can be processed independently, but managing the tree structures causes substantial practical problems for parallelization.

### 3.2 Potential Parallelism

The high computational requirements of solid modelling indicate the desirability of parallel processing. Earlier work explored this through the Mistral series of experimental parallel CSG systems [9, 10]. The most recent of these, Mistral-3, achieved over 80% efficiency for ray-tracing a spatially divided CSG model on 128 T800 transputers, including creating the spatially divided model in parallel [10]. Parallelism was obtained almost entirely by exploiting the D&C paradigm. Since the tree structures were typically highly unbalanced and developed dynamically, distributed dynamic load balancing techniques were required to gain this scalable performance.

These results demonstrate that excellent parallel performance is possible for CSG by exploiting the underlying data structures through D&C processing. The price paid, however, is the complexity of the software; most of the code (and effort) of Mistral-3 provided system-level infrastructure for parallelism, particularly dynamic load balancing and the movement of complex data structures. Arguably these should not be the responsibility of an application programmer; this motivates the desirability of a higher-level approach to free the programmer from these concerns. The recurring use of D&C algorithms provides a promising approach for investigation.

# 4 GEL: a prototype library

GEL (Geometric Evaluation Library) is a prototype library of higher order functions designed to study the systematic use of D&C operations for CSG and spatial subdivision. It has been used to explore the hypothesis that a realistic range of algorithms could be developed using such a restricted set of operations. A pure functional language, Hope+, was chosen to prototype GEL, since functional languages provide a natural means to define higher order functions.

Here we briefly outline the main features of GEL; a more comprehensive discussion can be found in [7]. Readers familiar with other higher-order functional languages should find no difficulty with the notations of Hope+.

### 4.1 Principles of GEL

The current version of GEL is based on the following principles:

- The main data structures are trees parameterized by an arbitrary geometric type, enabling the same operations to be carried out in different geometric domains.

- The primary skeletons are D&C operations on these data structures, which are all specialized variants of a general D&C operation *divacon* invoked as

```
divacon(data, leaf, divide, solve, combine);
```

with four customizing functions: *leaf* determines whether a problem is small enough to solve directly, *divide* splits a problem into a list of subproblems, *solve* computes the direct solution of a 'small' problem, *combine* combines the results of a list of subproblems.

- Variant forms of the primary skeletons are provided as a set of overloaded functions, disambiguated by the number and types of the parameters.

## 4.2 CSG Trees

CSG trees are binary trees with instances of primitive solids at the leaves and instances of boolean operators at interior nodes. Since CSG is a set-theoretic representation, there should be a means of denoting the empty set ($\emptyset$) and the universal set ($\Omega$) in a CSG system. These considerations lead to the following algebraic type definition, parameterized by *rho* and *chi*, the types for primitives and operators respectively:

```
data CSG(rho, chi) == Emptysolid ++ Fullsolid ++ Primitiv
(rho) ++ Compose (CSG(rho, chi) # chi # CSG(rho, chi));
```

Note that *chi* is an enumeration of the specific set of operators used, such as {*Intersection, Union, Difference*} or {*Union, Difference*}. Its inclusion as a parameter, rather than as a fixed enumeration, is motivated by the observation that CSG systems vary in both the number and specific kinds of boolean operations allowed. The actual implementation of these operations is carried out by combining functions.

The primary higher-order operation on CSG trees is an *evaluation* of the tree. This is a D&C traversal, suitable for the family of set membership classification problems noted in section 3. A typical invocation, to classify a point against a solid, is

```
CSGtraverse(point, tree, solve, combine);
```

where *solve* classifies a point against a primitive, and *combine* implements the boolean operations to combine classifications.

Note that a binary CSG tree may include $\Omega$ nodes (to model complementation as $\overline{P} = \Omega - P$), and trees with $\emptyset$ primitives may exist as intermediate steps. Also, there are situations in which there is no external 'query' data like the *point* above – a trivial example is an algorithm to count the number of primitives in a tree. These variants are implemented by overloading.

GEL also provides higher-order operations to input or output CSG trees. The customizing functions for *CSGget* require the programmer to specify how primitives and operators should be read from an input stream (lazy list of characters); *CSGput* uses corresponding customizing functions. For instance, to input a CSG tree and classify it against a point

```
let (tree, _) == CSGget(instream, get_hs, get_op) in
CSGtraverse(pt, tree, class, combine);
```

where *get_hs*, *get_op* are the customizing functions to input primitives and operators respectively. Only two higher-order functions and four (relatively straightforward) customizing functions have been needed, emphasizing the simplicity of the approach.

### 4.3 Geometric Decomposition Trees

Secondary solid representations based on octree-based spatial subdivision are general-ized to a *Geometric Decomposition Tree* (GDT). Noting that the interior nodes of the octree hold no geometric information, we parameterize GDTs by the type of geometric objects stored at the leaves, $\tau$.

```
data GDT(tau) == Terminal (tau) ++ Interior (list (GDT(tau)));
```

Two fundamental operations are needed for GDTs. *GDTcreate* builds a GDT from the primary solid representation. *GDTtraverse* is a D&C traversal of an existing GDT, analogous to *CSGtraverse*. For instance a GDT can be derived from a CSG tree by invoking

```
GDTcreate((cll,tr), leaf, divide, solve, 7);
```

where *leaf(cll, tr)* returns true if the number of primitives in *tr* is less than some threshold, and *divide(cll, tr)* creates eight subcells of *cll*, and prunes *tr* to each subcell. Pruning involves a further D&C operation, easily implemented using *CSGtraverse*. *Solve* is the identity if pruned trees are stored unchanged at terminal nodes, but might otherwise involve some transformation of the terminal geometry. The optional final parameter, again implemented by overloading, allows, a maximum subdivision depth to be specified.

An example of the use of *GDTtraverse* is the family of recursive integral property algorithms described in [14]. For instance, computing the mass of a solid represented in octree form invokes

```
GDTtraverse(gdt, solve, combine);
```

where *solve* computes the mass of a solid at a leaf of the octree and *combine* simply adds the result of subtrees. As with *CSGtraverse*, there is an optional parameter for an external object; for instance the moment of inertia of a solid about a point *pt* is computed by

```
GDTtraverse(gdt, pt, solve, combine);
```

where *solve* now computes the moment of inertia of the terminal tree about *pt*.

Like CSG trees, GDTs can be input or output by a single higher-order functions.

### 4.4 Using *divacon* directly

The original description of integral property algorithms in [14] does not explicitly create an octree but evaluates the result 'on-the-fly' as each branch of the subdivision terminates. This cannot directly be captured by the GDT operations, but can easily be described by a general *divacon* operation, which effectively combines the customizing functions from *GDTcreate* and *GDTtraverse*. Thus *divacon* acts as a 'safety net', catching D&C operations which do fall within the more specialized forms. In fact, all the CSG and GDT operations described above can be derived formally from *divacon* using 'fold-unfold' transformations.

Using *divacon* directly might have a performance benefit when only a single traversal of the GDT is required. Experiments with GEL, however, suggest that if the traversal is to be repeated only once more it is advantageous to create the GDT explicitly [7]. Where the GDT is re-used many times, as in ray-tracing, the performance benefits are very large.

## 4.5 Geometric extensibility

The key CSG and GDT operations intentionally do not depend on a specific geometric domain; in this sense GEL is 'geometry-independent'. Parameterization by an arbitrary geometric type allows the same algorithmic structures to be used in different domains. Indeed the main elements of GEL contain no geometric routines, other than support for basic entities such as points and vectors. This high level of polymorphism appears to be a significant strength of GEL. Domain-specific parts of geometric computations are isolated in type definitions and customizing functions. Since these aspects of computational geometry are well-known for difficulties with floating point accuracy, this isolation helps to localize such problems. In principle, it should be possible to import code from other geometric libraries, taking advantage of the extensive efforts on this area.

The first task for a user of GEL is therefore to customize it for the application's requirements by defining a suitable geometric domain. For instance, a collection of three-dimensional primitives can be defined by:

```
type SP_HS == real # POINT3; ! radius # centre type PL_HS == real #
VECTOR3; ! dist. from O # normal to plane ! similarly for CY_HS, CO_HS

data HS == sphere(SP_HS) ++ plane(PL_HS) ++ cyl(CY_HS) ++ cone(CO_HS);
data ROP == Union ++ Inter ++ Diff;

type SOLID == CSG(HS, ROP); ! using generic CSG type
```

Basic operations on these primitives, including I/O and classification, can then be written using a systematic pattern-matching approach.

Adding an additional primitive to an existing domain is also straightforward; an extra constructor is needed in the relevant type definition with a corresponding extra equation to match that constructor in each customizing function. Thus adding new geometry can be done in a simple, organized fashion. Effectively, GEL provides syntactic support for extensibility, with a flexible framework for developing geometric applications in different domains.

# 5 Parallel CSG

A parallel version of GEL would need to provide skeleton implementations of the main higher-order functions which can be parallelized through their D&C structure. In this section we consider the parallelization of *CSGtraverse*, using the earlier example of PMC as a case study. The next section shows how this may be extended to a generic skeleton.

An obstacle to parallelizing CSG traversals is the unpredictable and (usually) unbalanced structure of the tree. In Mistral-3 [10] CSG trees are stored in pointer-less postfix form, enabling easier migration between nodes than pointer-based versions. Terminal nodes include indices into an array of primitives. Parallel CSG operations are carried out by 'farming'; the array is partitioned into packages, these are sent on request to other processors for classification, and the results are returned. When all the primitives have been classified the results are combined sequentially using a conventional stack-based algorithm.

The main drawback of this method is that it is not possible to parallelize the combining stage. An alternative approach, described in [2], is based on the principle of *tree contraction*. Here the tree is stored in infix form in a global shared array with a separate array of primitives, stored in the natural left-to-right order. The array can be partitioned among the cooperating processes, all processes receiving approximately equal numbers of contiguous primitives. In parallel, all processes classify their segment of primitives. Then the tree is contracted from the bottom upwards, combining the classifications each time an operator is reached.

A problem arises when an operator is reached via one of its descendants (the left say,) while the other subtree is still not fully evaluated. This will lead to a delay while the other subtree is evaluated, and possible load imbalances.

There is an elegant solution to this problem, based on the *shunt* operation [2], provided the operators are limited to union and intersection. The same approach may be used for expression evaluation over any semi-ring which has $*$ and $+$ operators with identities [11].

Each node $N$ of the tree is labelled with a pair $(a_n, b_n)$, initialized to the identities for $*$ (intersection) and $+$ (union). For PMC these are IN and OUT respectively. Consider the situation when a node $U$ is an evaluated left subtree (with value $u$), of a node $F_u$ (with operator $Op$), and the sibling $S_u$ of $U$ is the root of an unevaluated right subtree $T_2$. Let the parent of $F_u$ be $G_u$, and assume that the other subtree $T_1$ of $G_u$ is unevaluated. This situation is shown in figure 1.

The shunt operation allows $F_u$ to be replaced by $S_u$ with a new label $(a_{s'}, b_{s'})$ given by

$$Op = * \qquad \left[ \begin{array}{l} a_{s'} = a_f * (a_u * u + b_u) * a_s \\ b_{s'} = a_f * ((a_u * u + b_u) * b_s) + b_f \end{array} \right.$$

$$Op = + \qquad \left[ \begin{array}{l} a_{s'} = a_f * a_s \\ b_{s'} = a_f * ((a_u * u + b_u) + b_s) + b_f \end{array} \right.$$

Thus each operator can be evaluated as it is reached, even if one subtree is not yet evaluated. Hence, effects of tree imbalance are eliminated and a naturally load-balanced algorithm is achieved. Fuller details can be found in [2] and the second author's forthcoming PhD thesis.

A parallel PMC program using this tree contraction technique was implemented in C. The target system was the WPRAM [16], a general-purpose scalable shared memory computational model developed at the University of Leeds. Currently the WPRAM exists only as a simulator, though an implementation using Inmos T9000 transputers is under way. The simulator includes a detailed performance model, parameterized

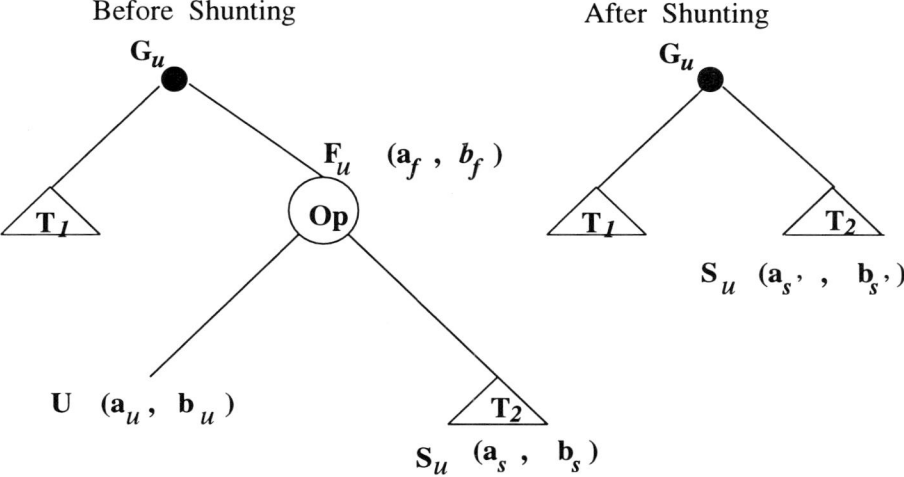

Fig. 1: The *Shunt* operation

by the characteristics of potential hardware components. Simulated execution times were obtained for up to 64 processors, based on parameters for Inmos T9000 and C104 components. Figure 2 shows the speedups obtained for trees with 1000 and 5000 primitives. These results are very positive in showing the potential performance gain from parallelizing CSG, with over 50% efficiency on 64 processors for both trees. They also compare very favourably with the results reported in [2] for a parallel implementation of line membership classification on a BBN Butterfly, where the best reported speedup was 6.9 on 16 processors for a tree with 1001 primitives.

## 6 A Parallel Skeleton

Transition to a general skeleton for D&C traversal of CSG trees is straightforward. The parallel algorithm for PMC is the same as was used in [2] for line membership classification. Thus the existing code provides a template into which customizing functions for *solve* and *combine* could be inserted. A higher order function could then be mapped onto this code template.

Moving to a parallel skeleton, however, would bring some differences from GEL.

- Since tree contraction with *shunt* depends on the semi-ring structure of the underlying domain, boolean operators would be confined to union and intersection. Thus it would be less general than the corresponding GEL operation, being restricted to positive forms of CSG tree.

- Since there are only two standard boolean operators it is simpler to have customizing functions for each of these, replacing the single *combine* function by *union* and *intersection* operators. Generic CSG trees need not be parameterized by an operator type.

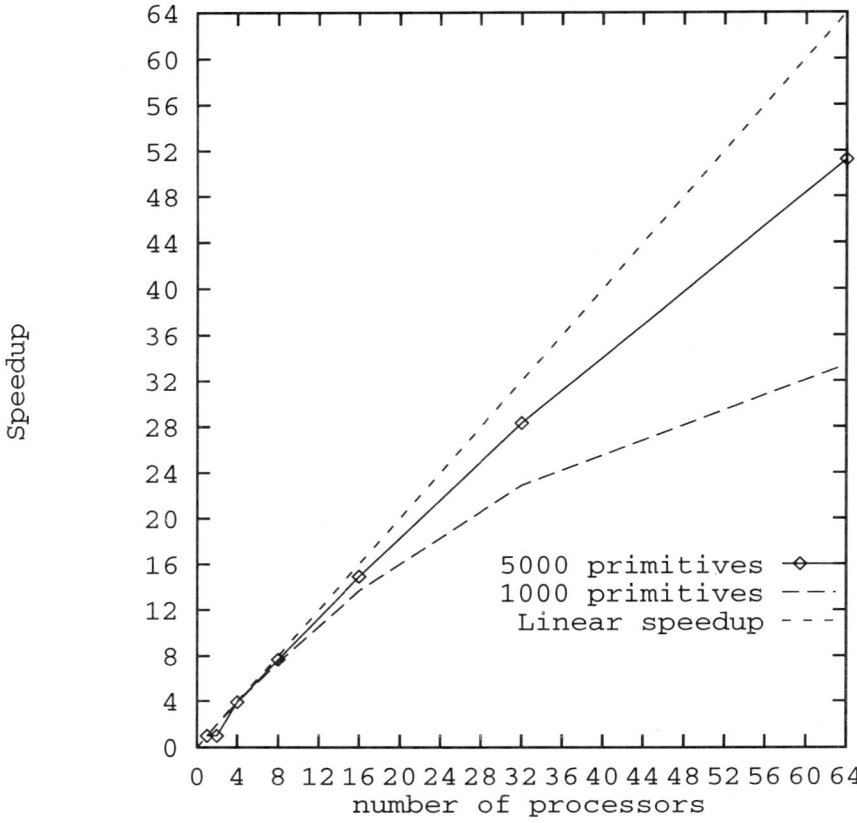

Fig. 2: Speedup of parallel PMC

- The tree contraction algorithm requires the identities for the values to be combined under the intersection and union operations. These depend on the particular task being performed, hence must be specified by the programmer when calling the higher-order function. Thus the interface might be modified to

```
CSGtraverse(query, tree, solve, intersect, union, I_intersect,
I_union);
```

## 7 Discussion

Though not yet complete, the current study provides enough evidence to begin to assess the potential for algorithmic skeletons in this domain. We shall consider the extent to which GEL is applicable within solid modelling and in a wider context, the practicality of programming with skeletons, the merits of a functional base language, and prospects for parallelization.

## 7.1 Applicability of GEL within solid modelling

GEL's initial scope was rather limited: D&C operations in CSG. Thus it does not currently provide the full functionality of solid modelling; amongst other omissions, alternative solid representations are not currently covered, including the important *boundary representation (B-rep)*.

The potential scope of GEL is, however, much wider than appears at first sight. The parameterization of the CSG type can capture the wide range of current or proposed CSG systems, which vary in both the formal properties of primitives, and in the specific sets of available primitives, as well as in the set of boolean operators used. CSG traversals directly model the important family of Set Membership Classification algorithms identified by Tilove [19]; they provide a utility operation which is of wide applicability in CSG modelling.

GDT operations directly model spatial subdivision. This widely used technique has also been used on other solid representations than CSG, including B-reps, polyhedral models and sweeps. Typically, trees are generated in which terminal nodes contain an exact or approximate representation of the model localized to the relevant subspace. Variants of this type have been called *octrees* (with the equivalent *quadtrees* in two dimensions), *polytrees* and *extended octrees*. A similar *bintree* structure has been proposed with a binary subdivision at each stage, cycling between the dimensions. All these structures can be modelled by the GDT type.

In addition to applications previously noted, spatial subdivision techniques have been used for wire-frame edge evaluation, NC program verification, collision detection, finite element mesh generation and boolean operations in polyhedral modellers. In view of this broad applicability, spatial subdivision can be seen as a fundamental approach to solid modelling applications.

On the other hand, the limitation to D&C means that not all possible algorithms on the types provided are currently included in GEL; for instance, ray-casting involves following a single path through an octree, which is not a D&C operation[1]. Such algorithms can of course be programmed directly using the constructors of the types concerned. Similarly, operations between two tree structures (for instance addition and subtraction of octrees) cannot currently be directly described in GEL. Further work is needed to determine whether these and other computations could usefully be captured as higher-order functions.

D&C methods are also widely applicable in other areas of computational geometry. Striptrees and similar multi-resolution structures are already covered by an extension of the GDT type [7]. Other examples include the construction of Voronoi diagrams and Delaunay triangulation, and the determination of convex hulls. While these cannot be expressed using the specialized CSG and GDT operations, they can, in principle, be solved using the general *divacon* function.

---

[1] Recall, however, that the motivation behind GEL was to exploit parallelism through recurring algorithmic patterns, which explains the emphasis on D&C. By contrast, the single-path traversal noted above appears inherently sequential.

It thus appears that the generic nature of D&C, and of geometric decomposition trees in particular, makes GEL applicable far beyond its initial aims.

## 7.2 A Complete Programming Paradigm?

It is clear that GEL does not cover the complete functionality required by applications making use of solid modelling. For instance, there is no support for the analysis or display of solid models. Hence GEL cannot be viewed as a general-purpose programming paradigm, even within the field of solid modelling.

Again, however, there is much scope for development beyond current limitations. Programming with skeletons is not restricted to a particular application domain. Skeletons remain an active research area, and many researchers are aiming to demonstrate an effective general-purpose paradigm. A number of general-purpose skeletons have been implemented, such as pipelines and farms. The *divacon* operation in GEL shows that such skeletons can be used alongside more specific operations, with the same potential to exploit parallelism. Thus the use of skeletons is not inherently limited to a narrow class of applications.

Arguably, however, application-specific skeletons have proved the most effective to date. They simplify programming through the use of specialized data types and may use detailed knowledge of the application to enable subtle optimizations within a compiler which application programmers may not realistically have the time to implement. This is demonstrated in the image processing language Apply, where programs generated from skeleton-like specifications often outperform hand-coded programs. Interestingly, recent work [13] has considered (parallel) skeletons for image display, suggesting that skeletons may have broader applicability within graphics.

## 7.3 Programming with skeletons

Programming with skeletons proved to have both benefits and drawbacks. There is a helpful discipline to facilitate program development, code is concise, and the low-level, error-prone geometric computations are isolated in a few customizing functions. On the other hand, the limited set of operations may lead to more imaginative and appropriate solutions being missed, or incur inefficiencies such as repeating computations in *leaf* and *solve* functions [7]. Moreover, 'short-cut' solutions, such as 'early-outs' may not fit into the higher order function framework; Tilove's work on generic CSG algorithms also pointed to this conflict between generality and efficiency [19]. Adding extra CSG and GDT operations for special cases may partly resolve this, but would conflict th the simplicity of using a small set of generic operations, without guaranteeing that no more special cases will occur. Of course it is still possible to code such special cases directly in Hope+ or any other base language used.

## 7.4 Appropriate base language for skeletons

Reasons for using a functional base language for GEL were noted in section 4. Skeletons are not, however, restricted to this paradigm, and the merits of functional programming in this context should therefore be assessed.

The arguments for and against functional programming have frequently been re-hearsed, and our experiences largely confirm established wisdom. Polymorphic types match the requirement to provide different geometric domains within the same generic structure. Higher-order functions successfully capture the computational structures initially identified and isolated low-level geometric details in customizing functions. In these respects functional languages show an excellent match to the nature of the problem.

On the other hand, multilinked structures are perceived as being much harder to de-scribe in functional languages [3]. This would become significant if GEL were extended to include B-reps, which require complex graph structures. Related difficulties were observed with the current version of GEL; for instance, we were unable to implement a *father-of* function to move back up a tree, precluding some of the efficient octree and quadtree traversal algorithms in the literature.

By reputation, functional languages are less efficient in runtime performance than imperative languages. We were therefore pleasantly surprised to find that GEL programs often outperformed the corresponding recursive C versions, a result of the efficient heap management techniques employed by Hope+, which aid fast tree construction. We have no evidence to suggest that Hope+ will generally outperform C over a wide spectrum of applications.

A second positive performance result was that the overheads of using higher-order functions (compared with a directly recursive Hope+ version) were mostly low, suggesting that the higher level of abstraction provided by GEL was obtained without undue performance penalty. This is important evidence supporting the use of skeletons.

On the other hand, we found several very unpredictable aspects of Hope+ performance, making optimization problematic. Details can be found in [7]. We have no specific evidence that such problems would occur with other functional languages, but our experience supports the view that performance prediction for functional programs is less tractable than with imperative languages.

## 7.5 Parallelism and GEL

While preliminary results for parallelizing CSG trees are positive, much work remains to be done. More experiments are needed to understand the implications of tree shape on the performance of parallel CSG. We also intend to port our code to a true parallel multiprocessor, to confirm the performance gains and assess whether speedup is significantly affected by the particular parallel platform.

Further development of this work will require parallel GDT skeletons. Unlike CSG trees, the tree structures will be developed dynamically at runtime, so dynamic load balancing will be needed to ensure efficient implementation.

We surmise that parallelizing the GDT operation should bring greater benefits than parallelizing CSG, for two reasons. First, it is more general, since it allows other solid representations to be parallelized, notably B-reps [12]. Second it provides a coarser grain of parallelism and therefore greater performance gain; in Mistral-3 most speedup was obtained from the (outer loop) octree computations, with smaller gains from parallelizing the (inner loop) CSG computation.

Probably the biggest challenge faced by parallel algorithmic skeletons is the effect of composition. Sequential composition occurs, for instance, when a *GDTcreate* skeleton is followed by *GDTtraverse*. Nesting occurs during octree creation, when a customizing function for *GDTcreate* invokes *CSGtraverse*.

In a sequential system such as GEL, such composition causes no practical problems, but composition of independent parallel skeleton implementations faces some difficulties. In particular, 'stand-alone' implementations of skeletons invoked in sequence might not be easily compatible. For instance, the data distribution at the end of one skeleton may not match that required by a subsequent skeleton. Also, an implementation of a skeleton which presupposes sole use of the machine may not be applicable if the skeleton is nested within another partially executed skeleton, particularly if multiple instances of the nested skeleton are invoked in parallel.

To develop a complete parallel application-specific language in this field will require a suitable framework to combine skeletons. Possible approaches can be found in [1] and [6]. The former allows nested and sequential compositions of a small set of general-purpose skeletons, using C++-based syntax. In the latter a high-level declarative framework is used to write programs composed of skeletons defined in standard languages such as Fortran. This appears to combine the conceptual clarity and desirable formal properties of functional languages with the more pragmatic benefits of procedural languages. For GEL it seems particularly desirable to retain the polymorphism which enables varying geometric domains to be handled within the same algorithmic framework.

# 8 Conclusions

The case study has shown several clear benefits of programming CSG (and other) applications using algorithmic skeletons. Though there still remain a number of areas to explore, we have not yet found any decisive counter-evidence of the feasibility of the paradigm in the sequential world.

Skeleton programming may be used with either sequential or parallel computers. It seems, however, that the advantages will be greater in the latter case. There is far more low-level complexity to hide from the programmer, and the potential for saving development time is much greater. Minor inefficiencies which might be incurred (noted in section 7.3) should be insignificant compared with the benefits of efficient pre-packaged parallel implementations.

The implementation of effective systems based on composing parallel skeletons still involves substantial research challenges. Thus, while the paradigm offers some promise, its ultimate potential as a serious development tool remains to be proved.

A functional language provided an elegant and natural base for prototyping GEL, but difficulties with multi-linked structures and performance analysis have led us to pursue further developments in a more conventional imperative framework.

**Acknowledgements**

Thanks are due to Professor Alan de Pennington and the Geometric Modelling Project at Leeds for their support, to Professor John Darlington of Imperial College for supplying the Hope+ compiler used, and to Jon Nash for use of the WPRAM simulator. The second author was supported by a studentship from the Iranian government.

# References

[1] B. Bacci, M. Danelutto, S. Orlando, S. Pelagatti, and M. Vanneschi. $P^3L$: a structured high-level parallel language, and its structured support. *Concurrency: Practice and Experience*, 7(3):225–255, May 1995.

[2] R Banerjee, V Goel, and A Mukherjee. Efficient parallel evaluation of CSG tree using fixed number of processors. In *Proc. 2nd ACM Symposium on Solid Modeling*, pages 137–145, May 1993.

[3] F. W. Burton and H-K Yang. Manipulating multilinked data structures in a pure functional language. *Software Practice and Experience*, 20(11):1167–1185, November 1990.

[4] M. Cole. *Algorithmic Skeletons: Structured Management of Parallel Computation*. Pitman/MIT Press, 1989.

[5] J. Darlington, A. J. Field, P. G. Harrison, P. H. J. Kelly, D. W. N. Sharp, Q. Wu, and R. L. While. Parallel programming using skeleton functions. In *Proceedings of PARLE 93*, 1993.

[6] J. Darlington, Y. Guo, H. W. To, Q. Wu, J. Yang, and M. Kohler. Fortran-S: a uniform functional interface to parallel imperative languages. Imperial College London, October 1994.

[7] J. R. Davy and P. M. Dew. A polymorphic library for constructive solid geometry. *Journal of Functional Programming*, 1995. forthcoming.

[8] H. Deldari, J. R. Davy, and P. M. Dew. The performance of parallel algorithmic skeletons. In *Proceedings of ZEUS'95*, pages 65–74. IOS Press, May 1995.

[9] N. S. Holliman, D. T. Morris, and P. M. Dew. An evaluation of the processor farm model for visualising constructive solid geometry. In P. M. Dew, R. A. Earnshaw, and T. R. Heywood, editors, *Parallel Processing for Computer Vision and Display*, pages 452–460. Addison Wesley, 1989.

[10] N. S. Holliman, C. M. Wang, and P. M. Dew. Mistral-3: Parallel solid modelling. *The Visual Computer*, 9(7):356–370, July 1993.

[11] R. M. Karp and V. Ramachandran. Parallel Algorithms for Shared Memory Machines. In J. van Leeuwen, editor, *Handbook of Theoretical Computer Science : Volume A, Algorithms and Complexity*, pages 869–941. North Holland, 1990.

[12] A. Kela and M. Wynn. Parallel computation of exact quadtree/octree approximations. In *4th Conference on Hypercube Concurrent Computers and Applications*, Monterey California, March 1989.

[13] M. Kesseler. Constructing skeletons in Clean: the bare bones. In *Proceedings HPFC95*, 1995.

[14] Y. T. Lee and A. A. G. Requicha. Algorithms for computing the volume and other integral properties of solids. ii. a family of algorithms based on representation conversion and cellular approximation. *Communications of the ACM*, 25(9):642–650, September 1982.

[15] D. Meagher. Geometric modeling using octree encoding. *Computer Graphics and Image Processing*, 19:129–147, 1982.

[16] J. M. Nash, P. M. Dew, M. E. Dyer, and J. R. Davy. Parallel algorithm design on the WPRAM model. In J. R. Davy and P. M. Dew, editors, *Abstract Machine Models for Highly Parallel Computers*, pages 83–102. Oxford University Press, 1995.

[17] A. A. G. Requicha. Representations for rigid solids: Theory, methods and systems. *ACM Computing Surveys*, 12(4):437–464, December 1980.

[18] T. Ruppelt and G. Wirtz. Automatic transformation of high-level object-oriented specifications into parallel programs. *Parallel Computing*, 10:15–28, 1989.

[19] R. B. Tilove. Set membership classification: A unified approach to geometric intersection problems. *IEEE Transactions on Computers*, C-29(10):874–883, October 1980.

[20] H. Wang, P. M. Dew, and J. Webb. Implementation of Apply. *Concurrency: Practice and Experience*, 3(1):43–54, February 1991.

[21] J. A. Webb. Steps toward architecture independent image processing. *IEEE Computer*, 25(2):21–31, February 1992.

# Composing Haggis

Sigbjørn Finne*and Simon Peyton Jones

Department of Computing Science, University of Glasgow,
Glasgow G12 8QQ, United Kingdom.
E-mail: {sof,simonpj}@dcs.glasgow.ac.uk

**Abstract**  Haggis is a purely-functional, multi-threaded user interface framework
for composing interactive applications.  It provides a compositional view of the
world of user interface applications, applying to all aspects of the interface the
principle of building a component from parts.  Interactive components are viewed
as *virtual* I/O devices that are composed together to make up complete applications.
To fully support this style of programming, Haggis makes good use of the integral
features of Haskell, a lazy, purely-functional language. The resulting system offers
an extensible, modular and simple programming model for writing user interface
applications at a high level of abstraction.

Two key ingredients that Haggis relies on to provide its compositional style
are concurrency and monads, making it possible to write multi-threaded functional
programs that interact with the Real World comfortably.

# 1 Introduction

Writing and maintaining user interface software can be a trying experience. Established
software engineering habits such as the modularization of code into different parts and
the composition of these to make up a complete system, do not currently carry over to the
user interface domain [14]. The servitude that the non-user interface parts has to endure
under the tyranny of the event-loop is well known, but the frameworks provided for
programming the user interface are also lacking. Instantiating and fitting together pre-
fabricated user interface objects is in most cases not too hard, but constructing new *first-
class* abstractions *within* these user interface frameworks is not well supported. Rather
than building new components by composing existing ones together, the programmer
is forced to adopt a completely different and lower level model of programming. The
result of having to violate the black box properties of an interactive component is that
extending the range of interactive components becomes hard, and programmers stick
to the predefined set rather than try to build a component that best fit the interaction at
hand.

This paper presents and explores the compositional mechanisms of Haggis (permu-
tation of: A Glasgow Haskell Graphical user Interface System), a functional, multi-
threaded user interface framework being developed at the University of Glasgow. Its
salient features are:

- *It is based on a functional language.* The framework is implemented in Haskell
  [9], a lazy, purely-functional language. Working in the context of a high level,

---

*Supported by Research Scholarship from the Norwegian Research Council declarative language allow us to make full use of features such as composition, higher-order functions, automatic storage management, static type checking, and the use of monads to structure I/O (Section 2)

- *It is compositional.* The central idea in Haggis is to view the construction of a user interface as a composition from parts. This compositional approach is similar to the object-oriented approaches of Interviews [12], and more recently Fresco [11], but differs in that Haggis provides *a unified programming model for writing both applications and new first-class interactive components*. The compositional mechanisms are described in detail in Section 3, and a discussion of the relationship to other systems can be found in Section 6.

- *It is extensible.* One consequence of using a functional language to provide a compositional style of programming is that writing an user interface application becomes indistinguishable from creating a new user interface abstraction. User defined abstractions are first-class and enjoy the same status as the primitive or predefined components that Haggis happens to already have. Section 4 looks at some of the standard 'devices', while Section 3 deals with the different techniques for extending existing components.

- *It is concurrent.* To be able to treat user interface components as black boxes that can be composed together, Haggis relies on the use of concurrency. It is implemented in Concurrent Haskell [16], an extension of standard Haskell with support for the dynamic creation of lightweight threads and, at the lowest level, shared memory synchronization primitives. Section 3.3 looks at where concurrency is required to maintain a compositional style, and briefly discusses the powerful abstraction technique that the separation of a program into several concurrently running threads offers for user interface applications in particular.

- *Virtual I/O devices.* Interactive objects are the medium by which application and user interact. Haggis extends the metaphor of devices and device handles to such objects, treating interactive components as *virtual* I/O devices where the user and application can exchange information (Section 2.3)

# 2 Overview

Haskell [9] is the standard non-strict, purely-functional programming language, and several high quality, freely available compilers already exist for it. It differs from mostly-functional languages such as Lisp and SML, in that non-strict languages deliberately do not specify evaluation order, and side-effecting constructs are outlawed.

## 2.1 Functional Input/Output

Avoiding side-effecting constructs in a functional language is attractive from a semantical point of view, but until recently, at the cost of making the expression of stateful, I/O-intensive programs complex and inefficient. The discovery of the applicability of monads to functional programming [22] has, amongst other things, provided a frame-work for writing interactive programs in a non-strict, purely-functional language. For the purposes of this paper, a monad provides a functional framework for expressing computations that side-effect without compromising features such as equational reason-ing.

A monad introduces computations or *actions* as values, which can manipulated just like any other value in the language. The fact that a value represents a monadic action is reflected in its type. In the case of the monad used for I/O, such values have type IO a. A value of type IO a represents an action that, when it is performed, may perform some I/O operations before returning a value of type a (lower-case identifiers in type expressions represent polymorphic type variables in Haskell.) So, in the case of simple character I/O operations we have:

```
putc :: Char -> IO ()
getc :: IO Char
```

putc 'a' is an action that, when performed, writes its argument to the standard output. Similarly for getc, it reads a character from standard input and returns it. Single actions are combined together to make up bigger ones using the following set of basic combinators:

```
thenIO    :: IO a -> (a -> IO b) -> IO b
seqIO     :: IO a -> IO b -> IO b
returnIO ::     a -> IO a
```

thenIO a1 (\ x -> a2) joins up two actions in such a way that when performed, the action a1 is executed first, binding its result to x before executing a2. seqIO is similar, differing only in that the value returned by a1 is simply thrown away before executing a2. returnIO is the simplest possible I/O action, as it performs none, just returning the value it was passed!

Armed with these combining forms, I/O 'scripts' can be constructed by stringing actions together. To illustrate, here is the function getLineIO which reads a line from standard input (back quoting is the Haskell syntax for infix operators):

```
getLineIO :: IO String
getLineIO =
  getc    `thenIO` \ ch ->
  if (ch==EOF) || (ch=='\n') then
     returnIO []
  else
     getLineIO    `thenIO` \ ls ->
        returnIO (ch:ls)
```

The standard input is read until either the end of file marker or a newline character is encountered, at which point the list of characters on the line is returned. These scripts of actions can be executed using the following two mechanisms:

- Through main :: IO (), which is the function that is first evaluated when a Haskell program is run. It can be thought of as given the state of the Real World, which it then proceeds to side-effect by executing a sequence of actions on it.

- In Concurrent Haskell [16], processes can be created dynamically using the forkIO construct (forkIO :: IO () -> IO ().) It eagerly starts to evaluate the action it is passed, concurrently with the context that executed the forkIO action.

The key point of the IO monad is that the combinators thenIO and seqIO serialize I/O operations. The evaluation order of the (side-effecting) actions becomes thus fixed, admitting not only an efficient implementation [17], but allows I/O performing, purely-functional programs to be expressed *without* sacrificing vital underlying language properties. Monadic techniques are used when we really want to be explicit the order that we want to perform actions on the outside world.

## 2.2 Monadic syntax

To aid a monadic style of programming, Haskell 1.3 introduces syntactic support that provides a more familiar style than the Haskell infix notation used above. The syntactic sugar is:

$$
\begin{aligned}
exp \quad &\rightarrow \quad do\ \{\ stmt\ \} \\
stmt \quad &\rightarrow \quad expr \\
&\mid \quad pat \leftarrow expr\ ;\ stmt \\
&\mid \quad expr\ ;\ stmt \\
&\mid \quad let\ decls\ ;\ stmt
\end{aligned}
$$

where *exp* and *pat* belong to the syntactic classes of expressions and patterns, respectively. The 'thenIO' and 'seqIO's are replaced by semicolons, and backarrows are used to bind result values of I/O actions to patterns. As an example, consider this 'sugared' version of getLineIO:[1]

```
getLineIO :: IO String
getLineIO =
 do
   ch <- getc
   if (ch==EOF) || (ch=='\n') then
       return []
   else
       ls <- getLineIO
       return (ch:ls)
```

## 2.3 User interface devices

The monadic I/O model allows the Haskell programmer to express simple file I/O in much the same way as you can in imperative languages, where it is the application

---

[1]Haskell's layout rules is used here to actually avoid using semicolons and braces to disambiguate the sequence of actions.

that drives the I/O. For example, a program that counts the number of characters in a file would use a loop to read characters from the file one by one until the end of file was reached. A useful advance introduced by UNIX was to present an interface to the program that hid whether the input came from a file, another program or the keyboard.

Haggis extends this device abstraction to include user interface components. This is not new and unique to Haggis [18], but this perspective differs distinctly from an event-driven system. Changing the input of the character counting program in an event-driven system to use a 'virtual keyboard' displayed on the screen would require the program structure to be turned inside out. The interface drives the application. Virtual key presses cause the invocation of action procedures/callbacks to increment the counter; the callback for end of file has to induce whatever actions are meant to follow the counting exercise. Not only is this structure undesirably different from the 'conventional' model, but it is non-compositional; how is a general-purpose counting program supposed to know what to do when a end of file is reached ?

In Haggis user interface components are instead regarded as typed, virtual I/O devices that can be queried, read, written, and closed, just like more conventional ones. Each type of device supports the common set of operations plus a set of device-specific operators, for example a label device supports the setting of a new string label. Representing the interactive components as devices have some advantages:[2]

- *Concrete representation.* In the same way as opening a file returns a file descriptor for the program to subsequently use to access a file, creating user interface components return a *handle* to that virtual device. The handles to virtual devices can be manipulated just like any other value, and new virtual devices can be created by composing existing ones. As a result of the uniform representation, a general-purpose counting program can now easily be written, just passing it a handle to a device.where it can read characters from.

- *Use of application control flow.* The application is in control of the interaction with the virtual devices, meaning that the application flow of control is used to encode the state of the application. This is not the case in an event-driven system, where the application state has to be explicitly updated and maintained between different event handlers.

For each type of user interface device there is a function for creating an instance of it; in the case of a push button:

```
mkButton :: String    -> a -> Widget (Button a)
disable  :: Button a -> Widget ()

pushB :: Widget (Button Bool)
pushB =
 do
  btn <- mkButton "On" True
  disable btn
  return btn
```

---

[2]We take the word 'device' to encompass both 'normal' devices and interactive components from here on.

`mkButton "On" True` creates a button device labelled On that will report the boolean value `True` each time it has been selected. The handle that `mkButton` returns, is used by the application to interact with it. In `pushB`, the button handle is used immediately to disable interaction.

To hide the low level interaction with the underlying window system from the programmer, a monadic abstraction, `Widget`, is introduced. A value of type `Widget` a represents an action that when it is performed, may interact with the underlying window system to create an interactive component, before returning a value of type a. Hiding the idiosyncrasies of the window system from the programmer cleans up the code, and avoids accidental 'plumbing' errors.

To make the metaphor of user interface components as virtual I/O devices work in all but the simplest of cases, Haggis and the underlying language has to provide a number of services:

- *Asynchronous forwarding of events to the correct device.* The character counting program does not have to be built around an event-loop, as Haggis takes care of forwarding events such as key presses to the virtual keyboard device. A program operates concurrently, interacting with user interface devices only when it needs to.

- *Support for multi-threaded programming.* The user normally interleaves interaction between different parts of an interface. If the application has to repeatedly check which device was last interacted with and then execute some appropriate action in response, event-loops at the level of devices have effectively been introduced. In Haggis, Concurrent Haskell's [16] lightweight processes are used to dynamically create processes to handle interaction with parts of the user interface. In the character counting example, a separate process can be created to handle interaction with the virtual keyboard, allowing other parts of the application to continue independently.

## 2.4 Realizing interfaces

To use a device, a program first has to open it. Virtual, interactive devices are realized or opened with `wopen`:

```
wopen :: Widget a -> IO (Window, a)
```

`wopen (mkButton "On" True)` creates a new top-level window containing a button labelled On, and returns a handle to the button device. The `Widget` value can be seen as a template, which `wopen` uses to create an instance inside a separate top-level window.

The handle for the window returned by `wopen` is used to reconfigure or close the top-level window, and as an example of how a virtual device can be incorporated into an application, consider the definition of a dialogue box in Figure 1. The message box `alert` consists of two buttons together with a label displaying a message (the operators used to compose the dialogue box are presented at length in Section 3.) To use this alert box abstraction in an application:

```
mkLabel  ::    String -> Widget Label
hBox     ::    Widget a -> Widget a
mkButton::    String -> a -> Widget (Button a)
space    ::    Int -> Widget ()
combineButtons ::    [Button a] -> IO (Button a)
getValue ::    Button a -> IO a

warning str = "Do you want to delete "++str++" ?"

alert ::    String -> Widget (Button Bool)
alert str =
 vBox (
 do
   space 5
   mkLabel (warning str)
   space 10
   hBox (
    do
      space 10
      yes <- mkButton "Yes" True
      space 20
      no <- mkButton "No" False
      space 10
      answer <- ioW (combineButtons [yes,no])
      return answer))
```

Fig. 1: Alert dialogue box

```
safe_delete :: String -> IO ()
safe_delete fname =
 do
   (w,d) <- wopen (alert fname)
   cfirm <- getValue d
   closeWindow w
   if cfirm then
      deleteFile fname
   else
      return ()
```

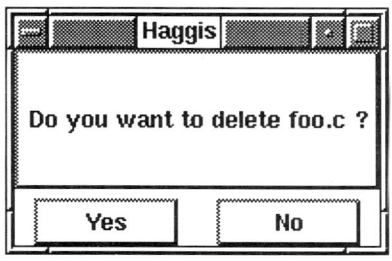

Executing wopen causes the dialogue box on the right to appear on the screen. The application then tries to read the user's response to the delete request, demanding a confirmation before possibly going ahead with the operation.[3] This trivial example

---

[3] The example code shown here does not create a modal interaction. Other windows on the screen can still be interacted with.

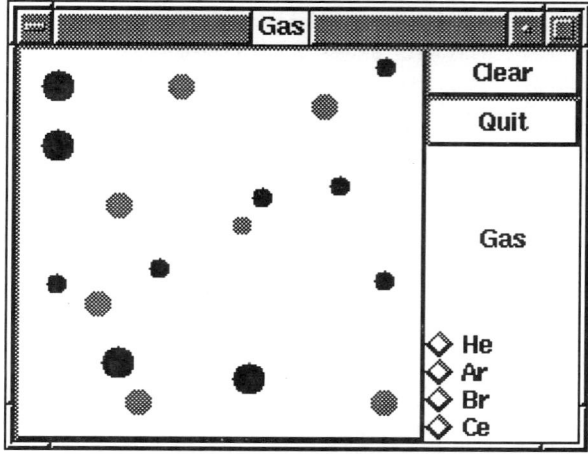

Fig. 2: Gas simulation chamber

highlights some features of Haggis:

- The dialogue box is built by composing together its constituent parts.

- Hiding window system details inside values of type `Widget` avoids esoterica at the level of use, hence there is no need to plumb window system details through the `safe_delete` function.

- Since the delivery of events is performed behind the scenes by Haggis, the program does not hand over control to a centralized run-time system like the event-loop after creating the dialogue box. The `safe_delete` action is free to continue to execute its thread of actions, interacting with the dialogue box only when it has to.

## 3 Composing the interface

Consider the user interface application in Figure 2, a toy simulation laboratory for visualizing the interaction between atoms in a chamber. Selecting an item in the radio group causes an atom of that type to be inserted into the chamber at a random location with an arbitrary velocity vector. The user can interact with the atoms by grabbing them and throwing them in a different direction, and the chamber can be cleared by pressing a command button. This toy interface is constructed using three separate types of composition:

- At the presentation level, the laboratory is composed out of two parts arranged horizontally, the chamber and the control area. The control area is again constructed out of two separate units, each of which have further internal structure.

*Physical composition* and how Haggis supports the composition of the visual aspects of a user interface is discussed in Section 3.1.

- The command button for clearing the chamber consist of a graphical output view and a *controller* that attaches interactive behaviour to that view. The controller catches mouse clicks and inverts the button view output and signals the completion of the button press by emitting a value via its device handle. *Behavioural composition* deals with interactive behaviour and how it can be attached to virtual I/O devices to augment or modify their existing behaviour (Section 3.2.)

- At an even deeper level than attributing interactive behaviour to graphical elements, the one-from-many choice provided by the radio group is also a composition. A set of buttons laid out in an arbitrary manner are combined to make up a 'bigger' component that allows only one of them to be selected at a time. *Semantic composition* is concerned with how handles to virtual devices can be combined together, and how application semantic properties such as the exclusive choice of the radio group can be attached to a device (Section 3.3.)

These three types of composition constitute the mechanisms that Haggis offers for building complete user interface applications. We consider each in turn.

## 3.1 Physical composition

How might we go about describing the visual layout of a collection of components? One way of describing it would be to have operators like:

```
beside  :: [Widget a] -> Widget [a]
```

beside takes a list of components, and aligns them all horizontally. The value returned by each component are collected into a list and returned. Unfortunately, this forces all the components laid out with beside to have uniform type. Haskell is a statically typed language, so even if beside does not inspect the values returned by its components, elements of the list have to be uniformly typed. The result is too tight a binding between interface and application, the physical layout demanding that only components of same type can be arranged. Instead of forcing the programmer to manually coerce the values of the widgets into a common type, we make Widget a a monadic type. Operations similar to those provided for gluing I/O actions are provided, this time working on Widget actions:

```
thenW   :: Widget a -> (a -> Widget b) -> Widget b
seqW    :: Widget a -> Widget b -> Widget b
returnW :: a -> Widget a
```

thenW w1 (\ x -> w2) combines two widget values together to create a larger component, such that when it is realized, w1 is created first, binding its returning value to x before creating w2. The default appearance of this composite component is w1 stacked on top of w2 in a pile:[4]

---

[4] Adopting the syntactic sugar of Section 2.2 to describe actions of type Widget from here on.

```
pile :: Widget ()
pile =
  do
    mkDiamond 50
    mkCircle 25

row :: Widget ()
row = hBox pile
```

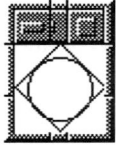

When `pile` is realized, a window with a diamond on top of a circle is created, as shown in the left figure. The combinators `thenW` and `seqW` allow arbitrary components to be piled on top of each other, including, of course, other piles. To get different visual layouts, a pile of components can be constrained by encapsulating it in a *container*. A container spreads the pile out flat, rearranging the components according to the layout scheme it is implementing. The `row` widget applies the `hBox` container to the pile, pulling the circle out from underneath the rectangle in the original pile and aligns them horizontally, as seen on the right. Upon resize of the box, the `hBox` container will calculate the new sizes for its children and resize them accordingly, so whatever internal layout the container has, is hidden from the outside.

What about the coupling between interface and application? The drawback with an operator like `beside` is avoided because the combining together of widgets is separated from attaching a particular layout scheme. Components of different type can be put together in a pile using `thenW` and `seqW`, and if required, later be encapsulated with a container like `hBox`.

Arbitrary layout schemes can be enforced via the encapsulation of `Widgets` inside containers, but by far the most common class of such layout schemes are the tiling operators. Haggis provides a set of tiling combinators based on the TEX model of boxes and glue:

```
hBox,  vBox  :: Widget a -> Widget a
pHBox, pVBox :: Length   -> Widget a -> Widget a
```

A pile of widgets is aligned vertically by `vBox` to construct a *box* which externally appears as one component. Resizing the `VBox` causes the components to be resized, distributing the change in size between them. The combinators `pHBox` and `pVBox` provide the equivalent of the `\parbox` construct in TEX, constraining the length of a box along its axis.

Inter-component void is captured through the component `space` which has no functionality except from laying claim to some screen real estate. The relative willingness of components to both stretch and shrink is finely adjustable through the setting of attributes similar to TEX'. A more substantial example of physical composition is the alert dialogue shown in Figure 1, having the layout structure shown in Figure 3.

For the buttons, an `HBox` is used to place them on a horizontal line, taking care to space them properly. This box is treated as a single component by `VBox`, using only the overall geometry of the line to compute the layout and size of the dialogue box. The structure of the code in Figure 1 reflects quite closely the layout of the realized dialogue

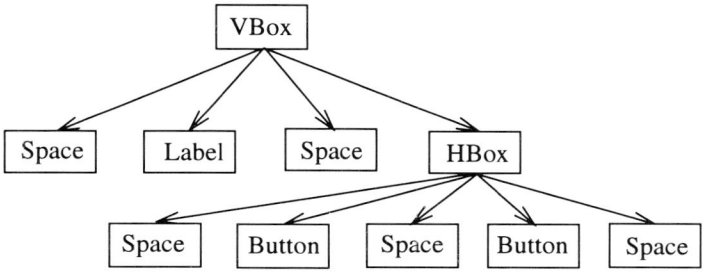

Fig. 3: Layout hierarchy of dialogue box

box, and a good estimate of how a component will be laid out can often be derived simply by looking at the code.

The construction of the physical presentation of a complete interface is achieved in Haggis by repeatedly encapsulating piles of widgets inside containers. A composite component is first-class as seen in the dialogue box example, where an HBox was used on equal terms with a primitive label inside a VBox.

### 3.2 Behavioural composition

To make the interface come alive, we need to be able to attach interactive behaviour to the components that were composed physically in the previous Section. *Behavioural composition* is concerned with building new components by adding to or modifying the interactive behaviour of an existing component. The push button of the example in Section 3 was constructed by encapsulating a basic output view inside a controller that catches and translates a mouse click into commands to highlight the output view. A user action such as a key press is ignored by the button controller and just passed on to the view. The basic construct for adding interactive behaviour to a component is encapsulate:

```
encapsulate :: (a -> Controller b)
               -> Widget a
               -> Widget b
mkGlyph :: Picture -> Widget Glyph

button :: String -> a -> Widget (Button a)
button str val =
  encapsulate (bCtrl)
              (mkGlyph (frame str))
  where
  bCtrl :: Glyph -> Controller (Button a)
```

encapsulate (ctrl) comp constructs a new component where the controlling function ctrl is put on top of component comp, intercepting all external actions performed on it. The command button is the encapsulation of a view inside the controller bCtrl, as shown on the right. The controller is passed the handle to the view, so that upon seeing mouse clicks it uses the handle to ask the view to change its current output. Note that the type of encapsulate is general in that any value of type Widget a can be encapsulated, not just simple views. As an example of this, a controller that interprets mouse clicks could also be attached to a general text editing device, so as to allow the mouse to be used for operations such as cursor movement and cutting and pasting.

The controller is also responsible for providing and maintaining an application view of the constructed device. Normally, the encapsulation of a device creates not just a device with modified or augmented interactive behaviour, but also returns a new type of device handle back. bCtrl returns a handle to a button device handle that provides the application interface to the new component, i.e. the application can change the button label or listen for button clicks via this handle.

The basic encapsulation or delegation mechanism does not specify how to express the controller itself. Different approaches to specifying interactive behaviour can be accommodated, such as the generic interactors used by [8, 13], where default behaviour can be overridden and adapted to fit context of use, or higher level notations such as the UAN [6]. Haggis does not dictate the manner in which the controllers should be expressed, but we are currently experimenting with an approach similar to that of Interactors[13], where the different types of interactions possible using mouse and keyboard are enumerated. As an example, a simple push button is an instance of a *trigger*, an abstract interaction object that will emit a value when some condition is met.

### 3.3 Semantic composition

Using the techniques of the previous two sections, hierarchies describing the behaviour and physical layout of interactive devices can easily be constructed. However, the story does not by any means end there. The motivating example in Section 3 used a radio group to provide the selection of an atom type. To express this one-from-many choice externally as a device, the hierarchical, top-down techniques of previous sections do not suffice. Using a controller to encapsulate the items in a one-from-many group wouldn't be a very good solution, for a couple of reasons. Firstly, the controller would have to fix the layout of the items of the group in order to be able to map events such as mouse clicks to individual items. Secondly, it would have to impose the same selection mechanism across all items, making it hard to combine items with different interaction behaviours together in a group. While these restrictions would not be such a high price to pay for a radio group, this top-down solution forces the controller to deal with issues of layout, behaviour and semantics all at once.

Picking an item from many is an operation at the semantic level of devices. The radio group will in response to output reported on any of the item handles, update its current selection and turn off the highlighting of the previous selection. In the case of button devices, this composition or merging of devices to create a composite one is performed by combineButtons:

```
combineButtons  ::  [Button a]  -> IO (Button a)
```

```
radio:: [Button Int]
      -> IO (Button Int)
radio ds =
 do
 cdev <- combineButtons ds
 forkIO (rCtrl Nothing ds cdev)
 return cdev

rCtrl :: Maybe Int
       -> [Button Int]
       -> Button Int
       -> IO ()
rCtrl state ds cdev =
 do
  val <- getValue cdev
  case state of
   Nothing ->
    rCtrl (Just v) ds cdev
   Just v ->
    if val==v then
     rCtrl (Just v) ds cdev
    else
     do
      deactivate (devs!v)
      rCtrl (Just val) ds cdev
```

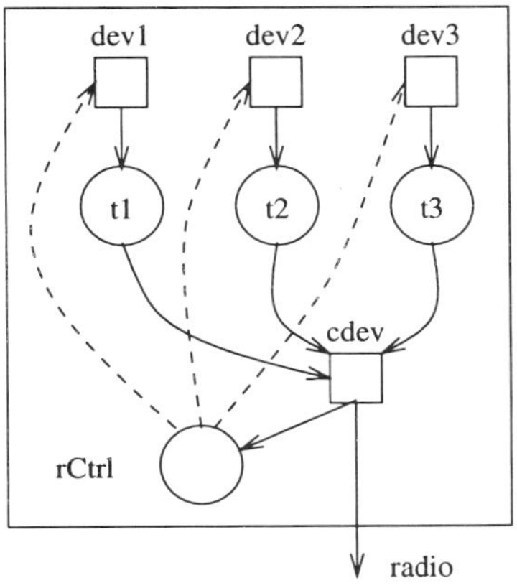

Fig. 4: Exclusive choice group

combineButtons takes a list of button device handles and returns a single one. This new device operates by echoing the values that the individual devices output, and is implemented by attaching a separate thread to each device. Each thread is a simple loop that runs independently, reading values from a button device using getValue and forwards them to the combined one. The combined device does not implement a radio group though, as the output from a device does not cause the previously selected item in the group to become de-selected. The exclusive semantics of the group can readily be attached though, the code implementing it can be seen in Figure 4.

radio takes a list of button devices which have been laid out in some manner, and for simplicity let us assume the numbers which the items output correspond to their position in the list (The restriction in type and value is made here to simplify the code somewhat, more expressive types would normally be used.) radio creates a combined device and a process to keep track of the current selection in the radio group, deactivating the previous selection whenever it sees a new one. This is illustrated on the right hand side, where devices are represented as squares and the threads that operate on them are pictured as circles. This example of an exclusive choice shows up some interesting points about Haggis:

- The representation of user interface components as virtual I/O devices was used to compose, using Haskell, a new device by combining existing ones (The implementation for `combineButtons` is not shown here, but it is of the same length and complexity to that of the `exclusive` definition above.)

- The construction of the radio group is not coupled to the user interface at all, as the `radio` function is just an I/O action. The one-from-many choice is now just the merging of input from a set of sources, taking care of notifying input devices that they have become unselected.

- Attaching the `exclusive` function to the combined device is an example of how application semantics can be linked into the user interface. By having a separate process executing `exclusive`, the invariant of only allowing one item to be selected is actively and independently maintained. Constructing an application in Haggis can be seen as the repeated use of such *semantic composition* to link larger and larger pieces of the application into the user interface. Using concurrency, the large and perhaps complex structure of these components can be hidden, as the computation required in response to user interaction will be handled independently to the rest of the application. The result is a modular and extensible application that is not centred around a single event loop.

## 4 Standard devices

Using the compositional mechanisms just presented, a number of common user interface abstractions have been constructed. To give a flavour of how they appear to the programmer, here are some of the type signatures:

```
mkSlider       :: Widget (Slider Float)
mkHScrollbar   :: Float   -> Widget (Scrollbar)
mkField        :: String -> Widget Field
mkViewport     :: Size -> Widget a -> Widget (a, Viewport)
catchMouseEv   :: Widget a -> Widget (a, Mouse)
scaleW         :: (Float,Float) -> Widget a -> Widget a
mkPopup        :: Widget a -> Widget (a, Popup)
printerW       :: Widget a -> Widget (a, Printer)
```

The combinator `printerW` encapsulates an arbitrary component for printing, so that when the action `printW printer "dump.ps"`

```
printW :: Printer -> String -> IO ()
```

is executed, a PostScript[5] [1] representation of the current graphical output for the encapsulated component is generated. This is made possible by the device-independent 2D graphics model used to describe graphical output [4], where pictures are described by composing parts, similar to that of [7, 20].

---

[5]PostScript is trademark of Adobe Systems Incorporated.

# 5 Implementation

Haggis is operational and currently only available for internal use at Glasgow. It will eventually be released as part of the Glasgow Haskell Compiler(ghc), which is available on a wide range of UNIX platforms.[6] Haggis runs under the X Window system (interfaces with Xlib), and uses the concurrency features supported by ghc.

Internally, concurrency is used to structure tasks such as the delivery of events, redisplay and the provision of servers to manage resources such as fonts and colours to provide a more convenient and declarative interface to the underlying window system. The windowing model is similar to Fresco's [11], and heavy use is made of lightweight display objects based on glyphs [2], which, in X terms, do not have a window associated with them. A consequence of having such a 'windowless' windowing model is that updates cannot be done by issuing drawing requests to X asynchronously, since a widget could be obscured by others. Rather than having a global redisplay thread which takes care of damage repair, Haggis distributes clipping regions to each component, so that asynchronous redisplay becomes possible.

# 6 Related Work

Haggis' use of composition as the main programming glue is to some degree used by Fresco [11]. Built on top of class-based, object oriented languages, Fresco provides a set of common user interface abstractions together with a *fixed* collection of operators for combining them. Composition and delegation is used to construct the *graphical* parts of a user interface, so building new abstractions by composing existing ones is possible. However, the model of composition does not extend to the interactive domain, creating new objects requires the abstraction that interactive components represents to be broken and the class hierarchy to be manually extended. Haggis differs in that it tries to provide a uniform programming model where the construction of a user interface is inseparable from the construction of new components. This uniform representation of the world is similar to LiveWorld [21], a prototype-based graphical programming system for experimenting with active objects. It has a uniform object model based on recursive containment, so the hierarchies constructed are similar to what Haggis creates. Although the two systems explore largely different issues, Haggis extends the use of hierarchical composition beyond the interface, providing semantic operations such as combineButtons.

The extension of the device abstraction to incorporate interactive components is also used by Acme [18], a concurrent window system that provide access to its windows via a file system interface. The resulting system has a simple, uniform application interface to the windowing capabilities, making its presence almost transparent to the programmer.

Haggis is most closely related to eXene [5], a multi-threaded framework written in Concurrent ML(CML) [19]. The use of concurrency to structure both the underlying implementation and application is common for both systems, but the current implementation of Haggis has a less fine-grained use of processes.

---

[6]Available by anonymous ftp from ftp://ftp.dcs.glasgow.ac.uk/pub/haskell/

Other functional approaches (notably Fudgets [3]) have been evaluated well else-where [15]; Haggis differs from these in its use of concurrency and monads to structure interaction with the outside world. Representing user interface components as virtual I/O devices is also a distinguishing feature, and the result is a cleaner separation between interface and application.

# 7 Conclusions and Future Work

We have in this paper presented Haggis, a compositional approach to user interface construction, describing the various forms of programmer glue that Haggis provides. Interactive components are treated like virtual I/O devices, and three different ways of composing them together were presented:

- *Physical composition.* - the presentational side of an application is described by arranging components in a layout hierarchy.

- *Behavioural composition.* - augmenting the interactive behaviour by encapsulating components inside a controlling layer.

- *Semantic composition.* - building larger semantic units by composing handles of different interactive components. Requires support for concurrency.

One area of further work is to look into ways of defining relationships between different types of interactive devices and operations over them. Haskell's type classes [9] are not expressive enough for defining these relationships, and we are currently investigating how the more powerful type system of constructor classes [10] can be put to use. Alas, it is out of the scope of this paper to go into detail here.

Haggis is operational and one near term goal is to release the system for others to try and evaluate. Although the emphasis is on providing a framework which is extensible through composition of parts, we recognize that a common set of interaction objects has to be provided, and a set of such abstractions is under development.

Currently, Haggis is being used in a compiler environment, and one natural direction of further work would be to integrate Haggis into an interpreter for Haskell, offering a more powerful environment for quickly prototyping and developing user interface applications by combining components together to make up complete applications.

# References

[1] Adobe Systems Inc. *PostScript language reference manual.* Addison Wesley, second edition, 1990.

[2] Paul R. Calder and Mark A. Linton. Glyphs: Flyweight objects for user interfaces. In *ACM Symposium on User Interface Software and Technology*, pages 92–101, 1990.

[3] Magnus Carlsson and Thomas Hallgren. FUDGETS – a graphical user interface in a lazy functional language. In *Proceedings of the 6th ACM Conference on Functional Programming and Computer Architecture*, pages 321 – 330. ACM Press, 1993.

[4] Sigbjorn Finne and Simon Peyton Jones. Pictures: A simple structured graphics model. In *Glasgow Functional Programming Workshop*, Ullapool, July 1995.

[5] Emden W. Gansner and John H. Reppy. eXene. In *Proceedings of the 1991 CMU Workshop on SML*, October 31 1991.

[6] H. R. Hartson, A. Siochi, and D. Hix. The UAN: A user-oriented representation for direct manipulation interface designs. *ACM Transactions on Information Systems*, 8(3):181–203, June 1990.

[7] Peter Henderson. Functional geometry. In *ACM Symposium on LISP and Functional Programming*, pages 179–187, 1982.

[8] Tyson R. Henry, Scott E. Hudson, and Gary L. Newell. Integrating gesture and snapping into a user interface toolkit. In *Proceedings of UIST'90*, pages 112–121, 1990.

[9] Paul Hudak et al. Report on the programming language haskell version 1.2. *ACM SIGPLAN Notices*, 27(5), May 1992.

[10] Mark P. Jones. A system of constructor classes: overloading and implicit higher-order polymorphism. In *Proceedings of the 6th ACM Conference on Functional Programming and Computer Architecture*, Copenhagen, June 1993. ACM Press.

[11] Mark Linton and Chuck Price. Building distributed user interfaces with fresco. In *Proceedings of the Seventh X Technical Conference*, pages 77–87, Boston, MA, January 1993.

[12] Mark A. Linton, J.M. Vlissides, and P.R. Calder. Composing user interfaces with InterViews. *IEEE Computer*, 22(2):8–22, February 1989.

[13] Brad A. Myers. A new model for handling input. *ACM Transactions on Information Systems*, 8(2):289–320, July 1990.

[14] Brad A. Myers. Why are human-computer interfaces difficult to design and implement? Technical Report CMU-CS-93-183, School of Computer Science, Carnegie-Mellon University, July 1993.

[15] Rob Noble and Colin Runciman. Functional languages and graphical user interfaces - a review and a case study. Technical Report 94-223, Department of Computer Science, University of York, February 1994.

[16] Simon Peyton Jones, Andrew Gordon, and Sigbjorn Finne. Concurrent Haskell. In *ACM Symposium on the Principles of Programming Languages*, St. Petersburg Beach, Florida, January 1996.

[17] Simon L. Peyton Jones and Philip Wadler. Imperative functional programming. In *ACM Conference on the Principles of Programming Languages*, pages 71 – 84. ACM Press, January 1993.

[18] Rob Pike. Acme: A user interface for programmers. In *Proceedings of the Winter 1994 USENIX Conference*, pages 223–234, San Francisco, 1994.

[19] John H. Reppy. CML: A higher-order concurrent language. *Proceedings of the ACM SIGPLAN'91 Conference on Programming Language Design and Implementation*, pages 293–305, 1991.

[20] Roger Took. Surface interaction: A paradigm and model for separating application and interface. In *Proceedings of the CHI'90*, pages 35–42, April 1990.

[21] Michael Travers. Recursive interfaces for reactive objects. In *Proceedings of CHI'94*, pages 379–385, Boston, MA, April 24-28 1994.

[22] Philip Wadler. The essence of functional programming. In *Proceedings of the ACM SIGPLAN 19th Annual Symposium on Principles of Programming Languages*, January 1992. Invited talk.

# Functional Specification of
# JPEG Decompression,
# and an Implementation for Free

Jeroen Fokker

Department of Computer Science, Utrecht University
P.O.Box 80.089, 3508 TB Utrecht, The Netherlands
E-mail: jeroen@cs.ruu.nl
URL: http:/www.cs.ruu.nl/~jeroen

**Abstract** A decoder for images compressed by the JPEG algorithm is stated in the pure functional programming language Gofer. The program can be regarded as a mathematical specification of the decompression algorithm; the concise description (which is included almost in full) is very suitable for learning about the algorithm. At the same time the 'specification' is an executable program, which shows the usefulness of a functional programming language as a prototyping tool for graphics algorithms.

All functions are defined as much as possible at the function level, i.e., as compositions of other functions. A tutorial on the important concept of a 'State Monad', which plays an important role in the program, is included. From a functional programming theoretical point of view, the new technique of currying a state monad, which is introduced, and its application in the program, are interesting.

## 1 Introduction

JPEG is a standard for compressing images that has become very popular recently. Unlike general purpose compression algorithms, it exploits redundancy resulting from the two-dimensional structure of pictures, and from the continuous nature of photographic colour images. Furthermore, it offers the possibility to let the compression lose some information, which is intended to be hardly noticeable by the human viewer. JPEG is named after its designer, the Joint (ISO and CCITT) Photographic Expert Group.

In the JPEG algorithm various techniques are combined: Huffman encoding, run-length encoding, differential encoding, quantization, cosine transform, and data reordering. A general introduction to the algorithm is given by Wallace [11] in a 17 page article. It contains a numeric example which is quite instructive; however the information is not intended to be detailed enough to be able to implement the algorithm. For that, you would need the official (draft) standard [7] (210 pages) and/or the book that explains it [8] (334 pages). The ISO description in the standard is not so nice as Wallace's article: algorithms are given by unstructured flowcharts, use fuzzy identifiers and lots of indices and pointers, and are laid out poorly.

In some circles, functional programming has the reputation of being an academic plaything, only useful for toy problems like 'fibonacci' and '8 queens' and maybe some AI applications. This might be true for the earlier functional languages, but certainly not for the modern, polymorphically typed and lazily evaluated languages like Haskell [3], Gofer [5] and Clean [9]. We will demonstrate this by giving an implementation of a JPEG decoder in the Gofer language. This article can serve as a:

- *Specification*. The program has the conciseness of a mathematical description, and thus can act as a 'functional specification'. Unlike other specification formalisms, the language has a well defined semantics, and an interpreter that can check type correctness.

- *Teaching text*. The JPEG format can be understood by studying the decoder. Due to the abstraction mechanisms in the language, various aspects of the algorithm can be isolated and understood separately.

- *Implementation*. The program is executable, and has been applied successfully to decode images. The program is very slow (it takes 14 minutes to decode a $384 \times 256$ image). Running time could be improved considerably by using a compiler instead of an experimental interpreter, and by optimizing some functions (the cosine transform function in section 4.2 is a good candidate for this). We have not done so, because we consider the specification aspect of the program more important.

- *Functional programming tutorial and case study*. Some interesting programming techniques are used and explained. It shows that a functional language can be used for real life problems in graphics. In particular, it shows that by using a 'state monad', input-consuming functions can be defined, while keeping the benefits of abstraction in a functional language.

This article assumes no knowledge of JPEG or any of its algorithms, nor of specialized functional programming techniques. Basic knowledge of functional programming (recursion, manipulation of lists and the use of types, as described in the first few chapters of e.g. [1] or [5]) may be helpful.

The rest of this article is divided in two parts. Sections 2–3 describe some general purpose functions, that are needed in the sequel and that happen not to be part of the standard prelude of most languages. In section 2 matrix manipulation, bit lists and binary trees are dealt with. In section 3 the notions of 'state function' and 'monad' are introduced, and some utilities to manipulate them. Experienced functional programmers may want to skip these sections, although they might want to take a look at the end of subsection 3.3, where the new technique of currying state functions is described.

The JPEG decoding algorithm proper is dealt with in sections 4–5. In section 4 the basic algorithms used by JPEG are defined: Huffman coding, the Discrete Cosine Transform (DCT), and quantization. In section 5 functions for parsing the interleaved image data, are defined. The parsing of the header, and the main program are outlined only; they are included in the full paper which is available from the http address above. Finally, section 6 reflects on the program and the methodology.

# 2 A functional library

## 2.1 Auxiliary functions

In the functions in this article, we will use standard functions on lists, like map, sum, concat, zipWith and transpose. These functions are defined in the standard prelude of most functional languages. Three functions of general nature that we need are not defined in the Gofer prelude. They are defined in this section, and may also serve as an introduction to the Gofer syntax.

In the type of functions, an arrow is written not only between the type of the parameters and the result, but also between the two parameters. The type $a \rightarrow b \rightarrow c$ is to be read as $a \rightarrow (b \rightarrow c)$, which stresses the fact that a function may also be partially parameterized with its first parameter only. This mechanism is known as 'Currying'. Partial parameterization is also used when defining functions. The function multi takes an integer $n$ and a list, and replicates each element of the list, which remains unnamed, $n$ times.

```
multi  :: Int -> [a] -> [a]
multi n = concat . map (copy n)
```

The function is defined as a functional composition (denoted by the standard operator 'dot') of the map (copy n) function (which turns every element into a list of length $n$) and the concat function (which concatenates all lists into one big list). The function multi could also have been defined by explicitly naming the second parameter: multi n xs = concat (map (copy n) xs). However, this is avoided whenever possible in order to not overwhelm the reader with unnecessary names. Occasionally, we will also need to compose functions of two parameters. As this is not a standard function, we will define it here. The function o may be used as an infix operator by writing its name in back quotes.

```
infixr 9 'o'
o :: (c->d) -> (a->b->c) -> (a->b->d)
(g 'o' f) x y = g (f x y)
```

In addition, we define an explicit denotation ap for functional application:

```
ap      :: (a->b) -> a -> b
ap f x  = f x
```

## 2.2 Matrix manipulation

Matrix manipulation is a rewarding area for functional programming, as the definitions of most operations are short and elegant and don't need lots of indices as in many other formalisms. More important, we will need these functions in section 4 for the DCT operation, and in section 5 for colour space conversion. A matrix is simply a list of lists, of which we will assume that the rows have equal length. The dimensions of a matrix can be indicated by a pair of two integers.

```
type Dim   = (Int,Int)
type Mat a = [[a]]
```

We provide a function matmap which applies a function to all elements of a matrix, a function matconcat which collapses a matrix of sub-matrices into one big matrix, and a function matzip which transforms a list of matrices into a matrix of lists of corresponding elements.

```
matmap :: (a->b) -> Mat a -> Mat b
matmap  = map . map

matconcat :: Mat (Mat a) -> Mat a
matconcat = concat . map (map concat . transpose)

matzip :: [Mat a] -> Mat [a]
matzip = map transpose . transpose
```

The classic operations from linear algebra (inner product of vectors and linear transformation of a vector by a matrix) presuppose the existence of arithmetical operations on the elements, which is indicated by the Num a predicate in front of the type.

```
inprod :: Num a  =>  [a] -> [a] -> a
inprod = sum 'o' zipWith (*)

matapply    :: Num a  =>  Mat a -> [a] -> [a]
matapply m v = map (inprod v) m
```

Inner product is defined as elementwise multiplication followed by summation; matrix application as calculating the inner product of a vector with all rows of the matrix.

## 2.3 Bit Streams and Binary Trees

Of a more mundane nature are some functions that address the individual bits in a byte, and by extension, in a string. In the same vein the function byte2nibs splits a byte in two four-bit nibbles. The standard function rem is used to calculate the remainder after division.

```
type Bits = [Bool]

byte2bits  :: Int -> Bits
byte2bits x = zipWith (>=) (map (rem x) pows) (tail pows)
        where pows = [256,128,64,32,16,8,4,2,1]

string2bits :: String -> Bits
string2bits = concat . map (byte2bits.ord)

byte2nibs  :: Int -> (Int,Int)
byte2nibs x = (x/16, x'rem'16)
```

Binary trees, which will be used to represent Huffman trees in section 4, are defined by an algebraic type definition. Information is stored in the Tips of the tree, there may be Nil ends, and in Bin branching points only two subtrees are given.

```
data Tree a  = Nil
             | Tip a
             | Bin (Tree a) (Tree a)
```

# 3 Modelling of State

## 3.1 State Functions

Modelling of state has long been a problem when using pure functional languages, which by their nature are side-effect free. However, recently it has been discovered that state can be adequately dealt with using so-called 'monads' [10, 4, 6].

A 'state function from $s$ to $r$', or StFun s r for short, is a function that operates on a type $s$ (the 'state') and yields not only a value of type $r$ (the 'result'), but also a value of type $s$ (the 'updated state'). An algebraic type definition, involving an explicit conversion ST is used rather than a type synonym definition, as state functions are to be regarded as an abstract data type, to be manipulated only by the functions below.

```
data StFun s r = SF (s -> (r,s))
```

Firstly, state functions are made an instance of Functor, the class of all types supporting the map function. where in this instance the map function applies a given function to the 'result' part of a state function:

```
instance Functor (StFun s) where
    map h (SF f)    = SF g
                where g s = (h x,s')
                        where (x,s') = f s
```

Furthermore, state functions are made an instance of the Monad class. For this, a function result and a function bind need to be defined that fulfil certain laws. In this instance, the result function constructs a state function which delivers some result $x$ without changing the state, and the bind function composes two state functions in an intricate way:

```
instance Monad (StFun s) where
    result x        = SF g
                where g s = (x,s)
    SF f 'bind' sfh = SF g
                where g s = h s'
                        where (x,s') = f s
                              SF h   = sfh x
```

We will not use the bind function explicitly in the sequel. Instead we make use of a syntactic sugaring known as 'monad comprehension', provided in the Gofer language [5], which is discussed in subsection 3.2. A state function can be applied to an initial state using the function st'apply. This yields the proper result only, and discards the final state.

```
st'apply :: StFun a b -> a -> b
st'apply (SF f) s   =   x
                where (x,_) = f s
```

## 3.2 Primitive State Functions

In the JPEG decoder, as a state we will basically use a list. We provide three primitive functions that operate on list states, from which the more involved ones can be constructed. The empty state function reports whether the list in the state is empty, and leaves the state unmodified. The item state function returns the first element of the list in the state (which is assumed to be non-empty), and removes that element from the list. The peekitem state function returns the first element without removing it from the list.

```
empty   ::  StFun [a] Bool
empty   =   SF f
    where   f [] = (True,  [])
            f xs = (False, xs)

item    ::  StFun [a] a
item    =   SF f
    where   f (x:xs) = (x, xs)

peekitem  ::  StFun [a] a
peekitem  =  SF f
        where   f ys@(x:xs) = (x, ys)
```

A fourth primitive function meets a more special purpose. In the JPEG format, a binary data stream is terminated by a two-byte marker consisting of an '\xFF' byte and a non-zero byte. If an '\xFF' byte occasionally occurs in a data stream, it is padded by an extra zero byte. The state function entropy below gets one segment of binary data, taking care of the padding, and leaves behind as final state a list that begins with the terminating marker.

```
entropy :: StFun String String
entropy = SF f
    where f ('\xFF':'\x00':xs) = let (as,bs) = f xs
                                 in  ('\xFF':as,bs)
          f ys@(    '\xFF':_ ) = ([],ys)
          f (          x:xs) = let (as,bs) = f xs
                               in  (x:as,bs)
```

The state function item gets one character from a string state, removing it from the state. The state function byte does the same, but yields its result as an integer rather than as a character. It can be defined as map ord item (where ord is the primitive char-to-int function). Recall that map was overloaded in subsection 3.1, so that map $h$ $f$ applies a function $h$ to the result part of a state function $f$. We write the definition however in the form:

```
byte :: StFun String Int
byte = [ ord c | c <- item ]

nibbles :: StFun String (Int,Int)
nibbles = [ byte2nibs a | a <- byte ]
```

These look like list comprehensions, but as map is overloaded to operate on arbitrary Functors, so is the comprehension notation. From the type in the expressions above it can be inferred that these comprehensions are actually 'string-state function comprehensions'. The comprehension notation is especially useful when more than one generator is being used:

```
word :: StFun String Int
word = [ a*256+b | a<-byte, b<-byte ]
```

Comprehensions with multiple generators may be used not only for lists, but for arbitrary Monads, and hence in particular for state functions. The semantics of comprehension like this is defined using the result and bind functions (see [5]), but can be more easily understood intuitively: a 16-bit word can be fetched from a string state by successively fetching two bytes and combining them arithmetically.

### 3.3 State Function Combinators

The generalized comprehension notation will be used in this subsection to define some transformation utilities ('combinators') for state functions. The function list transforms a list of state functions into one state function with a list as result. As it makes use of no particular property of state functions, the function is actually applicable to any monad (for the list monad, the list function boils down to transpose).

```
-- list     ::                [StFun s r] -> StFun s [r]
list         :: Monad m => [m        a] -> m        [a]
list []      = result []
list (f:fs) = [ x:xs | x<-f, xs<-list fs]
```

The function exactly transforms a state function into one that applies the original one a given number of times, and thus results in a list of values. The function matrix is parameterized with two integers, and constructs a matrix-valued state function. Just a list, the functions exactly and matrix are defined for any monad, but are used only for state functions in the sequel. You may therefore read StFun s instead of the arbitrary monad m in the definitions below.

```
exactly          :: Monad m => Int -> m a -> m [a]
exactly 0     f  = result []
exactly (n+1) f  = [ x:xs | x<-f, xs<-exactly n f ]

matrix        :: Monad m => Dim -> m a -> m (Mat a)
matrix (y,x) = exactly y . exactly x
```

A combinator that is specific for state functions that have a list as state is many, which applies a state function as many times as possible until the state has become the empty list.

```
many     :: StFun [a] b -> StFun [a] [b]
many f   = [ if b then [] else y:ys
           | b   <- empty
           , y   <- f
           , ys <- many f
           ]
```

The type 'state function' was defined as a function that operates on a state, and returns a result and an (updated) state. Now imagine the situation where in conjunction to applying a state function StFun a c, a function b->b has to be evaluated. This could be modelled in two ways:

- the type b is tupled with the state: StFun (a,b) c
- the type b is added as an extra parameter, and tupled with the result:
  b -> StFun a (b,c).

Both approaches are equivalent, in the sense that conversion functions between the two implementations can be written:

```
sf'curry  ::   StFun (a,b) c   ->   (b -> StFun a (b,c))
sf'curry (SF h) = f
          where f b = SF g
                  where g a = ((b',c),a')
                          where (c,(a',b')) = h (a,b)

sf'uncur  ::   (b -> StFun a (b,c))   ->   StFun (a,b) c
sf'uncur f = SF h
        where h (a,b) = (c, (a',b'))
                 where SF g        = f b
                       ((b',c),a') = g a
```

These transformations are the analogues for state functions of the curry and uncurry operations on normal functions. Note the nice symmetry in the definitions: the equations in sf'uncur are the same as in sf'curry, written right to left.

All functions defined thus far (except entropy) are quite abstract, and should really be part of a monad or state function library. They have been treated here to make this article self-contained. The implementation of the proper JPEG algorithm starts in the next section.

# 4 JPEG Fundamental Algorithms

## 4.1 Huffman Trees

A Huffman coding translates values with a higher probability of occurrence into codes of shorter length, thus reducing the overall length of a message. Huffman codes can be decoded if all possible values are stored in a binary tree. The bits in a code are used as navigating instructions in the tree; on arriving in a tip, the value found there is the value corresponding to the bits consumed. As the number of bits that make up one code is variable, the decoding function is best modelled as a state function, which consumes as many bits as necessary from a [Bool] (or Bits) state.

```
lookup                :: Tree a -> StFun Bits a
lookup (Tip x)        = result x
lookup (Bin lef rit) = [ x
                       | b <- item
                       , x <- lookup
                              (if b then rit else lef)
                       ]
```

In the JPEG algorithm, four different Huffman trees are used. Each of them is specified in the header of the file as a list of lists. These lists contain the values that have codes of equal length. The construction of the corresponding Huffman tree can be elegantly described by an inductively defined state function. The state type used is [(a,Int)], a list of values with associated code length. The initial state can be easily computed from the [[a]] representation:

```
huffTree :: [[a]] -> Tree a
huffTree = st'apply (build 0) . concat . zipWith f [1..16]
        where f s = map (\v->(v,s))

build  :: Int -> StFun [(a,Int)] (Tree a)
build n = [ if b then Nil else t
          | b   <- empty
          , (_,s) <- peekitem
          , t   <- if   n==s
                   then [Tip v   | (v,_) <- item]
                   else [Bin x y | x<-build (n+1)
                                 , y<-build (n+1)]
          ]
```

In the JPEG algorithm, Huffman coding is not used to code values directly, but instead to code the *number of bits* that is used to store values. Given its number of bits, a value can be fetched from a bit-stream by the function receive.

```
receive       :: Int -> StFun Bits Int
receive 0     = result 0
receive (k+1) = [ 2*n + (if b then 1 else 0)
                | n <- receive k
                , b <- item
                ]
```

The decoding of a value is thus a two-stage process: first some bits are consumed to find a number of bits in the Huffman tree, and next that number of bits is received from the state. Before yielding the value, the function extend is applied to it. This function cares about negative numbers. For example with $s = 5$, the numbers 16 to 31 stand for themselves, but numbers 0 to 15 stand for $-32$ to $-16$. The numbers 0 to 15 could have been described in less than 5 bits, after all.

```
dcdecode   :: Tree Int -> StFun Bits Int
dcdecode t = [ extend v s
             | s <- lookup t
             , v <- receive s
             ]

extend v s | s==0      = 0
           | v>=half   = v
           | otherwise = v + 1 - 2*half
                where  half = 2^(s-1)
```

The function dcdecode could be repeatedly used to fetch multiple numbers. However, in practice long sequences of zeroes are to be expected in the data, and to code them even with a 1-bit Huffman code would be a waste of space. Instead, the mechanism described above is combined with run-length encoding of sequences of zeroes. For this situation, a different Huffman tree is used, which stores not only a code size $s$ but also a zero-run length $r$. Decoding now first involves consuming enough bits from the state to find an $(r, s)$ pair in the Huffman tree. Next, a value $x$ is `received` and `extended`, but it is prepended with $r$ copies of zero in the result. Finally, the function is called recursively to get even more values. An extra parameter $k$ is used to stop the recursion when 63 values have been accumulated. A special case is when both $r$ and $s$ are zero, which is a signal that only zeroes should be appended to complete a batch of 63 values.

```
acdecode :: Tree (Int,Int) -> Int -> StFun Bits [Int]
acdecode t k
  = [ x
    | (r,s) <- lookup t
    , x    <- let k' =  k + r + 1
              in  if   r==0 && s==0
                  then [ copy (64-k) 0 ]
                  else [ copy r 0 ++ (extend x s : xs)
                       | x  <- receive s
                       , xs <- if   k'>=64
                               then [[]]
                               else acdecode t k'
                       ]
    ]
```

Both the function `dcdecode` and the function `acdecode` will be used in subsection 5.1. The names 'dc' and 'ac' are used frequently in the JPEG literature, as the interpretation of the values will turn out to be vaguely reminiscent of 'direct current' and 'alternating current' in electricity.

## 4.2 Discrete Cosine Transform

The key to the high compression ratios of JPEG compression is that the image data is not compressed directly, but first transformed by a mathematical operator known as the 'Discrete Cosine Transform' (DCT). The cosine transform amounts to expressing a continuous function as a sum of (infinitely many) cosine functions with increasing frequencies. In the discrete version, the function is sampled at a number of points (JPEG uses 8 sampling points), and only that number of cosine functions are needed. The correspondence between samples $s$ and their transformations $t$ is:

$$t(u) = \sum_{x=0}^{7} \frac{C(u)}{2} s(x) \cos\left((2x+1) u \pi/16\right)$$
$$s(x) = \sum_{u=0}^{7} \frac{C(u)}{2} t(u) \cos\left((2x+1) u \pi/16\right)$$

where $C(0) = 1/\sqrt{2}$ and $C(u) = 1$ for $u \neq 0$. For the inverse transformation the second relation can be directly coded into Gofer

```
idct1 :: [Float] -> [Float]
idct1 = matapply cosinuses

cosinuses :: Mat Float
```

```
cosinuses  = map f [1,3..15]
       where f x = map g [0..7]
             where g 0 = 0.5 / sqrt 2.0
                   g u = 0.5 * cos(fromInt(x*u)*(pi/16.0))
```

In JPEG a two-dimensional version of the DCT is used, which transforms an $8 \times 8$ block of data into $8 \times 8$ DCT coefficients. A two-dimensional DCT can be performed by first transforming each row, and then transforming each column of the resulting 8 rows of coefficients:

```
idct2 :: Mat Float -> Mat Float
idct2  = transpose . map idct1 . transpose . map idct1
```

In the resulting block of coefficients, the upper left value can be interpreted as the average of the original data (if you know enough of electricity this may justify the name 'd(irect) c(urrent) coefficient'). The other 63 values ('ac coefficients') represent higher and higher harmonics as the bottom right is approached.

The function idct1 performs 64 multiplications, and hence idct2 requires $(8 + 8) \times 64 = 1024$ multiplications. Various clever schemes, which exploit the symmetry in the cosine matrix to bring down the number of multiplications, are summarized by Pennebaker and Mitchel [8]. Hartel and Vree [2] discuss how fast algorithms for the related Fourier transform (FFT) can be implemented and optimized in a functional language.

### 4.3 Quantization and Downsampling

The DCT as such does not bring in any data reduction, as an $8 \times 8$ block of image data is transformed into an $8 \times 8$ block of DCT coefficients. However, in continuous-tone images, such as scanned photographs, higher harmonics tend to be absent. Sequences of zeroes in the DCT coefficients are coded very efficiently by the run-length encoding described in subsection 4.1. To encourage the presence of zeroes, the DCT coefficients are *quantized* during encoding, i.e. mapped to a smaller interval, by dividing by a constant and rounding to an integer. Small coefficients will vanish, and larger coefficients lose unnecessary precision. The quantization factor can be specified for each coefficient separately. Thus the unimportant higher harmonics can be quantized more than the lower harmonics. The quantization factors are determined during encoding (typically by a user selecting a 'quality'), and stored in the image header. During decoding, which we deal with here, the coefficients are multiplied again by the quantization factors.

The coefficients in the 2-dimensional matrix of coefficients are not stored in row or column order, but in a zigzag order, which again promotes long sequences of zeroes, especially at the end if the list (bottom-right of the matrix) of coefficients. The function dequant below takes a list of 64 quantization factors and a list of 64 quantized coefficients, multiplies them together, constructs a matrix in zigzag order, and then performs a 2-dimensional inverse DCT.

```
type QuaTab = [Int]

dequant ::QuaTab -> [Int] -> Mat Int
```

```
dequant = matmap truncate 'o' idct2 'o' zigzag 'o'
            map fromInteger 'o' zipWith (*)
```

The function `zigzag` puts the 64 elements of a list in the desired order in a matrix:

```
zigzag xs = matmap (xs!!) [[ 0, 1, 5, 6,14,15,27,28]
                          ,[ 2, 4, 7,13,16,26,29,42]
                          ,[ 3, 8,12,17,25,30,41,43]
                          ,[ 9,11,18,24,31,40,44,53]
                          ,[10,19,23,32,39,45,52,54]
                          ,[20,22,33,38,46,51,55,60]
                          ,[21,34,37,47,50,56,59,61]
                          ,[35,36,48,49,57,58,62,63]
                          ]
```

During compression, an image can optionally be 'downsampled' by averaging over a (e.g. $2 \times 2$) block of pixels, and treating them as one pixel. It is common practice to decompose an image in a grey-value ('luminance') component and two components describing colour information ('chrominance'), and downsample the two chrominance components to half their resolution. This immediately reduces the size of the image to $(1 + \frac{1}{4} + \frac{1}{4}) / 3 = 50\%$ of the original size. During decoding the chrominance components are 'upsampled' again by:

```
upsamp        :: Dim -> Mat a -> Mat a
upsamp (1,1) = id
upsamp (x,y) = multi y . map (multi x)
```

# 5 JPEG Data Organization

## 5.1 Decoding Units

The DCT transformation operates on an $8 \times 8$ block of integers. However, a picture is usually bigger, and consists of more components (e.g., red/green/blue or luminance/twice chrominance). In this subsection we will compose the blocks together.

First, let's formalize how one $8 \times 8$ block is processed. The function `dataunit` is basically a state function, which consumes bits from the state and returns a `DataUnit` (a matrix of integers). The function is parameterized by upsampling factors, a quantization table, and two Huffman trees, which are conveniently grouped together in a four-tuple called `DataSpec`. The function uses `dcdecode` to fetch a 'dc' coefficient from the bits in the state. As a final optimization this is not the value of the dc coefficient itself, but the difference from the dc coefficient of the previous block. Therefore, the function has an additional integer parameter which specifies the previous dc coefficient, and returns the new coefficient as part of the result for use in the next block. After the dc coefficient, the ac coefficients are fetched form the bits state. Together, the coefficients are dequantized, DCTransformed and upsampled by the functions defined in subsection 4.3.

```
type DataUnit =  Mat Int
type DataSpec =  (Dim, QuaTab, Tree Int, Tree (Int,Int))
```

```
dataunit ::  DataSpec -> Int -> StFun Bits (Int,DataUnit)
dataunit (u,q,dc,ac) x
    = [ let y=x+dx
         in  (y, upsamp u (dequant q (y:xs)))
       | dx <- dcdecode dc
       , xs <- acdecode ac 1
       ]
```

To process more than one dataunit, we need a way to communicate the dc coefficient that was part of the result of the first block to the next block. It would be convenient if it was part of the state, so that it could be 'modified' after processing each dataunit. Careful inspection of the type of dataunit reveals that this is possible: the extra Int parameter to the state function and the Int part of its result can be attached to the state by the st'uncur combinator from section 3.3. Another combinator, matrix, can be used to transform the StFun (Bits,Int) DataUnit state function into one that returns a *matrix* of DataUnits instead of just one: StFun (Bits,Int) (Mat DataUnit). However, we immediately let this matrix collapse to one big DataUnit by applying matconcat to the result of the state function (using map in its state function result transforming role). All together, we have a state function that fetches a block (of which the dimensions are given by dim) of 8 × 8 blocks:

```
units     :: Dim -> DataSpec -> StFun (Bits,Int) DataUnit
units dim = map matconcat . matrix dim . sf'uncur . dataunit
```

A group of such big blocks, one for each image component, is called a *minimum coding unit* (MCU) in JPEG terminology. Imagine the case that luminance information is not downsampled, and chrominance components are downsampled by factors 2 × 2 and 4 × 4, respectively. Then we need 16 luminance units, and 4 and 1 chrominance units to make up one MCU. Indeed, the units of the various components are interleaved in this order during encoding. The development of the state function mcu, which fetches an entire MCU from a bit stream, is driven mainly by inspecting the types involved.

First, we construct a version of units in which the Int is detached from the state again, and in which the Dim and DataSpec parameter are tupled together:

```
units':: (Dim,DataSpec) -> Int -> StFun Bits (Int,DataUnit)
units' = sf'curry . uncurry units
```

Our first approximation of the mcu function is to apply units' to a (Dim,DataSpec) combination for each component:

```
type MCUSpec  =  [(Dim, DataSpec)]
mcu    :: MCUSpec -> [ Int -> StFun Bits (Int,DataUnit) ]
mcu    = map units'
```

The list of functions that is the result of mcu could be applied elementwise to a list of integers:

```
mcu'   :: MCUSpec -> [Int] -> [ StFun Bits (Int,DataUnit) ]
mcu'   = zipWith ap . mcu
```

A list of state functions can be transformed into a state function for a list by the list combinator from section 3.3. Then we have a state function of type StFun Bits [(Int,DataUnit)]. The result part of this can be unzipped. For the functional composition, we use `o`, because mcu' has two additional parameters:

```
mcu'' :: MCUSpec -> [Int] -> StFun Bits ([Int],[DataUnit])
mcu'' = map unzip `o` list `o` mcu'
```

Now we are almost done. The [Int] which appears both as a parameter and as part of the result is attached to the state again, and the list of matrices in the result is matzipped to a matrix of lists:

```
type Picture = Mat [Int]
mcu'''':: MCUSpec -> StFun (Bits,[Int]) Picture
mcu''' = map matzip . sf'uncur . mcu''
```

The function is now in its ideal form. The state consists of bits that contain the compressed image, and a list of integers that contains the last dc coefficient seen (one for each component). The result is a picture, which is a matrix with for each pixel information about all the components.

What remains to be done is repeatedly fetch MCU's in order to make a complete picture. Note that, as it is part of the state, the list of 'last dc seen' is passed silently from one MCU to the next.

```
picture :: Dim -> MCUSpec -> StFun (Bits,[Int]) Picture
picture dim = map matconcat . matrix dim . mcu'''
```

All these auxiliary functions can be summarized by the following two definitions, which capture the entire JPEG interleaving scheme in a few lines:

```
units dim =  map matconcat  . matrix dim   .
             sf'uncur        . dataunit
pict dim  =  map matconcat   . matrix dim   .
             map matzip       . sf'uncur     .
             map unzip       `o` list        `o` zipWith ap  .
             map (sf'curry   . uncurry units)
```

## 5.2 JPEG Header structure

What remains to be dealt with, is parsing the JPEG image header in order to collect the various Huffman tables, quantization factors and other parameters. Again, state functions considerably facilitate parsing. For example, a quantization table and its identifier are fetched from the header by the following parser:

```
qtabCompo = [ (id,qt)
            | (p,id) <- nibbles
            , qt <- exactly 64
                   (if p==0 then byte else word)
            ]
```

In the full paper three more pages are spend to define parsers for the various parts of the header (using the primitive parsers byte, nibbles and entropy from 3.2), and for combining them in a function

```
jpegDecode :: String -> Picture
```

This function takes a compressed picture and transforms it into picture, that is a matrix of pixels. Each pixel consists of a list of integer components with values in the range

−128 to 127. The interpretation of the components is left unspecified by JPEG, but most often they represent luminance, chrominance blue, and chrominance red. These values can be converted to the more widely used RGB coordinates by the following linear transformation:

```
yCbCr2rgb  =  matmap f
       where  f =  map ( (+128).(/15) )
                .  matapply [ [15,  0, 24]
                            , [15, -5,-12]
                            , [15, 30,  0]
                            ]
```

The resulting matrices of RGB values can be easily converted to other picture formats.

## 6 Conclusion and Future Work

We have shown that functional programming can be successfully used to implement a complicated algorithm in graphics. We hope that the reader agrees with us that the algorithms needed can be formulated quite concisely and elegantly, and that the borderline between 'specification' and 'implementation' is fading: the correctness of the specification can be demonstrated informally by executing it, and the specification can be used as a prototype implementation of which component functions can be optimized.

The technique of using 'state functions' has been used in the program on three occasions: fetching segments from a character string (section 5.2), fetching Huffman codes and other compressed information from a bit list (section 5.1) and as an auxiliary function for constructing a Huffman tree (section 4.1). The last one shows that 'state' need not be confined to a 'global program state', but that the state function technique can also be used locally.

In the program we have implemented the so-called 'baseline' variant of the JPEG standard, and even from that left out a few less commonly used features, such as 'restart markers'. The program could be easily extended to include these and non-baseline features such as:

- a progressive mode, in which multiple scans per picture frame are allowed;
- allowing for multiple frames;
- an implementation of 'arithmetical coding' instead of Huffman coding.

Another interesting project is to write a JPEG *en*coder in the same style. This has been done by my students Arjan van IJzendoorn and Dennis Gruijs. They had as input only a draft of this article, which they inverted function by function. Their program could be extended constructing Huffman tables optimized for a particular picture. Construction of Huffman tables is actually a functional programming classic (see [1]). The reader may well imagine that collecting the necessary frequency information from the image is just a matter of a few maps and concats.

Finally, it would be interesting to provide the program of an interactive interface, for which functional programming techniques have become available recently (e.g. in the

Clean language [9]). The very efficient code produced by the Clean compiler could speed up the program dramatically, especially if the `zigzag` and `dct` functions are implemented using arrays instead of lists. We have not done so yet, because the Clean language lacks monad comprehensions, and thus would make the functions less understandable to the human reader.

# References

[1] Richard Bird and Philip Wadler. *Introduction to functional programming*. New York: Prentice Hall, 1988.

[2] Pieter Hartel and Willem Vree. 'Arrays in a lazy functional language – a case study: the Fast Fourier Transform'. In: *2nd Arrays, functional languages, and parallel systems* (G. Hains, ed.). Montréal: Dept. d'informatique, Université de Montréal (publication 841), 1992, pp. 52–66.
also: ftp.fwi.uva.nl/pub/computer-systems/functional/reports/ATABLE92_fft.ps.Z.

[3] Hudak and Fasel. 'A gentle introduction to Haskell'. *ACM Sigplan Notices* 27, 5 (may 1992), pp. T1–T53.
also: haskell.cs.yale.edu/pub/haskell/tutorial.

[4] Mark P. Jones. 'A system of constructor classes: overloading and implicit higher-order polymorphism'. In: *FPCA '93: Conference on Functional Programming and Computer Architecture*. New York: ACM Press, 1993.
also: www.cs.nott.ac.uk/Department/Staff/mpj/fpca93.html.

[5] Mark P. Jones. *Gofer 2.30 release notes*.
ftp.cs.nott.ac.uk/nott-fp/languages/gofer.

[6] Mark P. Jones. 'Functional programming with overloading and higher-order polymorphism'. In: *Lecture Notes of the 1st International Spring School on Advanced Functional Programming Techniques* (Johan Jeuring and Erik Meijer, eds). Berlin: Springer, 1995 (LNCS 925).

[7] International Standards Organization. *Digital compression and coding of continuous-tone still images*. Draft International Standard DIS 10918-1. (reprinted in [8]).

[8] William Pennebaker and Joan Mitchell. *JPEG still image data compression standard*. New York: Van Nostrand Reinhold, 1993.

[9] Rinus Plasmeijer and Marko van Eekelen. *Concurrent Clean Language Report*. Nijmegen: Dept. of Computer Science, University of Nijmegen, the Netherlands, 1995 (to appear).
ftp.cs.kun.nl/pub/Clean.

[10] Philip Wadler. 'The Essence of Functional Programming'. In: *19th Annual ACM SIGPLAN Symposium on Principles of Programming Languages*. Santa Fe, 1992 (pp. 1–14).
also: ftp.dcs.glasgow.ac.uk/pub/glasgow-fp/papers/essence-of-fp.ps.Z.

[11] Gregory Wallace. 'The JPEG still picture compression standard'. *Communications of the ACM* **34**,4, 1991 (pp. 30–44).
also: ftp.uu.net/graphics/jpeg/wallace.ps.gz.

# Part IV: Multi-Paradigm

# The "No-Paradigm" Programming Paradigm for Information Visualization

E.H. Blake and H.A. Goosen

Computer Science, University of Cape Town
Rondebosch 7700, South Africa
E-mail: {edwin,goosen}@cs.uct.ac.za

**Abstract** We describe our exploratory visualization environment, the interactive Inventor Shell (iIsh), and the fact that no single programming paradigm underlies it. IIsh is an environment for interactive exploration of large databases of multidimensional abstract data, an application known as *Information Visualization*. This environment has been used in a number of areas but is still evolving — this flexibility is a key feature. IIsh is built around the Tcl scripting language and the Inventor[1] three-dimensional graphics toolkit, and simplifies the creation of interactive three-dimensional visualizations of abstract data. A particular feature of iIsh is that the interaction behavior of the system can be easily modified at run-time. We have used iIsh to construct a variety of visualization applications in fields ranging from computer architecture to medical insurance, and we describe our experience.

## 1 Introduction

The interactive Inventor Shell (iIsh) is an environment for Exploratory Multidimensional Abstract Data Visualization or *Information Visualization*. We have developed this environment for the interactive exploration of large databases of abstract information. We have used iIsh for visualizing shared-memory parallel program performance, manufacturing scheduling information, an astronomical database of galaxy information, medical insurance claim information, financial market data, and teletraffic data.

The design space of information visualization systems is even larger than that of Scientific Visualization systems because there are no physical objects to ground the concepts portrayed. The requirements of Information Visualization place a high premium on fast modification of systems, the maintenance of multiple versions reflecting different possible solutions to problems, and the ability to generate diverse high quality graphical interfaces.

IIsh uses interactive three-dimensional (3D) graphics techniques to display large amounts of data, enabling the human visual system to derive insights from the spatial, color, and texture information in the images. The use of three dimensions is important for two reasons. First, it enables us to display a much larger amount of data than would be possible in two dimensions. Second, it provides an extra dimension in which we can display interesting correlations. The interactive nature of the user interface complements the 3D aspect by allowing the user to focus in on interesting aspects of the data, while ignoring irrelevant detail, further improving our ability to display large amounts of data.

---

[1] Inventor is a trademark of Silicon Graphics Incorporated.

In this paper we describe our visualization environment, and the programming paradigms that underlie it. A theme of the paper is that we are presenting a snapshot of a system and a field that is in rapid development. As such the emphasis of a system has to be on flexibility and extensibility rather than on structure and formalism. We are convinced that only once the subject matter is better understood can more supportive but restrictive methodologies (let alone "paradigms"!) be formulated. As a result of our experience we can present design criteria (Section 2.1) that in a presentation, such as this paper, belong before the discussion of the system but which were of course uncovered as we performed our experiments.

The organization of the paper is as follows. First there is a general discussion of the programming requirements of information visualization systems (Section 2). We then briefly discuss previous approaches to visualization programming in this context (Section 3). Our system, iIsh, is then introduced in two stages, firstly (Section 4) its design and salient features of the implementation, and then (Section 5) a few highlights of our experience in using iIsh. This experience is then discussed in Section 6 "No Paradigm or Multi-Paradigm?". This is followed by a few concluding remarks and pointers to further work.

## 2 The Programming Requirements of Information Visualization Systems

In its present state of development, the field of information visualization has no fixed methodologies, nor established problem areas with recognized solutions. This essential characteristic carries a number of implications when experimenting with visualization systems and developing visualization solutions. One has to be able to explore multiple solutions in parallel and to design new systems in an iterative design-implement-evaluate cycle. A further ramification is that there is no clear distinction between development-cum-experimentation systems and "production" systems. As a result there is also a need for the distinction between user and application programmer to be blurred.

In visualization, the importance of the user is always recognized. The whole aim of the visualization is to create an internal representation of the information in the mind of the user.

A visualization processing pipeline is presented in Figure 1. The first two stages, data modelling or acquisition followed by processing, are common to graphics pipelines. The need for flexibility means that the nature of the third, display, stage is not fixed and that it can be easily changed. Various forms and degrees of preprocessing can be applied to the data. There isn't any notion of graphical "realism", instead the ideal of truth in representing the underlying data is maintained. It is acknowledged that prettiness may stand in the way of insight. The addition of the final step, that is, decoding by the user, is an emphatic difference with standard graphics pipelines. The role of interaction is emphasized by the feedback loop.

There has been surprisingly little published on systems that allow three-dimensional graphics and interactive exploration techniques to be employed for information visualization. Partly this is due to a lack of suitable tools. The scientific visualization packages like AVS, Explorer, etc, have poor support for more abstract information, focusing in-

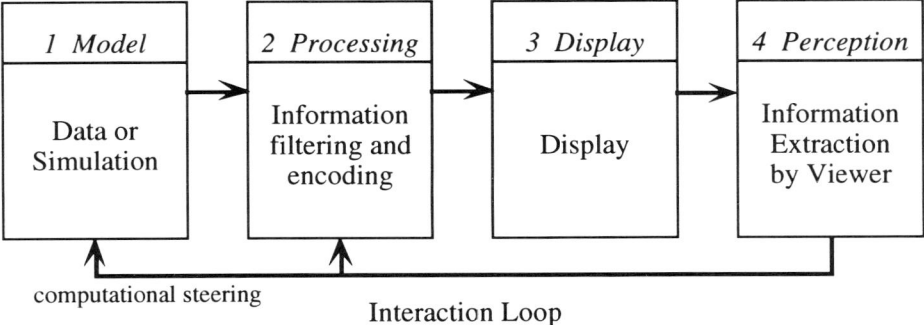

Fig. 1: A visualization pipeline.
The role of the viewer and computational steering is indicated in this diagram.

stead on continuous fields and support for more traditional scientific and engineering representations. Also, scientific visualization packages typically do not provide good support for interaction and particularly new forms of interaction. In our experience, it is difficult to extend these packages to include the required features for information visualization.

## 2.1 Key Design Criteria and Concepts

During a process of implementation, testing, and progressive refinement of ideas, we developed the following set of criteria (which are not independent) to support the design:

*Immersive manipulation* — the user interacts directly in 3D (by using a pointing device) with an immediate graphical representation of the data or data attributes, without the intervention of agents like 2D controls (scrollbars and other traditional direct manipulation tools), or 3D widgets that are separate from the data representation.

This is an extension of the original formulation of direct manipulation [13], and is in contrast with interfaces based on 3D widgets [17]. The VIEW system supports a similar notion of direct interaction with the image [2].

*Input-output coupling* — browsing of the display (output) image, and then using it as an input tool for the refinement of queries. The output of the browsing operation can be used as the input of another browser on a different set of attributes, and so on to any level of nesting [1].

*Flexibility, power, and extensibility* — these are not directly supported by the interface of the system, instead being provided by the underlying programming constructs. These are certainly vital to the success of a visualization system, but we consider that current attempts to provide these in the interface have not succeeded. The users of visualization systems are not professional programmers though they are competent and sophisticated professionals. These users combine needs in terms of ease of use and protection from their mistakes as novice programmers with the needs of flexibility, power and extensibility.

*Dynamic embedded spreadsheet* — the spreadsheet model of user-level programming has been proven to be accessible to general users (especially in the business community), and offers a concise and powerful and comprehensible programming model. While much of user-programmable system design makes use of visual programming techniques (e.g., the data-flow diagrams of AVS, etc.), the spreadsheet model and dataflow visual models are functionally equivalent.

*Focus* — related to browsing and refinement of queries. Focusing (or filtering) helps us to get rid of meaningless clutter, by reducing the amount of data displayed.

*Correlative linking* — techniques to make it easy to create correlation views. Interactive visual correlation allows one to have different displays relating to the same information. Shneiderman calls this tight coupling, referring to the extension of direct manipulation.

*Generality* — provided by the ease of modifying the specialized system. An analogy is a shifting spanner, which is specialized for one nut, but can easily be changed to accommodate different sizes.

*Computational steering* — while visualization systems have always recognized the importance of the user as *viewer* they have been less accommodating of the user as *interactor*. A user interaction loop which goes back to the model is given a special name, "computational steering".

*Standard building blocks* — we created our environment for interactive exploration by combining two widely available tools: Tcl, an extensible scripting language, and Inventor (based on OpenGL, which is fast becoming a standard for interactive 3D graphics). The environment is familiar to many users, powerful, and designed to be easily extensible. Because it is based on Tcl, iIsh can easily be incorporated as a building-block into other Tcl-based tools.

Finally, when these criteria, and particularly the central importance of interaction tools, are taken into account, then the standard visualization pipeline presented above, for all its novelty, becomes too restrictive. It seems better to regard the various aspects of a visualization system not as stages in a pipeline but as a collection of cooperating processes that act on a common pool of data ([16]). Once more the benefit of this is to emphasize flexibility. Figure 2 shows the various stages of the visualization pipeline arranged round a common cloud of dynamically changing data. The viewer is dependent on display and input devices for interaction with the data.

# 3 Previous Approaches to Visualization Programming

In this section we discuss the basic enabling technologies that contributed to our iIsh system.

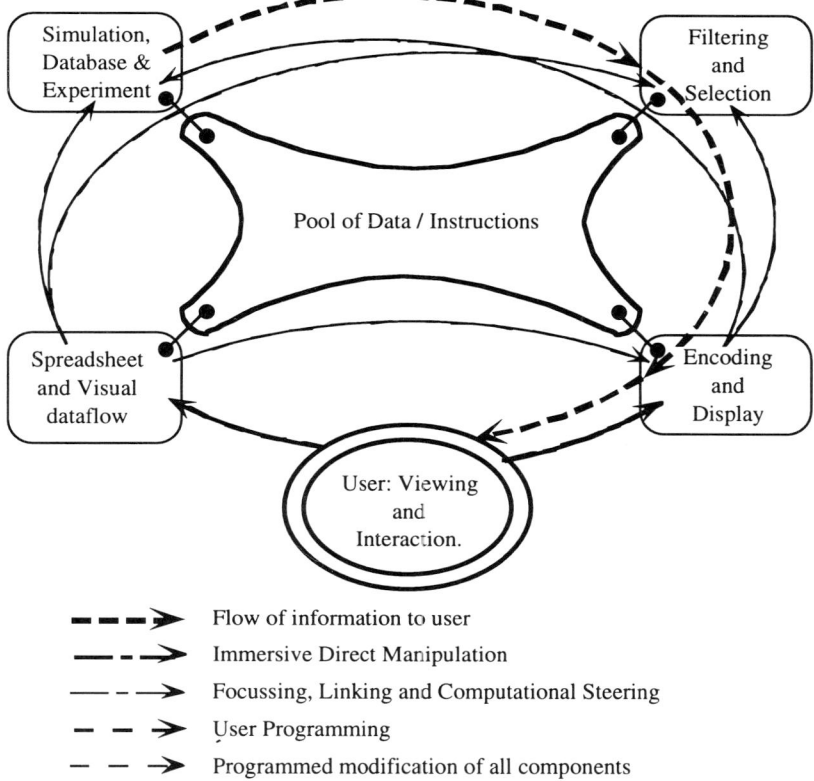

Fig. 2: A Conceptual Model of a Visualization System.
Visualization systems allow the user to view complex data. They also allow sophisticated interaction with many aspects of the data and the models. The notion of plugable processing, output
and input modules should be contrasted with that of a pipeline with a feedback loop.

### The Contribution of Graphics Programming Methodologies

The Eurographics workshop series on Object-Oriented Graphics has reflected a certain
'eminence' of object-orientation in interactive systems, graphics, and computer animation [3, 10]. The *Doré* system, which was already well established by the time it was
presented at the first workshop, was a major first success of object-oriented graphics.

The ilsh system is (by its very name — interactive Inventor Shell) based on the
Inventor C++ toolkit from Silicon Graphics [15]. Inventor is an object-oriented toolkit
that supports the programming of direct manipulation interfaces in the immersive sense
— allowing the user to interact directly with the displayed 3D objects in the same
window as the display and without having to seek recourse to manipulation widgets.

The Inventor library provides a collection of retained high-level 3D objects and makes them available for building interactive interfaces. The contrast is with earlier interactive graphics systems where rendering of 3D objects was the prime focus and "picking" of objects was the most sophisticated user input action possible.

An Inventor 3D scene and associated interactions are stored as a direct acyclic graph of nodes (it is analogous to traditional display lists). There are *shape nodes* for the geometry, *property nodes* for attributes, and other nodes for *interaction* to act on events.

The philosophy of Inventor is that flexibility is the overriding concern. Questions of efficiency are important but secondary, while structure and policy enforcement are considered least important. Inventor is object oriented, but with many extensions. The 3D scene graph is a mixture of aggregation relations that build up 3D objects, attribute inheritance trees, procedural rendering instructions[2] and asynchronous event handling code.

Objects in Inventor come in two guises: *nodes* which are open objects storing state, and objects representing single *actions*, with possibly some associated state information. This extension of object-orientation provides the user with the ability to design new actions (methods) for existing system classes without having to create subclasses of the existing classes. An action can be applied to objects in a scene graph and it then processes the nodes in the graph. The state held by the action object provides the inheritance and accumulation of attributes during traversal of the scene graph.

Inventor also introduces *node kits*. The previous paragraph described how Inventor extends object-orientation to provide methods divorced from classes (the *actions*) and opens up the internal state of an object to allow various useful features. The node kit should be seen then as a re-introduction of many of the traditional encapsulation and enclosed methods associated with object-oriented programming. The node kit provides a collection of subgraph nodes that "relate to 'objects' (chairs, bicycles) in the 3D scene" [15, p. 346]. Thus a node kit in many ways reassumes the role associated with classes in object-oriented programming.

### Scripting Languages

Tcl (Tool Command Language) is a popular and flexible scripting language [12]. Tk extends Tcl to support the writing of graphical user interfaces. Languages like Tcl are now frequently used in visualization systems (for example, VIEW mentioned earlier uses a language modelled on Smalltalk-80 [2]). In accordance with our desire for flexibility, we have opted for one of the least structured of these languages, believing that in the absence of clear guidance on what our user will require we want to start off providing the maximum flexibility.

Tcl is interpreted and the interpreter can be *embedded* in the application. Tcl can be regarded as providing a powerful command interface to the application. Alternatively the application can be regarded as extending the Tcl language with application specific semantics. These views are equivalent. The power of the conceptual model is further that the user's Unix shell interface is extended (since Tcl provides the capabilities of a shell) to become the interface to the application. Tk adds window management and event handling to this powerful interface. Finally, the Tcl/Tk user communities is expanding rapidly and providing further enhancements to the toolkits.

---

[2]The nature of a displayable object depends on its parents and preceding siblings.

The limitations of Tcl are an excess of its strength: flexibility. Tcl provides only two data types: strings, and associative arrays. There are also built-in commands to manipulate lists. Multidimensional arrays have to be simulated, and arithmetic is inefficient because numbers have to be converted between string and internal representations.

### Spreadsheets

Our application building environment incorporates a spreadsheet module to augment the standard data-flow models used in systems like AVS and Iris Explorer. Our spreadsheet is embedded in a dataflow environment, with the dataflow relationships specifying the inputs and the outputs to the spreadsheet. Unlike conventional spreadsheets that are loaded up with static data, our spreadsheet is part of a processing pipeline, and dynamically fires when new data becomes available.

Spreadsheets have made their appearance in computer graphics [11, 9]. Levoy's system uses spreadsheets where the individual cells contain graphics, and the formulae are programmed with Tcl [11]. He cites the limitations of dataflow visualization system in terms of expressive power and scalability to motivate the use of spreadsheets. We have chosen to separate the spreadsheet interface model from the graphical direct manipulation style of interaction.

Hudson discusses the advantages of spreadsheets as user interfaces and points out that spreadsheets embody a kind of dataflow computation [9, p211]. One might prefer to say that both dataflow and spreadsheets embody many aspects of the declarative or functional programming paradigm.

Spreadsheets have a distinct declarative feel, in the sense that the user specifies relationships that have to be maintained between cells. In addition, a spreadsheet spreads the problem out in space, in a declarative fashion, rather than in time sequence (or procedural fashion).

Dataflow derives meaning purely from geometrical relationships. If the graph gets complex, the user gets lost. Spreadsheets retain the declarative feel and the spatial localization, but adds naming, to control the visual complexity.

## 4 Design and Implementation of iIsh

IIsh is an interpretive environment for creating interactive 3D visualizations of abstract data. It includes a scripting language, a visual programming system, and 3D viewers that support immersive manipulation.

A user interacts with iIsh in one of three ways. First, iIsh provides a window into a three-dimensional space populated by 3D view objects. Zooming, panning, camera rotation, camera translation, and selection can all be done using only a mouse within the 3D window, and without requiring 2D or 3D widgets as intermediaries. Selection can be either on view objects as a whole, or else on components of view objects, for example, on an individual face or vertex.

Second, a two-dimensional drawing editor, called Vizion, is used to specify which view objects should be drawn, and what the relationship between the input database and each view object is. Vizion supports a visual programming system based on

128

dataflow diagrams (much like that used in Iris Explorer or AVS), using functional blocks interconnected by lines indicating the dataflow relationships. However, the dataflow diagram is *not* intended to be the primary way of programming the visualization. Instead, Vizion provides an *embedded spreadsheet* functional block that accepts arbitrary iIsh scripts as formulas. Unlike more conventional spreadsheets that have cells containing static values, the embedded spreadsheet module has input and ports that are connected to data sources. The input ports feed into cells, and cells can contain lists of values. Cells can also be connected to output ports, supplying data to the rest of the system, in particular to the view modules.

Third, an interpretive shell allows the user to program the system by entering iIsh scripting language commands. This general programming interface supports features that we have not yet decided how to provide in the Vizion programming system, for example, the binding of event handling scripts to events. Figure 3 shows the iIsh 3D viewer (displaying a cone) and the Vizion visual programming window with a spreadsheet module.

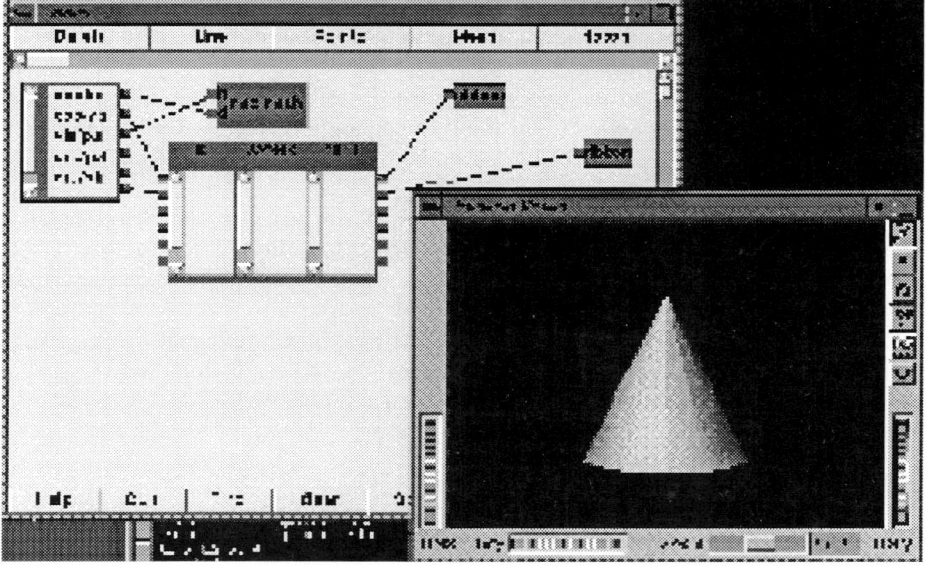

Fig. 3: iIsh windows.
The iIsh 3D window displaying a cone, and the Vizion visual programming editor with a spread-sheet module.

IIsh achieves its functionality by creating and manipulating Inventor scene graphs through an interpreted scripting language. It supports an event binding mechanism that allows iIsh scripts to be dynamically bound to scene graph components.

Compared to more traditional programming tools based on compiled programming languages and libraries, the iIsh scripting language provides

- a short write and test cycle,

- an easy learning curve, and

- a convenient and compact way of storing different versions of a visualization program.

## 4.1 Design

The iIsh scene graph structure is considerably simpler than the Inventor scene graph structure. As in Inventor, a scene graph consist of nodes that are connected to form a directed acyclic graph. There are two kinds of nodes: shape nodes, and group nodes. The shape nodes represent simple graphical shapes (cubes, spheres, cylinders, or cones) or more complex shapes (meshes, text, or nurbs surfaces). Because iIsh nodes are based on Inventor node kits (mentioned above), the material properties, coordinate transformations, and other information required to render the shapes are all contained within the iIsh node itself, and we do not require property or transformation nodes as in Inventor.

An iIsh scene graph can be active or inactive. When a scene graph is activated, it will be rendered, and the active graph also automatically supports the dynamic binding of iIsh scripts to scene elements.

There are five basic iIsh commands to enable node creation, scene graph composition, setting of graphical attributes (for example material properties of shapes), the binding of iIsh scripts to graphical components, and the activation of scene graphs.

For example, the iIsh command line

```
iCreate Cube my_cube
```

consist of three strings. The first string, iCreate, is the name of the iIsh command to create a node. The second string, Cube, tells iIsh what kind of node to create (in this case a cube). The third string, my_cube, is the name we give to the node, so that we can refer to the cube node later in the program.

The various types of iIsh commands can be summarized as follows:

- iCreate node_type node_name — node_type specifies which node to create, and node_name associates a name with the node.

- iAddChild parent_name child_name — parent_name is the name of the parent node, and child_name is the name of the child node that will be attached to the parent node.

- iSet node_name attribute_string — The attribute_string will be passed to the node identified by node_name. The underlying Inventor node kit mechanism supports the use of such strings to set the values of parts contained in the node kit.

- iBind node_name event_specifier script_string —node_name identifies the graphic element[3] we want to interact with, event_specifier

---

[3]Note that this is not the same as a node, because a single node can represent many graphic elements, uniquely identified by giving a path name to the node representing the graphic element.

specifies an event, and `script_string` is a string which will be interpreted by iIsh when the specified event occurs. The `script_string` can contain special character combinations that are replaced by event-specific information before the script is interpreted, as described below.

- `iSetSceneGraph node_name` — node_name identifies the node that should be considered the root of the active scene graph.

For example, here is a complete iIsh program that creates a green cube named my_cube, a red cone named my_cone, and draws the cone 2 units away from the cube. When the left button is pressed on the cube, "mouse button pressed on green cube" will be printed on the standard output, when the left mouse button is pressed on the cone, "mouse button pressed on red cone" will be printed on the standard output, and when the left button is pressed anywhere else in the display area, "mouse button pressed on nothing" will be printed on the standard output.

```
iCreate Cube my_cube
iCreate Cone my_cone
iSet my_cube "material {diffuseColor 0 1 0}"
iSet my_cone "material {diffuseColor 1 0 0} \
        transform {translation 2 0 0}"
iBind .my_cube down1 {puts "mouse button pressed on green cube"}
iBind .my_cube.my_cone down1 {puts "mouse button pressed on red con
iBind . down1 {puts "mouse button pressed on nothing"}
iAddChild my_cube my_cone
iSetSceneGraph my_cube
```

## 4.2 Implementation

IIsh is an extension of Tcl to support interactive three-dimensional graphics, in much the same way that Tk extends Tcl to support the writing of graphical user interfaces. The implementation of iIsh borrows heavily from the Tk implementation. The three-dimensional graphics primitives used in iIsh is supplied by the Silicon Graphics Inventor library (see above). IIsh supports the standard Inventor file formats for input and output of scene graphs.

The iIsh implementation is based on an interpretive interface to the Inventor node kit mechanism. Node kits allow text strings to be used to set attribute values, greatly simplifying the interpretive interface. For example, iIsh does not have to support all the member functions used to set the values of fields in Inventor node classes. Instead, a single command (`iSet`) is used to pass text strings to the node kit `set` member function.

Tcl (Tool command language) is an extensible interpreter developed at the University of California, Berkeley. It is freely available, and many extensions are have been developed to support application requirements like graphical user interfaces (Tk), distributed programming (Tcl-DP), and database access (Tcl-SQL). Tcl provides basic facilities like variables, associative arrays, string processing, and procedure calls.

IIsh is a simple extension to Tcl/Tk. All the Tcl/Tk commands are available in iIsh. IIsh node names reside in a separate name space from Tcl variables. IIsh supports an explicitly controlled stack of name spaces, which helps to keep name space pollution under control in procedure calls, but without requiring modification to the Tcl interpreter. The iIsh name space stack is implemented using a linked list of hash tables.

The binding of iIsh scripts to graphical components is based strongly on the Tk binding mechanism. An arbitrary iIsh script can be bound to a specific event on a graphical element. A number of special replacement character sequences can be included in the script: appropriate values based on event information will be substituted for these characters before the script is executed. For example, the character sequence "%w" will be replaced by the window position, in pixels, of the mouse pointer when the event occurred.

Graphical elements are specified by composing a path name to the graphical element. Each path name element is the name of the node that has to be traversed to get to the shape node representing that element. The node names are separated by "." characters. The path name "." will match an event occurring anywhere in the display area.

The event binding mechanism is implemented using a hash table that stores *(path, event, script)* tuples. When an event occurs, a path name is generated for the graphical element associated with the event. For example, if the event is a left mouse button down event that occurs on the red cone in the above example, the path `.my_cube.my_cone` would be generated. The hash table is then scanned for tuples matching the path and the event. If no tuple is found, the trailing path element (`.my_cone`) is removed, and the hash table scanned again for a match. The search for a handler continues until the "." path has been checked. If a matching handler is found, the script associated with that handler is scanned for substitutions, and then the script is interpreted by the Tcl interpreter.

In addition to the iIsh extensions to the Tcl interpreter, we have also implemented a collection of C++ classes to encapsulate view objects that we have found useful. These classes allow the concise specification of a view object, based on the quantitative data we want to display. For example, our `VoMesh` object takes a list of name-value pairs, and creates a square mesh with the heights proportional to the values, and the names available for use in callback functions that support correlative linking to other view objects.

The three-dimensional viewing area in iIsh is provided by the Inventor SceneViewer, that already provides camera movement, rotation, and zooming features. The Vizion drawing editor to support visual programming is implemented entirely in Tcl/Tk, with iIsh providing the three-dimensional graphics primitives.

# 5 Experience with Using iIsh

IIsh was developed in an experimental environment, in the course of building several information visualization systems. These are presented below, in chronological order, to present our experience and reasons for particular design decisions.

## 5.1 Chiron Parallel Program Visualization

The original application we were interested in was the analysis of traces of parallel architecture behavior. We had constructed an execution-driven simulator that provides detailed information about parallel architecture behavior (especially cache memory system behavior) when executing programs, and visualization seemed a powerful tool to help us understand the behavior, given the large volumes of data generated by a simulator. Our initial experience with scientific visualization tools convinced us that we needed something more flexible, and we started implementing our visualization system, Chiron [8, 7] using Inventor, a C++ toolkit for implementing interactive 3D graphics programs.

Chiron displays several views of performance data associated with lines of source code and objects in the parallel program. Our primary focus was on providing fine-grain information about the behavior of individual objects, source lines, and cache lines in the program. The information included both temporal event information, and also summary information accumulated over selected time periods.

We designed several interactive views to represent this information. Each view is a 3D shape that can be individually manipulated. We also support the linking together of different views, so that the mouse selection of a particular point on one view can be correlatively linked to the graphical representations presented in the other views.

We have evaluated Chiron using several parallel applications [8, 7]. Although space does not permit a complete discussion of Chiron features, Figure 4 (in the colour plate appendix) show an example of Chiron views.

In the course of the Chiron development, we needed to maintain multiple versions of the program to experiment with. Apart from the cumbersome implement-compile cycle, we found several other problems:

- Object and executable files are large and consume significant amounts of disk space.

- It was difficult to maintain multiple versions of source files, synchronized to the executables, and to make sure that arbitrary features could be combined in one compilable executable.

- To keep track of the features in a particular version of the executable creates a significant documentation problem.

These problems motivated us to look for an alternative that would retain the flexibility of our C++/Inventor system, but that would eliminate these significant obstacles to experimentation. An extensible interpretive environment seemed like a natural solution. Tcl/Tk was chosen because it was fast, well-implemented, well-documented, and had a large user community.

## 5.2 Manufacturing

We developed a visualization system to assist the master scheduler in a manufacturing plant. The plant is run using a management information system implementing the MRP-II (materials requirements planning) methodology. The visualization system was implemented in six weeks by two COBOL programmers who had no previous experience of computer graphics or C programming. The application required a custom COBOL interface to extract data from a database of manufacturing information. This data was then forwarded to our visualization module.

Two visualization modules supported the MRP-II functions of rough-cut capacity planning, and capacity requirements planning. A third module represented sales history data. Figure 5 (in the colour plate appendix) shows the rough-cut capacity planning module. The ribbons represent the available capacity, measured in machine hours, of each work center on a weekly basis. For each week, a colored cube indicates the total capacity required of that work center. The vertical position of the cube indicates the required capacity relative to the available capacity. In addition to the position, the cube is colored red if the required capacity exceeds the available capacity, and green otherwise.

To get more information, the user can click on a particular cube. That brings up a display of all the orders that were scheduled on the work center for the week in question.

### 5.3 Other Applications

Several other applications have either been completed or are under construction, and we briefly discuss these here. The Astronomy Department at the University of Cape Town does research on the large-scale structure of the universe. A database of all known galaxies in the Southern Sky has been compiled, and we implemented a visualization system for displaying this database. The system has been used to discover new types of large-scale structures [6, 5], and also to make video and slide shows for use in planetaria. Although this application does not require much interaction, it demonstrates the flexibility of our environment.

A second application we are working on is visualizing medical insurance data. Medical insurance companies collect large amounts of information relating to claims. This information is potentially valuable for designing fee structures, and also for discovering fraudulent use of benefits. However, there are few suitable tools available for exploring such databases, with the result that often the data is not fully exploited. The dataflow programming interface to iIsh allows the user to rapidly switch between different datasets, to view multiple datasets at the same time, or to link features on one data set to the representation of another dataset.

We are also exploring the visualization of financial market data. This is a demanding application area that could make good use of animation to show the real-time behavior of financial instruments. iIsh does not currently support the easy specification of animation behavior, and we are therefore working on animation extensions.

# 6 No Paradigm or Multi-Paradigm?

How did object-orientation fare under iIsh? As we have seen iIsh uses Iris Inventor as its underlying interactive graphics system. In general we found that *node kits* were needed to prevent our users from being overwhelmed by the flexibility provided by Inventor. Therefore to the extent that node kits mark a return to class inheritance and encapsulation this represents a step back towards object-oriented orthodoxy from the potential for freedom from structuring inherent in Inventor.

As we have pointed out, both spreadsheets and visual dataflow provide essentially functional programming facilities. We have extended this with a full procedural language. However unlike Levoy [11] we do contain the imperative programming within the spreadsheet cells (in the same way that visual dataflow allows state in the individual modules), spreadsheet cells are not allowed to have side-effects on other spread-sheet cells. This greatly aid the understanding of users and controls some of the complexity of the spreadsheet.

## 6.1 Interaction

We believe that support for the flexible specification of interactive behavior is essential in an information visualization system. In information visualization applications, the relationship between data items are often non-linear. The dimensionality of the data is often much greater than in typical scientific data sets, increasing the need for examining many different types of correlation between data items. Our experience with trying to use traditional scientific visualization systems for information visualization leads us to conclude that more support for interaction is needed. Often the types of interaction that the user may require cannot realistically be anticipated by the designer of the visualization system, arguing for a programming interface to interaction specification.

The most basic kind of interaction is to query a visual representation, to find out more about the underlying data relating to a specific part of the image. For example, consider the visualization representing work centers in the manufacturing plant showed in Figure 5. The user of such a system may notice a particular week in which the needed capacity is particularly high, and would like to see, for example, detailed information on the order which is responsible for the high demand that week . This data is stored in a database, and to get the information, the system has to query this database, based on a user action (like mouse selection).

## 6.2 Interactive Correlation

A more complex interaction that we have found useful in our work is interactive correlation. For an example, refer to Figure 4, showing two surfaces. The surface on the left represents the execution time of individual lines of code in a program, while the surface on the right represents the execution time spent waiting for individual objects to be accessed in memory. To optimize the performance of the program, it may be useful to know which objects are accessed by which lines of code in the program. By selecting a source code line on the left surface (using the mouse), we can highlight all objects accessed by that line of source code on the right surface. In the same way, by selecting an object on the right surface, we can highlight all lines of source code that access that object on the left surface. The user is in effect browsing a database of correlation information, getting rapid visual feedback on the relative cost of different selections. These operations require access to a database of correlation information, and then modifying the images to show the correlation information.

# 7 Concluding Remarks

We believe it is too early for a programming paradigm (i.e., set of abstractions) for Information Visualization systems. Instead, we opted for a relatively unstructured collection of concepts, each appropriate to a particular need that we perceived. A summary of these needs and concepts are:

*Exploration* — Supported by immersive manipulation and correlative linking to browse the data space, and dataflow connections to select particular data sources and appropriate view objects.

*Filtering* — We provide an embedded spreadsheet module to program general filtering and data processing. The spreadsheet formulas are written in the Tcl scripting language.

*Interaction* — By binding Tcl/iIsh scripts to events and view objects, the user can change the interaction behavior to suit the particular needs of a data set.

Our initial experience with iIsh has been favorable, and we are continuing our experimental evaluation by building more information visualization systems, and getting people to use them. We are also extending iIsh as we discover new requirements that challenge the existing implementation.

Many issues are still unclear. First, it is difficult to find the proper balance between the use of 2D and 3D graphics for visualization. There are many cases where the use of 3D allows the display of more information, and where the position of objects in space can give clues about the underlying process one is analysing. However, it is also often the case that 3D confuses the user by presenting too much data that becomes simply confusing, or that a particular 3D display is difficult to interpret because background parts of the image is obscured by foreground features.

Another problem is the choice of an appropriate display method before one has seen the data displayed, as often happens in an exploratory environment. For example, a particular data set may be too large to display in a given format, given the limited performance of a particular machine. This can be frustrating in a supposedly interactive, exploratory environment. We are therefore examining features to allow iIsh to remain responsive and controllable while data is being processed, so that commands can be aborted or modified as the user receives incremental information.

Our spreadsheet module (in common with most existing spreadsheets) has a shortcoming in that it only supports a global namespace and therefore is not suitable for implementing large problems. We are investigating the use of a hierarchical spreadsheet model to address this.

# Acknowledgements

This work was supported in part by the Foundation for Research Development (South Africa) and the University Research Committee of the University of Cape Town, South Africa. We would like to thank Dieter Polzin, Wayne Paverd, Matthew Shaer, Grant

136

Kauffman, Philip Machanick, and Peter Hinz for implementing and using various parts of Chiron, iIsh, and Vizion. Explorer and Inventor are trademarks of Silicon Graphics Inc., Mountain View, California.

# References

[1] C. Ahlberg and B. Shneiderman. Visual information seeking: Tight coupling of dynamic query filters with starfield displays. In B. Adelson, S. Dumais, and J. Olson, editors, *Proceedings of CHI*, pages 313–317. ACM, 1994. (Boston, MA, USA, April 24-28, 1994).

[2] L. D. Bergman, J. S. Richardson, D. C. Richardson, and J. Frederick P. Brooks. VIEW — an exploratory molecular visualization system with user-definable interaction sequences. In SIGGRAPH '93 [14], pages 117–126.

[3] E. H. Blake and P. Wißkirchen, editors. *Advances in Object-Oriented Graphics, I*. Springer-Verlag. Berlin, 1991.

[4] W. S. Cleveland. *The Elements of Graphing Data*. Wadsworth & Brooks/Cole, Pacific Grove, California, 1985.

[5] A. P. Fairall and W. R. Paverd. Large-scale structure in the southern sky to 0.1c. In *35th Herstmonceux Conference on Wide-field Spectroscopy and the Distant Universe*. World Scientific Publishing Company, 1994. In press.

[6] A. P. Fairall, W. R. Paverd, and R. Ashley. Visualization of nearby large-scale structures. In C. Balkowski and R. Kraan-Koorteweg, editors, *Unveiling Large-Scale Structures Behind the Milky Way*. Astronomical Society of the Pacific Conference Series, October 1994.

[7] H. A. Goosen, P. Hinz, and D. W. Polzin. Experience using the chiron parallel program performance visualization system. 1995. Submitted for publication.

[8] H. A. Goosen, A. R. Karlin, D. R. Cheriton, and D. W. Polzin. The chiron parallel program performance visualization system. *Computer-Aided Design*, 26(12):899–906, December 1994.

[9] S. E. Hudson. User interface specification using an enhanced spreadsheet model. *ACM Transactions on Graphics*, 13(3):209–239, 1994.

[10] C. Laffra, E. Blake, V. deMey, and X. Pintado, editors. *Object-Oriented Programming for Graphics*. Springer-Verlag, Berlin, 1995. To appear early 1995.

[11] M. Levoy. Spreadsheets for images. In *SIGGRAPH '94*, Computer Graphics Proceedings, Annual Conference, pages 139–146, Orlando, Florida, 24-29 July 1994. ACM SIGGRAPH.

[12] J. K. Ousterhout. *Tcl and the Tk Toolkit*. Addison-Wesley, 1994.

[13] B. Shneiderman. Direct manipulation: A step beyond programming languages. *IEEE Computer*, 16(8):57–69, 1983.

[14] *SIGGRAPH '93*, Computer Graphics Proceedings, Annual Conference, Anaheim, California, 1-6 August 1993. ACM SIGGRAPH.

[15] P. S. Strauss and R. Carey. An object-oriented 3d graphics toolkit. *Computer Graphics*, 26(2):341–349, July 1992. SIGGRAPH'92, Chicago.

[16] J. J. van Wijk and R. van Liere. An environment for computational steering. Technical Report CS-R9448, Centrum voor Wiskunde en Informatica—CWI, Amsterdam, 1994.

[17] R. C. Zeleznik, K. P. Herndon, D. C. Robbins, N. Huang, T. Meyer, N. Parker, and J. F. Hughes. An interactive 3d toolkit for constructing 3d widgets. In SIGGRAPH '93 [14], pages 81–84.

**Editors' Note: see Appendix, p. 171 for coloured figures of this paper**

# Reactivity, Concurrency, Data-flow and Hierarchical Preemption for Behavioural Animation

Stéphane Donikian and Éric Rutten

IRISA, F-35042 RENNES, France
E-mail: donikian@irisa.fr, rutten@irisa.fr

**Abstract** Behavioural models offer the ability to simulate autonomous entities. Such entities perceive their environment, and communicate and decide actions to execute, on themselves or on their environment. These reactive systems treat flows of data to and from the environment in a complex way. They need modularity, concurrency and hierarchy, and involve task control and preemption. We examine the adequacy for decision making of the behavioural model in the following programming paradigms: reactivity, concurrency, data-flow and hierarchical preemption.

Reactive languages provide complete design environments. The specification of concurrent behaviours is naturally supported in the synchronous languages, and they address control intensive applications (sequencing and preempting tasks) as well as computation intensive applications (data-flow). SIGNAL*GTi* is an extension of the language SIGNAL where data-flow processes can be composed into nested preemptive tasks.

An application in the simulation of a transportation system shows how these programming paradigms can be of use, and how SIGNAL*GTi* can support their implementation.

## 1 Introduction

**Context.** Behavioural animation consists of a high level motion control of dynamic objects, which offers the ability to simulate autonomous entities like organisms and living beings. Such entities are able to perceive their environment, to communicate with other creatures and to execute some actions either on themselves or on their environment. This requires to make a deliberative choice of the behaviour, and for that we have to design a *reactive system* continuously in communication with the environment (*data-flow*). The behaviour of a creature, even for the simplest, is composed of different activity lines (*modularity*) which can be completely distinct but also *concurrent*). *Hierarchy* and *preemption* are some other important notions for such a system, because they enable users to construct them in a modular and re-usable way, defining behaviours from sub-behaviours, sequenced, interrupted or suspended by preemption.

Reactive languages (and particularly synchronous ones) handle these programming paradigms in different forms. Additionally, they open up perspectives concerning the formal verification of safety-critical behaviours and the distributed compilation of applications. However each does so by concentrating on one or two paradigms, not integrating them all. The tasking extension of SIGNAL called SIGNAL*GTi* integrates the concurrency and data-flow reactivity of SIGNAL with notions of sequencing and hierarchical preemption of tasks. Hence, it is a fitting candidate for programming our class of applications.

**Behavioural animation.** The objective of animation is the calculation of an image sequence corresponding to discrete time states of an evolving system. Animation consists at first of expressing relationships linking successive states (specification phase) and then evaluating them (execution phase). Motion control models are the heart of any animation/simulation system and determine the friendliness of the user interface, the class of motions and deformations produced, and the application fields. Motion control models can be classified into three general families : descriptive, generative and behavioural models [14]. Descriptive models are used to reproduce an effect without any knowledge about its cause. Unlike preceding models, generative models offer a causal description of objects movement (describe the cause which produces the effects), for instance, their mechanics. In this case, the user control consists of applying torques and forces on the physical model. Thus, it is not easy to determine causes which can impose some effects onto the mechanical structure to produce a desired motion. Two kinds of tools have been designed for the motion control problem: loosely and tightly coupled control. Motion control tools provide the user with a set of elementary actions, but it is difficult to control simultaneously a large number of dynamic entities. The solution is to add a higher level which controls the set of elementary actions [5, 6]. This requires making a deliberate choice of the object behaviour, and is done by the third model named *behavioural*. The goal of the behavioural model is to simulate autonomous entities like organisms and living beings. A behavioural entity possesses the following capabilities: perception of its environment, decision, action and communication. The paradigms needed for programming a *realistic* behavioural model are reactivity, data-flow, modularity, concurrency and hierarchical preemption.

**Synchronous reactive languages, SIGNAL and SIGNAL*GTi*.** *Reactive systems* are characterized by the fact that they perform actions only in reaction to the occurrence of an event: their pace is determined by discrete events to which they react. The *synchronous languages* are dedicated to the programming of such systems [7, 13]. These languages have a notion of simultaneous events, and synchronous communications allow processes to synchronize their transitions on shared instants. This model of time is the basis of clear semantics, a model of concurrency easier to handle than the asynchronous one, and efficient analysis tools. Their aim is to support the design of safety critical applications, especially those involving signal processing and process control. The synchronous approach guarantees the determinism of the specified systems, and supports techniques for formal verification (like the detection of causality cycles and logical incoherencies). A family of languages is based on this approach [13], featuring ESTEREL, LUSTRE, SIGNAL, ARGOS and also STATECHARTS. SIGNAL [16] is a data-flow language, with a declarative style, and an environment supporting automated formal verification. A recent extension to SIGNAL provides constructs for the specification of the preemption (i.e., abortion or suspension) of *nested tasks* on intervals of time [20]. This extension is implemented in SIGNAL*GTi* (which stands for *Gestion de Tâches et d' intervalles*, the french for: tasks and intervals management), a pre-processor to SIGNAL, fully compatible with the tools in the environment, and hence benefitting from their functionalities such as proof, code generation in various languages.

**Organization of the paper.** The nature of behavioural animation is presented in the following section. Section 3 presents an application which requires *Realistic* Behaviours. In Section 4, a set of characteristics needed for the specification of a virtual driver are listed and a Modular and Hierarchical Behavioural Model integrating these characteristics is presented. Section 5 gives a presentation of the synchronous reactive data-flow language SIGNAL, and of its extension with hierarchical preemptive tasks SIGNAL*GTi*. Next, Section 6 discusses the adequacy of the paradigms proposed by SIGNAL*GTi* for the description of our behavioural model, with the example of a driving simulation system.

# 2 Behavioural Animation

Behavioural models are based on two kinds of relationships between the object and its environment: perception and action (see Figure 1). The temporal dependency relation of the state of an entity $E(t_i)$ at the time $t_i$ is globally expressed by a function $f(E(t_{i-l}), \ldots, E(t_{i-1}), P(t'_{j-k}, \ldots, t'_j), C(t_i), t_i)$, where $C(t_i)$ is the set of messages received by the entity at time $t_i$ and $P$ represents the environment perception function during the temporal interval $[t'_{j-k}, \ldots, t'_j]$, with $t'_j \leq t_i$. Different approaches have

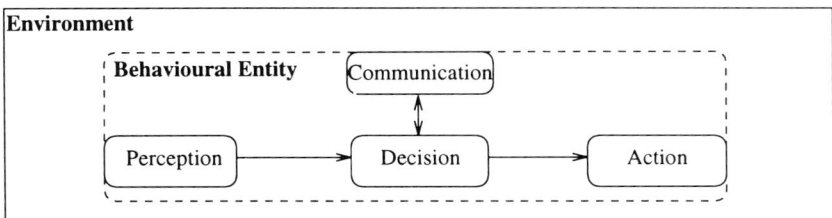

Fig. 1: A behavioural agent immersed in its environment.

been studied for the decision part of these models [9]:

**Sensor-effector Approach** The behaviour of objects is defined by sensors, effectors and a neural network which connects them. The way an object behaves in the environment depends on how the environment is sensed, and how this information is passed through the neural network to the effectors that produce the motion of the object. The same neural network can produce different kinds of motion depending on the parameterization of nodes and on the weight of connections (see e.g. [22]).

**Behaviour Rule Approach** Like the previous approach, it takes sensed information as its input and motor controls as its output, but the behaviour of the object is controlled by a set of behaviour rules. The possible behaviours can be represented by a decision tree in which each branch represents one alternative behaviour (see e.g. [21]). This method offers a higher level of description than the preceding one, but the difficulty results from the choice of the rating strategy.

**Predefined Environment Approach** This approach is based on the fact that the environment is predefined and static: thus, all possible paths from the initial position to the goal position can be explored. It is easy to determine an optimal solution inside the set of enumerated solutions, according to behaviour criteria, but on the other hand a little change in the environment implies a complete recomputation of the motion (see e.g. [19]).

**Finite Automaton Approach** In this approach, the behaviour of an object is either controlled by one finite automaton or by combining elementary behaviours and designing a supervisor for the resulting composite behaviour. The use of a single automaton is not convenient: firstly making conceptually simple changes in behaviours requires widespread modification of the finite state machine, secondly it is difficult to express concurrent constraints on control processes [8]. Modularity, hierarchy and concurrency can be obtained by using Hierarchical Concurrent State Machines (HCSM) [1] or Hierarchical Parallel Transition Systems [3].

Most of these systems have been designed for particular examples, in which modularity and concurrency are not necessary. This is because entities possess only one activity line and because possible interactions between an object and its environment are very simple: sensors and actuators are reduced to minimal capabilities which, mostly, permit only avoidance of obstacles in a 2D or 3D world. A notion of time is generally not treated. In a system mixing different objects described by different kinds of models (descriptive, generative and behavioural), it is necessary to take into account the explicit management of time, either during the specification phase (memorization, prediction, action duration) or during the execution phase (synchronization of objects with different internal times).

# 3 Driving Simulation for the Praxitele Project

## 3.1 The Praxitele Project

The Praxitele project combines the efforts of two large government research institutes, one in transportation technologies (INRETS), the other in computer science and automation (INRIA), in cooperation with large industrial companies (RENAULT, EDF, CGEA). This project designs a novel transportation system based on a fleet of small electric public cars under supervision from a central computer. These public cars are driven by their users but their operation can be automated in specific instances. The system proposed should bring a solution to the congestion and pollution in most cities through the entire world. The concept of a public transport system based on a fleet of small electric vehicles has already been the subject of experiments several times but with poor results. The failure of these experiments can be traced to one main factor: poor availability of the vehicles when a customer needs one. To solve this main problem, Praxitele project develops and implements automated cooperative driving of a platoon of vehicles, only the first car is driven by a human operator [18]. This function is essential to move easily the empty vehicles from one location to another. The realization of such a project requires experiments of the behaviour of autonomous vehicles in an urban environment. Because of the danger of this kind of experiments in a real site, it is necessary to design a virtual urban environment in which simulations can be done. Our simulation platform permits to simulate a platoon of vehicles evolving in a virtual urban environment and so to test control algorithms of the automated cars.

## 3.2 A Simulation Platform

With the intention of making the three kinds of motion control models work together, we have been interested in their integration into a single system and we have proposed the architecture of a simulation platform. The simulation platform is composed of a set of *agents/actors* whose synchronization and communication are managed by a real-time kernel. The main part of this kernel is the general controller. Communication between the agents is both synchronous and asynchronous. The synchronous part is data-flow based where each agent has its own frequency and is managed by the general controller. So, the data-flow communication channels include all the mechanisms to adapt to the local frequency of the sender and receiver agents (over-sampling, sub-sampling, interpolation, extrapolation). The asynchronous part is based on two mechanisms: event based communication between agents and the general controller, and global data-structure updating and accessing mechanisms. A first version of the simulation platform has been performed [11]. PVM is used to define the real-time kernel which is in charge of communication and synchronization between different processes, while SIGNAL is used to assume internal management of each process (see Colour Figure 9 in appendix).

## 3.3 Simulation of an Urban Environment

An urban environment is composed of many dynamic entities evolving in a static scene. These dynamic entities have to be both autonomous and controllable and also realistic in term of behaviour. It is necessary to combine the three motion control models to describe dynamic entities of the environment. For example, to describe traffic lights it is not necessary to use a generative model when a descriptive model (finite state automata) is sufficient. On the other hand, for a realistic car driving, we need both generative and behavioural models (the first one to simulate the dynamics of the vehicle and the second one to simulate the driver).

**The static scene.** As we want to control entities evolving, we need to link dynamic entities with the static scene in which they are moving. This link requires a semantic knowledge on the scene. If we want to simulate as completely as possible the life of a city, we need a lot of semantic information. Information required for the simulation are : geometric (geometry of the town, roadsigns), topologic (the road network, a grid of visibility) and semantic (meaning of roadsigns, colour of traffic lights, qualitative aspect of the road and city information like the name of streets and of particular buildings). To describe such a scene, an urban modelling system is currently in development. This system is an extension of the Scriptography (Declarative Design System) [12], in which all these information are mixed.

**Dynamic objects.**   To take into account natural phenomena, the first work is to choose a physical model to represent the object. A vehicle is an articulated rigid object structure if we do not consider the deformations of the tires and the component flexibility [4]. From a high level description of articulated rigid body systems, a simulation blackbox is generated whose inputs are two torques (motor and guidance) and outputs are position and orientation parameters. We have now to determine how to control this physical model that is to say, depending on the actual state of the entity what kind of torque must we apply to it to obtain the desired motion ? In the case of an automatic motion control, this question can be decomposed into two parts: how to control the physical model, and what is the desired motion? The answer to the first question consists of using motion control algorithms well known in the automatic and robotic communities, which can permit to build a library of elementary actions. The behavioural model tries to answer to the second question by defining actions and reactions of an entity [21, 10, 15].

# 4 A Virtual Driver

## 4.1 A Modular and Hierarchical Behavioural Model

We have chosen to define a modular and hierarchical behavioural model, as shown in the Figure 2, to specify the behaviour of a car driver. This model is decomposed into a set of specialized agents who use themselves some experts to reconstruct the new state of the world, before proposing their diagnosis to the decisional agent. Therefore, the supervisor decides to activate some of the specialized agents and this decision depends on its own state and on sensor data. The *road signs* module is, at the moment, in charge of determining the value of three parameters: speed limitation (real value), overtaking (YES | NO) and crossroads priority (right of way | priority to the right way | stop | traffic lights). The *itinerary* module is in charge of determining the new direction at each crossroads, so this module is only activated when the vehicle is near one of them. The *obstacle detection* module has to determine if there are some possible intersections between the vehicle desired trajectory and predicted trajectories of other vehicles, and if so to propose a new trajectory. Actions managed by the *state feedback control* module consist of determining the guidance torque (follow a desired trajectory) and the motor torque (accelerate, brake, stop). In order to simplify calculation, the human vision is not completely simulated but is replaced by a global knowledge on the scene geometry and on the location of objects, then by using visual sensors we obtain qualitative information about objects in the vision cone.

The work of the decisional model is to compare and mix different possible behaviours according to the desired behaviour and then to make a decision of the adopted behaviour. To deal with complex and concurrent behaviours, we have proposed to use hierarchical parallel transition systems to describe the decisional model of the driver. The use of hierarchical parallel transition systems allows us to take into account concurrency and abstraction in the description of the behaviour, like Kearney et al. with their hierarchical

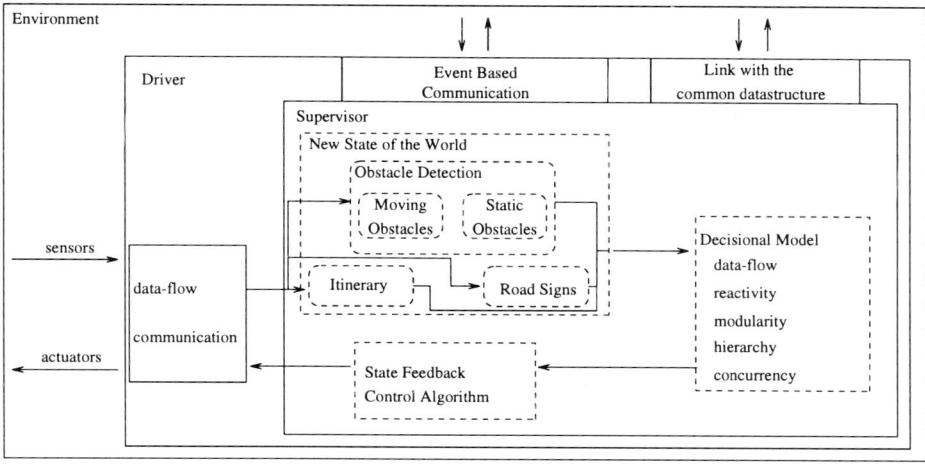

Fig. 2: Modular and hierarchical structure of the driver.

concurrent state machines [15, 1]. Because of the integration of our behavioural model in a simulation platform, we have also the ability to deal with real time during the specification and the execution phases.

## 4.2 Hierarchical parallel transition systems for decision

The Decisional model consists of a reactive system, which is composed of a hierarchy of state machines (possible behaviours). Each state machine of the system can be viewed as a blackbox with an In/Out data-flow and a set of control parameters. It can be defined by the following tuple $< S, \Gamma, IS, OS, CP, LV, IF >$ in which:

**S** : is a set of sub-state machines,      **CP** : is a set of Control Parameters,

$\Gamma$ : is the activity function,      **LV** : is a set of Local Variables,

**IS** : is a set of Input Signals,      **IF** : is the integration function.

**OS** : is a set of Output Signals,

**State Machine.** Each state machine of the system is either an atomic state machine ($S = \emptyset$), or a composite state machine. An activity parameter is associated to each state machine which corresponds to the current status of this machine. This parameter is accessible by using the function *status(state,instant)*, which has five possible values:

$$(\forall s \in S)(\forall k \in \mathcal{N}), \; status(s, t_k) \in \{started, active, suspended, terminated, idle\}$$

**The activity function.** Activity of a state evolves during the simulation, and this is determined by an activity function $\Gamma$. This function possesses four parameters and returns the new status:

$$(\forall s \in S)(\forall k \in \mathcal{N}^*), \; status(s, t_k) = \Gamma(status(s, t_{k-1}), IS, CP, LV)$$

This function permits to represent some transitions between different sub-state machines, but more than one sub-state can be active at each instant (concurrency). For example, in the Figure 3, *Driving* and *Road Shape* sub-state machines work in parallel. This function handles also hierarchical preemption, by the fact that one argument of the function is a set of Control Parameters (CP) which permits to deal with internal events as "substate *i* is *terminated* " or external events as *"an ambulance is coming"*.

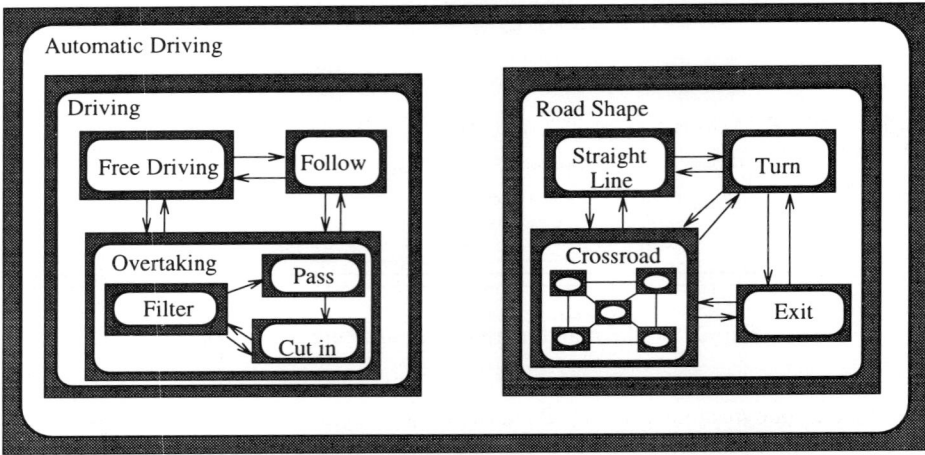

Fig. 3: State transition aspect of the state machine.

**Input / Output parameters.** Input and output parameters correspond to continuous signals of standard type (e.g. integer, real, boolean). The value of an Output signal is undetermined when the state machine is *idle* or *suspended*. For the driver example, some of the input signals of the *Automatic Driving* State Machine and of its sub-state machines are shown on the Figure 4. In this example, there are two output signals: *Guidance action* and *Motor action*; the first one determines what lane has to be followed and actions are for example *turn left* or *filter to the right*, while the second one determines what kind of action must be applied to the vehicle motor and can be for example *brake* or *cover(distance, delay)*.

**Local variables.** Local variables are some variables of standard type, whose value is computed by using the $\Omega$ function. Local variables can either retain their values between activations or be reinitialized on each reactivation (*started* status):

$$(\forall v \in V)(\forall k \in \mathcal{N}^*), \; value(v, t_k) = \Omega(value(v, t_{k-1}), status(s, t_{k-1}), IS, CP)$$

**Control parameters.** Control parameters permit to modulate the behaviour of an entity, depending on external or internal decision. The type of a control parameter is either boolean or interval (*value* $\in [Vmin, Vmax]$). For example, a sub process can inform its parent process that its status become *terminated*, while a process can notify another subprocess that it has to be *started*.

**The integration function.**   The integration function has to manage the coherence of the actions proposed by the different sub-processes, and make a synthesis of them. This is in fact a function which takes as inputs the outputs of all sub-processes and delivers the value of the process outputs. In the case of concurrent behaviours proposed by different sub-state machines, this function has to make a choice and to deliver a unified behaviour as output of the state machine (cf Figure 4). Let E be $< S, \Gamma, IS, OS, CP, LV, F >$.

$$OS = IF(output(S), LV, CP)$$

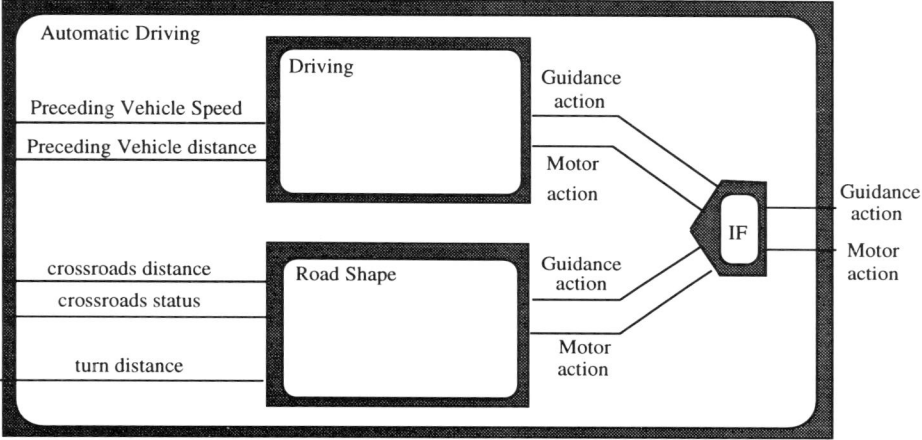

Fig. 4: Data-flow aspect of the state machine.

## 4.3 Conclusion

Characteristics needed for the specification and for a high level programming of the behavioural model are:

- reactivity, which encompasses sporadic or asynchronous events and exceptions,

- modularity in the behaviour description, which allows for parallelism and con-currency of sub-behaviours,

- data-flow, for the specification of the communication between different modules,

- hierarchical structuring of the behaviour, which means the possibility of preempt-ing sub-behaviours on transitions in the meta-behaviour, as a kind of exception or interruption. It means also that sub-behaviours can notify the meta-behaviour of their activity.

This combination of data-flow and event-driven features is not present in many languages; MANIFOLD is one of them, a language for the coordination of processes through a data-flow network, which can change state as a result of the occurrence of an event. Its behaviour is asynchronous, and can be defined in terms of transition systems [2]. In the synchronous approach to reactive systems, there exists a combination of the languages LUSTRE and ARGOS [13] into ARGOLUS, where a state in the hierarchical automata language ARGOS can be refined into a data-flow process in LUSTRE, and in a LUSTRE data-flow network, a node can be refined into an ARGOS automaton. In our approach, we chose the data-flow synchronous language SIGNAL, and its extension with hierarchical preemption tasks: SIGNAL*GTi*, both presented in the next section. In section 6, we will illustrate that this language can answer most of the requirements of a behavioural model combining the preceding characteristics.

# 5 Data-flow with preemption: SIGNAL*GTi*

## 5.1 The synchronous reactive data-flow language SIGNAL

SIGNAL is a synchronous real-time language, data flow oriented (i.e., declarative) and built around a minimal kernel of operators [16]. It manipulates signals, which are unbounded series of typed values (e.g., `integer`, `logical`). They have an associated clock determining the instants where values are present. Given a signal X, its clock is CX obtained by `CX := event X`, giving the event present simultaneously with X. The constructs of the language can be used to specify, in an equational style, relations or constraints of clock inclusion or equality between signals. Systems of equations on signals are built using composition.

The kernel of SIGNAL comprises the following *primitive processes*:

**Functions** $\boxed{\texttt{Y := f\{ X1, X2, ... , Xn\}}}$ e.g., boolean negation: `not E`.

**Delay** $\boxed{\texttt{ZX := X\$1 init V0}}$ gives the past value of $X$ (with initial value $V_0$).

**Selection** $\boxed{\texttt{Y := X when C}}$ according to a boolean condition.

**Deterministic merge** $\boxed{\texttt{Z := X default Y}}$ (with priority to X).

**Parallel composition** $\boxed{\texttt{( | } P_1 \texttt{ | } P_2 \texttt{ | )}}$ union of the systems of equations.

**Restriction** $\boxed{\texttt{P / X}}$ making X local to $P$.

The following table illustrates each of the primitives with a trace:

| X | -1 | 2 | 6 | 3 | -5 | 12 | 7 | -3 | -8 | 13 | ... |
|---|----|---|---|---|----|----|---|----|----|----|-----|
| Y := X + 1 | 0 | 3 | 7 | 4 | -4 | 13 | 8 | -2 | -7 | 14 | ... |
| ZY := Y$1 init 0 | 0 | 0 | 3 | 7 | 4 | -4 | 13 | 8 | -2 | -7 | ... |
| PY := ZY when ZY>0 | | | 3 | 7 | 4 | | 13 | 8 | | | ... |
| Z := PY default (0 when (event X)) | 0 | 0 | 3 | 7 | 4 | 0 | 13 | 8 | 0 | 0 | ... |

The rest of the language is built upon this kernel. A structuring mechanism is proposed in the form of `process` schemes. Instances of processes in a program are expanded by a pre-processor of the compiler. Derived operators have been defined from the primitive operators, providing programming comfort. E.g., synchro{X,Y} constrains the signals X and Y to be synchronous, i.e. their clocks to be equal. The process CB := when B gives the clock CB of occurrences of the logical signal B at the value true. The process Y := X cell B memorizes values of X and outputs them when B is true. In the process C := # X, C is an integer counter of the occurrences of signal X. Delays can be made of N instants, or on windows of M past values. Arrays of signals and of processes are available as well. The SIGNAL compiler performs the analysis of the consistency of the system of equations (absence of causal cycles), and determines whether the synchronization constraints between the signals are verified or not. Executable code can be produced automatically (in C, FORTRAN or ADA).

As a small example, a filter defined by equation $y_t = \frac{x_t + x_{t-1} + x_{t-2}}{3}$ is written in a style very close to this in SIGNAL: Y := (X + X$1 + X$2)/3. Another example is that of a memory cell, of which the value is read on signal V, and modified (i.e., written) by signal V_IN. It can be specified as follows:

```
process CELL= (V_0) {?V_IN, Clk !V}
   (| V := V_IN default (V$1 init V_0) | synchro{V, V_IN default Clk} |)
end
```

The first equation specifies that the output (read) value V is equal to the input (write) value V_IN when there is one and otherwise to the former value V$1. It is initialized at the parameter value V_0. As such, this equation does not specify V completely: the instants at which it is present are the *union* (by the operator default) of those at which it is written and those at which it is read. However, the clock of the readings is needed in order to know the clock of V; therefore, the CELL has a second input Clk, and the second equation defines the presence of V by the synchro operation. This process is in fact the expansion of the SIGNAL operator cell, more precisely V := V_IN cell Clk. This example shows how state information can be memorized and managed. Combined with the selection operator, it does enable the suspension or activation of reactions depending on the state, hence the specification of sequential behaviours in SIGNAL.

## 5.2 Time intervals and nested preemptive tasks in SIGNAL*GTi*

SIGNAL*GTi* extends SIGNAL with constructs for the activation, triggering, suspension and interruption of data-flow processes. We propose a language-level integration of the data flow and preemption paradigms, by extending SIGNAL with two kinds of *tasks* (suspendable or interruptible) which associate a process with the *time interval* on which it is active [20]. This extension is integrated to the SIGNAL environment as a pre-processor to the compiler. It has been applied to an active robot vision system and a control system for a power transformer station [17].

A new type is introduced in the language: interval. It can take two values: inside or outside. The purpose of intervals is to sub-divide the global interval of an application: ]$\alpha,\omega$] into *slices of time* (see Figure 5). The construction of an interval with initial value I0 is noted: $\boxed{\text{I := ]B,E] init I0}}$, where B and E are begin and end events. Repeatedly, I opens at the first occurrence of B, and is inside until it closes at the next occurrence of E, and then it is outside until the next opening, and so forth.

148

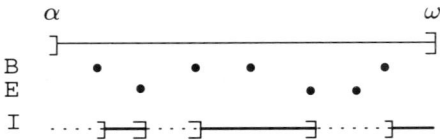

Fig. 5: Time intervals.

Bounding events are given by, respectively: $\boxed{\texttt{O := open I}}$ and $\boxed{\texttt{C := close I}}$.
Intervals are *left-open / right-closed*: transitions (going in and out of the interval) occur
in reaction to an event, and depending on the current state, resulting in the new state only
*after* the reaction instant (like in reactive automata). Time intervals can be composed in
expressions such as union $\boxed{\texttt{I := I1 union I2}}$, complement $\boxed{\texttt{I := comp J}}$,
or intersection $\boxed{\texttt{I := I1 inter I2}}$. The restriction of signal X to time intervals is
$\boxed{\texttt{XI := X in I}}$ for occurrences of X inside I, and $\boxed{\texttt{XO := X out I}}$ for those
outside I. Note that `X out I` is `X in (comp I)`, and that `open I` is `B out I`,
and `close I` is `E in I`.

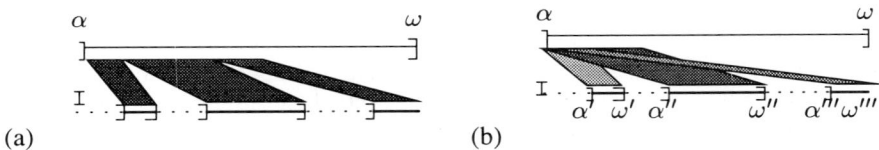

(a)            (b)

Fig. 6: Tasks on (*splitting* time) and `each` (*replicating* time) interval I.

Time intervals and processes are associated to form *tasks*. The process is *active*
inside the time interval, it is *triggered* by the opening event. Outside the time interval,
it is absent (in a sense, it is out of time: its clock is cut off). When the interval re-opens,
the process re-starts; it can do so in one of the two following ways:

**suspendable tasks** are noted $\boxed{P \text{ on } I}$, where the process $P$ is *suspended* on each
closing of I, and on its opening it re-starts from the *current state* of its state
variables. The behaviour of $P$ is *split* on windows in time where I is `inside`
(as illustrated by Figure 6(a)).

**interruptible tasks** are noted $\boxed{P \text{ each } I}$, where a process $P$ is *interrupted* on each
closing of I, and on its opening it re-starts from the *initial state* of its state
variables (according to their declaration). The behaviour of $P$ is *replicated* on
each time window inside I. (see Figure 6(b)).

The process in a task can be decomposed into sub-processes, which can be tasks
themselves. Hierarchies of tasks and sub-tasks can be built that way. In particular, when
a task is built with `each`, re-entering the interval involves re-initializing all sub-intervals
and all sub-tasks recursively.

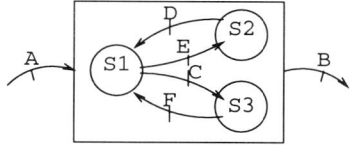

```
(| S1 := ](D in S2) default (F in S3),
                 E default C] init inside
 | S2 := ]E in S1, D] init outside
 | S3 := ]C in S1, F] init outside
 |) each ]A, B] init outside
```

Fig. 7: Sequencing, concurrency and nested preemption in SIGNAL*GTi*.

*Parallelism* between several tasks is obtained naturally using the composition "|" when tasks share the same interval, or overlapping intervals. *Sequencing tasks* then amounts to constraining the intervals of the tasks, by constraining their bounding events. Each time interval holds some state information, and events cause transitions between these states. With hierarchies of tasks, it is then possible to specify hierarchical parallel place/transition systems. For example, in the behaviour illustrated in Figure 7, a transition leads from the initial place S1 to place S2 on the occurrence of an event E, except if the event C occurs before, leading in place S3. If E and C happen synchronously or are constrained to be equal, then both places S2 and S3 are entered. This is a sub-behaviour attached to a place entered upon event A and left upon event B. This can be coded by a task and intervals such that the closing of the one is the opening of the other, as in Figure 7. This last example illustrates a hierarchy of tasks and intervals; it could also have featured data-flow equations. This is the advantage of embedding such constructs into a data-flow language and environment: it enables the integration of the two aspects for the specification of hybrid applications.

# 6 Using SIGNAL*GTi* for behavioural animation

### 6.1 Data-flow between perception, decision and action

At the global level, where the loop of *perception-decision-action* is handled, SIGNAL provides naturally the data-flow structures needed, especially through its graphical editing interface.

Across the levels, data-flow processes in SIGNAL can be organized in hierarchies, where a process is decomposed into a network of connected subprocesses itself. The driver is decomposed into sub-processes managing each one a particular aspect of the model (itinerary, obstacle detection, decisional part), as shown in Figure 2. Also, the possibility is given to declare process models, that can be instantiated in different places in a program, thus introducing re-usability.

The specification of multi-rate computations is handled by the multi-clocked aspect in SIGNAL: signals can be under-sampled and merged, hence leading to the presence of signals and computations on them having different clocks. This can be achieved as the decomposition of a basic clock into sub-clocks for the activation of sub-modules at different frequencies. However it should be noted that the SIGNAL compiler performs a resolution of clocks where they are ordered into an inclusion hierarchy; therefore, the global clock or base clock can be *synthesized* by the compiler, and does not have to be managed by the programmer. For example, in the driving simulation system, the frequency of the driver module is 10 Hz while the one of the vehicle model is 50 Hz, thus each value of the motor and guidance torques is used five times.

In a network of data-flow processes, the activation of computations in a process $P_1$ depends on the presence of the inputs, which can be themselves outputs of another process $P_0$. In that case there should be a sequencing of $P_0$ *before* $P_1$. This kind of sequencing of computations *within* a reaction is motivated by data dependencies but not by a real temporal precedence (from one instant to the other). This is scheduled by the compiler on the base of a graph representing actual data-dependencies between operations.

In SIGNAL programs, it is possible to call external functions; that is, some of the processes in the data flow network can be declared as being externally defined: only their interface (inputs, outputs and parameters) has to be known. This way, SIGNAL programs are open, and enable links with external modules written in C or in FORTRAN (e.g. numerical functions generated by mathematical systems, operating systems, windowing systems).

## 6.2 SIGNAL*GTi* for hierarchical parallel transition systems and concurrent data-flow tasks

An example featuring sequencing, concurrency and nested preemption in SIGNAL*GTi* was presented in Figure 7. It must be noted that in synchronous languages, the concepts of "asynchronous" events is handled in a way perfectly coherent with the general notion of events; therefore they should preferably be called *sporadic* events instead, in our framework. The reactive aspect of transitions is handled in the same way as the data-flow aspect.

Transition systems are given by time intervals and the constraints between their bounds. Indeed, each interval holds some partial state information. Leaving one interval and opening another one on the occurrence of the same event constitutes a sequencing from the one to the other. The fact that time intervals are inherently parallel makes that constrained time intervals support the definition of place/transition systems (*à la* Petri nets) rather than state/transition systems (sequential finite state automata).

The construction of hierarchies of behaviours, featuring definitive or temporary preemption of sub-tasks, is handled by the constructors on and each. They can be used to specify the re-initialization of local modules or agents upon the occurrence of events from the global controller: this is a case for the application of the each constructor, where the task interval is entered upon this event from the global controller. It must be noted that events can come as well from inside of the agents as from outside them.

Some behaviours require to first have a given data-flow network, continuously treating data in a certain way. Then, the occurrence of an event causes a change. This event can be either received from the external environment or caused by an internal event, like reaching a threshold. A new data-flow network, i.e. a new continuous interaction with the environment has to be installed. This sequencing of tasks *between* configurations of the network, involving a transition between states, is obtained simply by associating the processes of these tasks with intervals constrained accordingly.

These tasks can be connected in a data-flow network; their outputs and inputs can be shared, provided this does not impose incoherent constraints on their presence. E.g., in the driving simulation application, part of the driver requires the "integration" of the flows of results "proposed" by various concurrent tasks.

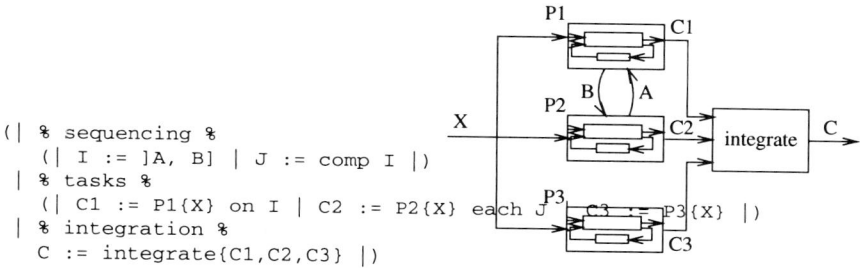

```
(| % sequencing %
   (| I := ]A, B] | J := comp I |)
 | % tasks %
   (| C1 := P1{X} on I | C2 := P2{X} each J | C3 := P3{X} |)
 | % integration %
   C := integrate{C1,C2,C3} |)
```

Fig. 8: Structural separation between sequencing, data-flow, and integration.

The specification of such behaviours in SIGNAL*GTi* provides a methodologically clean separation between the following aspects, that are specified in parallel:

- the sequencing of tasks, which is achieved by the constraining of time intervals (see Section 4.2)

- the data-flow processes, associated to the intervals into tasks using on or each, and connected into a network

- the integration processes taking as inputs the flows of results of the tasks, which may have overlapping time intervals. The integration process composes them in order to produce the unique result for the upper level (e.g. choice, average, sum, max)

Figure 8 gives a sketch of how SIGNAL*GTi* code can be structured this way. There can be an arbitrary recursive interleaving of data-flow and sequencing, i.e. data-flows between communicating automata or transitions between data-flow processes. This is because processes and tasks are unified into a coherent language framework.

# 7 Conclusions and perspectives

We have presented in this paper the behavioural model, and more precisely the decisional part of this model. A formal model of a Hierarchical Parallel Transition System has been presented to describe *Realistic* behaviours, which requires different programming paradigms: reactivity, concurrency, data-flow and hierarchical preemption. These paradigms are all integrated in SIGNAL*GTi* which is a tasking extension of the declarative synchronous language SIGNAL and we have outlined how this model can be described in SIGNAL*GTi* considering this work is currently in progress.

This model will allow us to describe, in a same way, different kinds of living beings, and to simulate them in the same virtual environment, while most of behavioural models are actually restricted to the animation of one model in a specific environment. Another important point is that our behavioural model has been constructed to generate dynamic entities which are both autonomous and controllable, allowing us to use the same model in different contexts and moreover with different level of control.

Perspectives for SIGNAL and SIGNAL*GTi* that are relevant to the domain of behavioural animation systems concern both the specification and the implementation aspects. On the side of the programming language and implementation of the systems: It would be interesting to be able to declare external tasks "driven" from *GTi* (asynchronous tasks started, stopped, suspended, resumed upon the occurrence of corresponding events); this would enable the linking with external tasks written in other languages. The former could be done by connecting *GTi* to a real-time operating system, taking advantage of lower-level functionalities for the preemption of external tasks. Work is currently in progress around SIGNAL in order to compile programs so as to produce distributed executable code; given the complexity of computations involved in graphics, it is beneficial to have a distributed implementation of systems. In the SIGNAL approach, the semantical equivalence between specification and distributed implementation would be guaranteed, which constitutes a great help for ensuring program correctness.

Another aspect of the synchronous approach, although also based on its formal grounds, is that the environments include tools for the automated analysis of formal properties of the specified systems and their behaviour (absence of deadlocks, reachability of states, or on the contrary non-reachability of a "bad" state). This point is important for development purposes: it is a complement to tests in the debugging phase, in order to verify that the systems really has the expected or required behaviour. It is also valuable for the certification of the safety of the controllers and behaviours, which is particularly meaningful regarding safety-critical applications like in the domain of transportation.

# References

[1] O. Ahmad, J. Cremer, S. Hansen, J. Kearney, and P. Willemsen. Hierarchical, concurrent state machines for behavior modeling and scenario control. In *Conference on AI, Planning, and Simulation in High Autonomy Systems*, Gainesville, Florida, USA, 1994.

[2] F. Arbab and E. Rutten. MANIFOLD: a programming model for massive parallelism. In *Proceedings of the Working Conference on Massively Parallel Programming Models*, pages 151–159, IEEE, Berlin, German, September 1993.

[3] B. Arnaldi, R. Cozot, and S. Donikian. Virtual urban environment for the simulation of an automated electrical cars platoon in the praxitele project. In *Second Eurographics Workshop on Virtual Environments*, Monte Carlo, January 1995.

[4] B. Arnaldi and G. Dumont. Vehicle simulation versus vehicle animation. In *Third Eurographics Workshop on Animation and Simulation*, Cambridge, September 1992.

[5] N. I. Badler, C. B. Phillips, and B. L. Webber. *Simulating Humans : Computer Graphics Animation and Control*. Oxford University Press, 1993.

[6] Norman I. Badler, Bonnie L. Webber, Jugal Kalita, and Jeffrey Esakov, editors. *Making them move: mechanics, control, and animation of articulated figures*. Morgan Kaufmann, 1991.

[7] A. Benveniste and G. Berry. The synchronous approach to reactive and real-time systems. *Proceedings of the IEEE*, 79(9):1270–1282, September 1991.

[8] M. Booth, J. Cremer, and J. Kearney. Scenario control for real-time driving simulation. In *Fourth Eurographics Workshop on Animation and Simulation*, pages 103–119, Politechnical University of Catalonia, September 1993.

[9] S. Donikian. Les modèles comportementaux pour la génération du mouvement d'objets dans une scène. *Revue Internationale de CFAO et d'Infographie*, 9(6):847–871, 1994. Numéro Spécial 1re journées AFIG Groplan.

[10] S. Donikian and B. Arnaldi. Complexity and concurrency for behavioral animation and simulation. In G. Hégron and O. Fahlander, editors, *Fifth Eurographics Workshop on Animation and Simulation*, Oslo, Norvège, September 1994.

[11] S. Donikian and R. Cozot. General animation and simulation platform. In D. Terzopoulos and D. Thalmann, editors, *Computer Animation and Simulation'95*, pages 197–209, Springer-Verlag, 1995.

[12] S. Donikian and G. Hégron. A declarative design method for 3d scene sketch modeling. In *EUROGRAPHICS'93 Conference Proceedings*, Barcelona, Spain, September 1993.

[13] N. Halbwachs. *Synchronous programming of reactive systems*. Kluwer, 1993.

[14] G. Hégron and B. Arnaldi. *Computer Animation : Motion and Deformation Control*. Eurographics'92 Tutorial Notes, Eurographics Technical Report Series, Cambridge (Grande-Bretagne), September 1992.

[15] J. Kearney, J. Cremer, and S. Hansen. Motion control through communicating, hierarchical state machines. In G. Hegron and O. Fahlander, editors, *Fifth Eurographics Workshop on Animation and Simulation*, Oslo, Norway, September 1994.

[16] P. Le Guernic, M. Le Borgne, T. Gautier, and C. Le Maire. Programming real time application with SIGNAL. *Proceedings of the IEEE*, 79(9):1321–1336, September 1991.

[17] H. Marchand, E. Rutten, and M. Samaan. *Specifying and verifying a transformer station in* SIGNAL *and* SIGNAL*GTi*. Research Report 2521, INRIA, March 1995. (ftp ftp.inria.fr, file /INRIA/publication/RR/RR-2521.ps.gz).

[18] M. Parent and P. Daviet. Automatic driving for small public urban vehicles. In *Intelligent Vehicle Symposium*, Tokyo, Japon, July 1993.

[19] Gary Ridsdale and Tom Calvert. Animating microworlds from scripts and relational constraints. In N. Magnenat-Thalmann and D. Thalmann, editors, *Computer Animation '90 (Second workshop on Computer Animation)*, pages 107–118, Springer-Verlag, April 1990.

[20] E. Rutten and P. Le Guernic. The sequencing of data flow tasks in SIGNAL. In *Proceedings of the ACM SIGPLAN Workshop on Language, Compiler and Tool Support for Real-Time Systems*, Orlando, Florida, June 1994.

[21] Xiaoyuan Tu and Demetri Terzopoulos. Artificial fishes: physics, locomotion, perception, behavior. In *Computer Graphics (SIGGRAPH'94 Proceedings)*, pages 43–50, Orlando, Florida, July 1994.

[22] Michiel van de Panne and Eugene Fiume. Sensor-actuator networks. In James T. Kajiya, editor, *Computer Graphics (SIGGRAPH '93 Proceedings)*, pages 335–342, August 1993.

**Editors' Note: see Appendix, p. 169 for coloured figure of this paper**

# A Dual-Paradigm Approach to Database Generation for Visual Simulation

M. D. J. McNeill, S. J. Lambourn, P. F. Lister and R. L. Grimsdale

Centre for VLSI and Computer Graphics, University of Sussex,
Falmer, Brighton BN1 9QT, UK
E-mail: m.d.j.mcneill@sussex.ac.uk

**Abstract** The generation of three-dimensional (3D) databases for visual simulation is traditionally a lengthy manual task. We introduce the GEN system, which generates high quality 3D databases for visual simulation using a combination of declarative and procedural techniques. This dual-paradigm approach offers the benefits of rapid database generation and the ability to control the generation of databases for different countries of the world from high level knowledge. Real world data is enhanced by the addition of synthetic data in order to produce rich databases. The system can generate databases suitable for flight simulation, driving simulation and virtual environments

## 1 Introduction

Traditionally three-dimensional (3D) databases for high quality visual simulation are generated manually [19]. A grid of spot heights, or digital elevation map (DEM) [9], representing terrain, is either generated synthetically or from maps or satellite data [5, 3]. Visual simulation is concerned with real-time visualization of such data, typically using special (polygon-based) hardware [19]. A first step in the visualization process is therefore to polygonize the elevation data. Although this can be achieved using well-known triangulation algorithms [12], it is more common for a modeller to generate ground surface polygons manually. This is due to the large number of polygons generated using automatic techniques, which are beyond the capability of current visual systems. To complete the visual scenario the modeller must colour and texture the ground surface polygons, and add 3D models representing features such as rivers, roads, forests and urban regions. These features, or *culture*, are necessary for realistic simulation—buildings, trees, electricity pylons and similar features which 'stand out' from the ground surface give important height cues to pilots. Certain features such as airports must be modelled accurately, and therefore the use of real world data (when available) is often important. Colouring and texturing terrain polygons and representing culture with appropriate 3D models are typical of the tasks performed manually by a modeller.

The generation of 3D databases for visual simulation is therefore a fairly laborious process, and a database can typically take several man-months to prepare [19]. Currently all this effort must be duplicated for each database produced. In addition, culture data can be sparse, leading to large vacant areas in the database. The GEN project is concerned with automation of the generation process, and enhancement of the database where real world data is not known.

Section 2 discusses the motivation for the work. Section 3 describes the system architecture, and details the structure of the knowledge base. Techniques used for the generation of urban areas are detailed in Section 4. Conclusions are presented in Section 5. Sample images are shown in Figure 4 (see Appendix).

# 2 Motivation

A primary objective of the GEN project is to produce a system capable of taking a combination of real world terrain and culture data and generating a coloured, textured, 3D database suitable for direct visualization. The system would require minimal human interaction, and be able to target different application areas such as visual simulation and virtual environment modelling. We hoped that the system could be generic and flexible enough to be used in real applications and generate rich 3D databases much faster than existing methods.

Two main application areas were targeted: *flight simulation*, where the objective is the generation of a database consisting of terrain and culture features such as rivers, roads, forests, electricity pylons and (low-detail) urban areas; and *driving simulation*, where the objective is the allocation of land in urban areas and the population of these areas with suitable roads, buildings and road signs, etc. An important element of the system would be the use of real world culture where available, and the generation of synthetic culture where real world data was not available or was sparse. We hope that the methodology adopted would provide insight into the viability of knowledge-based techniques for other graphics applications.

## 2.1 The generation process

Real world terrain and culture data is available from a number of sources, including MIL-STD-1851 [11]. Errors are often introduced during the digitizing process [20] which can result in visual imperfections, such as roads appearing in the sea, or rivers crossing roads. In addition, there may be areas where there is no culture data, resulting in large vacant regions of the landscape. Urban areas present more problems, where typically the only real world data available may be just the geometric outline of the town.

MIL-STD-1851 format, an industry standard for simulation databases, represents terrain as a height field, and culture data as ordered 2D points—no height is specified. Linear features such as rivers and roads are represented as sets of points defining the path, area features such as urban regions and forests are defined only by their boundary, and point features such as large buildings and electricity pylons are defined by position.

GEN reads the terrain and culture data input, automatically generates 3D polygons representing the terrain and transforms suitable 3D models, representing culture, into the database. Where multi-resolution models are available GEN can transform these into the database as *LevelOfDetail* nodes [21]. The task of adding additional culture where it is sparse is seen as a major activity of GEN for two reasons. Firstly the addition of such culture significantly adds to the realism of the database and would require a large amount of manual effort. The generation of this synthetic culture is constrained by the need to integrate it with known real-world culture. Secondly, this capability enables the creation of completely 'virtual worlds' where no real world data is available. We anticipated that information about the sort of features likely to be found in the world, and rules governing their placement could be encapsulated in a knowledge base.

### 2.2 Knowledge-based techniques in computer graphics

There are many applications in computer graphics where artificial intelligence (AI) and knowledge based techniques have been successfully applied. Computer animation, for example, has used AI techniques for several years in the specification and control of dynamic (physical) systems [1, 17]. Rule-based systems have also proved popular in spatial planning and computer animation [14, 7]. Further applications of such techniques include virtual reality [13] and urban planning [6].

The success of expert systems in spatial (and urban) planning is well documented [7]. Systems have been constraint-based [15], goal-based [14] and relational [16]. Such systems promote the specification of *relationships* between physical entities in a fairly natural way, for example, 'houses are placed to the side of roads'. *Constraints* can also be expressed in a high level manner, for example, 'hospitals are not placed in industrial areas'.

We propose a system where knowledge about the world is stored using a combination of hierarchical frames [10] and spatial relations [14]. The system deduces information from this knowledge domain in the context of the current country or region of the world using production rules [14]. The knowledge domain is extendible by the addition of more rules, which may contain knowledge specific to a part of the world, particular entities such as airports or urban areas or even a particular application area. The GEN system is now described in detail.

## 3 The GEN system

The main elements of the system (Figure 1) are the input data routines, the knowledge domain, the geometric functions and user interaction with the system.

Input to GEN has been detailed above, and consists of terrain and culture data. The GEN knowledge domain contains various facts about the type of cultural features found in the world, in order that suitable choices can be made about colours, textures and 3D models to accurately represent the area. In addition, it contains rules governing the placement of features. Geometric functions are called which transform 3D models from libraries into the database. These models are placed according to the rules in the knowledge base.

Output from GEN is a rich 3D database suitable for direct visualization on a graphics workstation or immediate transformation onto a simulation system.

### 3.1 The GEN run-time environment

The knowledge domain of GEN is implemented in Flex [18], an expert system toolkit from Logic Programming Associates (LPA). Flex is an expressive, hybrid expert system

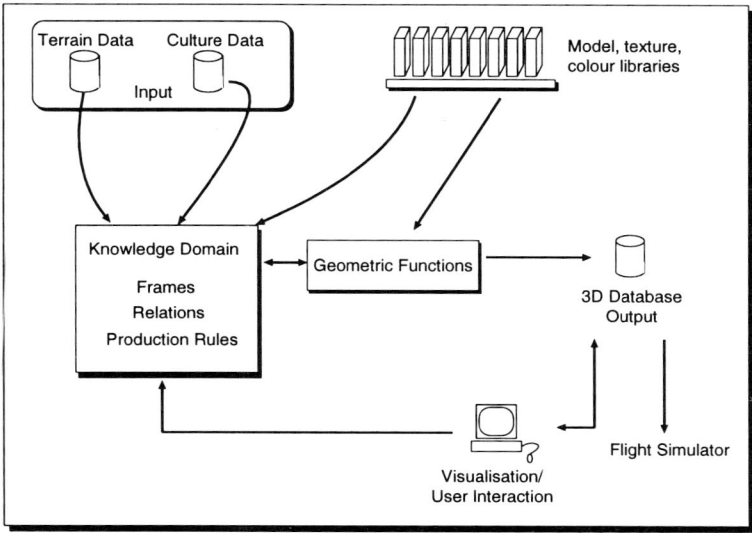

Fig. 1: GEN System Overview

toolkit that offers a number of programming paradigms—frame-based, data driven and rule-based. It is fully integrated into a Prolog environment, and we take advantage of the Poplog system [8], developed at the University of Sussex. Poplog incorporates Pop-11, Common Lisp and Prolog, and allows external calls to C functions. Flex provides an English-like Knowledge Specification Language (KSL) for expert system development, where knowledge can be stated in a natural manner.

Other features of Flex include a frame hierarchy with multiple inheritance, interleaved forward and backward chaining rules, and an automatic question and answer subsystem. Explanations, data-driven programming via daemons and a full GUI development environment which includes a syntax analyzer are also provided. Graphical entity browsers and spy points allow the user to interrogate the knowledge domain.

This sophisticated programming environment offers the advantages of an expert system toolkit containing production rules, frames, relations and rule agendas, combined with the numerical manipulation and processing capabilities of Pop-11 and C. GEN uses Flex to store information about the nature of the geographical region and the physical rules governing object placement. Included is information relating to the types of culture likely to be found and details about model colouring and texturing. Once the knowledge domain is built for a particular region, low level Pop-11 and C functions are called to transform the 3D models from model libraries and perform the floating point computations necessary for placement. Queries into the knowledge domain from geometric functions are possible, as is the triggering of individual rules or rule sets. The overall programming environment is therefore rich, with the user able to use both expert system constructs and procedural functions to store and manipulate data efficiently.

## 3.2 Architecture of the knowledge domain

The GEN knowledge domain comprises frames, relations and production rules containing a range of facts about the world and how entities are related to each other. Concepts and facts pertinent to the geographical area are stored in hierarchical frames; relations and production rules provide means of storing spatial relationships and facts. A suitable rule agenda can be used to influence the rule triggering algorithm [18]. GEN uses the knowledge domain to select suitable 3D models to accurately represent the features in the current region. English houses, for example, look different to Spanish houses, and the types of trees and crops found in the two countries are significantly different. The knowledge base attempts to encapsulate such information in order to accurately model the landscape of the particular country.

**Frames** Frames can be used in order to store several kinds of information [10]. In GEN, facts coded as frames include information about the appearance of the landscape particular to the geographical area—for example the cultural features likely to be found in that region. Flex also provides a means of specifying default values for frame slots, which may be changed as a result of a rule being fired. An example of the kind of knowledge represented as a frame is shown below (Knowledge Specification Language reserved words are shown in *italics*):

*frame* england *is a kind of* country ;
    *default* suburban_house_roof_slope *is* pitched *and*
    *default* crops *are* {barley, wheat, grass, rapeseed} *and*
    *default* land_use *is* {crops,ploughed,setaside,forest,heathland} *and*
    *default* trees *are* {sycamore, oak, larch} .


Frames offer a natural and high level means of encapsulating knowledge about physical entities, (the *object* in object-oriented systems is a similar concept). Modellers using GEN can extend the knowledge base by adding additional frames as necessary; suitable browsing tools are available to view frame hierarchies and slot values.

**Relations** Many types of spatial relations exist between objects which are used during the model selection and placement phase. In GEN, relations are used to specify physical rules which determine the way in which objects are to be placed, and also to constrain the placement of objects where appropriate. This functionality allows GEN to flag data it suspects is wrong—for example if a road juts out into the sea. Before placing any feature, GEN will check that relations concerning that feature are not violated. A typical statement would be 'roads cannot be placed in the sea'. Relations are an intrinsic feature of spatial planning systems where land use and population are important, and are returned to in Section 4.

**Production rules** In GEN, production rules are used for three purposes.

1. to store facts about the *cultural features* of the region; for example to specify typical features which may be found in an English town,

*rule* england
> *if the* population *of the* town *is greater than* 50000
> *then include* {suburban_area,industrial_area,
> commercial_area,parkland} *in the* contents *of the* town .

2. to specify the *appearance of the terrain*; for example the colours and textures appropriate to crops, country and season,

*rule* season
> *if* country *is* england *and*
> *the* season *is* summer
> *then include* {corn,grass} *in the* fields *of* england *and*
> *the* corn_colour *of* england *becomes* yellow *and*
> *the* corn_texture *of* england *becomes* "cornfield.rgb" .

3. to specify *constraints* on the size and number of particular features; for example the percentage of corn fields found in a typical region,

*rule* crop_percentages
> *if* country *is* england *and*
> corn *is included in the* crops *of* england
> *then the* corn_fraction *of* england *becomes* 0.3 .

GEN will enhance the real-world culture where appropriate; for example it will add bridges when rivers and roads cross, and add electricity pylons between industrial towns or telegraph poles between smaller towns as appropriate. Rules governing the representation of such features and the placement of features are contained in the knowledge base. The user can visualize the output on the GEN workstation and can then interact with the database at a number of levels. The database can be edited directly, and colours, textures or models can be changed as required. Alternatively, the user can change existing rules or relations in the knowledge domain, or add new knowledge (see Section 3.4). In the latter case care must be taken to avoid conflict with existing rules.

### 3.3 Geometric functions

The process of transforming 3D models into the database involves intensive floating point number manipulation and processing, and is handled by a large suite of geometric functions, coded in Pop-11 and C. These functions provide the ability to clip objects against one another, and to scale, rotate and translate models to the appropriate place in the database. Frequent queries to the knowledge domain are made from these geometric

160

functions, requesting frame-slot values and triggering rules as necessary. It is important to standardize the models contained in the libraries, in order, for example, to ensure that model placement satisfies the relations expressed in the knowledge domain. Houses, typically placed next to roads, may be declared in the knowledge domain as *facing towards* the road, or *facing away from* some other feature. In order for GEN to interpret the relational concept *facing towards* correctly, it must be able to distinguish the front of the house from the back. Models are therefore stored in a consistent manner, oriented along the z-axis. In this way GEN can translate high level relational concepts into 3D transformation matrices in Cartesian coordinate space.

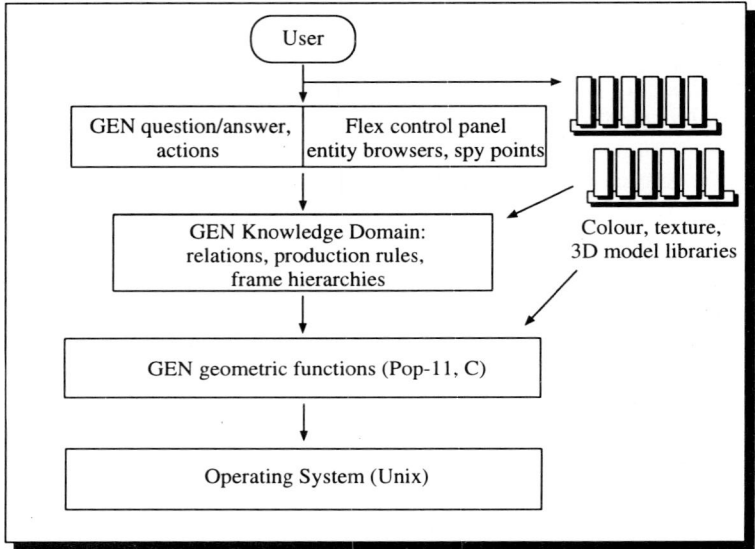

Fig. 2: The GEN programming interface

### 3.4 User interaction

The advantages of this dual paradigm approach are several. The use of the Flex expert system tool allows concepts, facts and rules to be coded within an environment which supports many facilities designed to store, manipulate, browse and debug high-level information. The language adopted, while ideal for such high level information processing, does not support many of the functions required for the complex numerical processing necessary to manipulate 3D models in Cartesian coordinate space. These functions are more efficiently implemented in Pop-11 and C, and this layer of software can remain hidden from the user. The modeller can, if he wishes, interact only with the knowledge base (Figure 2), and is free to adapt and extend this for the current application. There is no need to learn a traditional large, complex programming language.

The modeller can interact with GEN in several ways, including editing the 3D database directly. Straightforward textual substitution in the Knowledge Specification

Language code can be used in order to control the choice and placement of features. By changing the *default country* from *england* to *spain*, for example, GEN will output a significantly different database, useful for creating families of databases for training purposes. Similarly, the modeller is free to alter relations and production rules and build knowledge domains for particular applications. An experienced Flex programmer can, of course, extend the knowledge base by writing new frames, relations and production rules. GEN has been designed to allow the layer of geometric functions to remain hidden from the modeller, who is typically not a programmer.

# 4 Urban generation

One of the most interesting features of GEN is the generation of synthetic urban regions. High level culture data is often sparse, and many features must be present in an urban scene for realistic visualization. Rule sets which aid the generation of urban areas have proved difficult to build, due to the complexity of the factors involved. Many diverse elements have influenced the growth of real towns. These elements have changed with time, and the evolution of a town with only a short history is likely to have been subject to many different influences. Geographical factors such as proximity to the sea or a river have placed obvious physical constraints on urban growth, but in addition, waterways, roads and railways, as communication paths, have had significant influences on the development of urban areas. A detailed account of the growth of urban areas can be found in [2]. Expert systems for urban planning have been well documented [14, 15] and GEN specifies layout and determines space allocation in urban regions using typical space planning algorithms.

Three main elements which are important for realistic urban area generation have been identified:

- Site selection

- Site partitioning and space allocation

- Choice of appropriate styles of roads, buildings and other urban features

## 4.1 Site selection

The locations of real world urban regions may be available, but GEN can choose an appropriate site where such information is not available. In this case the terrain height and gradient, underlying soil type (if known) and surrounding natural features such as rivers and lakes can all contribute to the selection process. Proximity to communication links (roads, railways) and other urban areas also influence the decision process.

## 4.2 Site partitioning and space allocation

Many people have published work in the area of site partitioning and land use planning. In [4], three models of urban land use are presented: the *Concentric Ring Model*, with commercial, industrial and suburban rings at various distances from the centre; the *Sector Zone Model*, a variation of the Concentric Ring Model which takes account of transportation links such as rivers and roads; and the *Multiple Nuclei Model*, where the town is built up by an engulfment of smaller urban areas.

GEN currently implements the Multiple Nuclei Model, in which there are potentially a large number of nuclei which, over the course of the generation of the area, grow to fill the available space. Each nucleus represents a particular land usage, such as housing, industrial, commercial or parkland. Each can be configured to grow at a different rate, and may be constrained to follow or avoid certain features, such as existing roads or rivers. This is important for MIL-STD-1851 data, which often contains real-world data about rivers, main roads and urban boundaries but no information about the buildings inside the urban areas. In this case GEN can be used to populate the urban region with appropriate models for trees, secondary roads, houses and factories, etc.

### 4.3 Local culture

Once the nuclei have grown to fill the available space, GEN populates each nucleus with roads, trees and buildings. More detailed culture such as road markings, signposts and traffic lights suitable for each particular area can also be generated. Appropriate knowledge about the choice and placement of these features is contained in the knowledge base, and this allows for automatic placement of signposts on the right-hand or left-hand side of the road as appropriate to the country.

A sample urban area, consisting of a combination of real world culture data and synthetic data is shown in Figure 3. The known culture is a river, shown flowing top to bottom, and two road segments, one of which crosses the river. These features have constrained the selection, placement and growth of nuclei. The top left image shows the placement of the nuclei. In the top-right image all the nuclei have been left to grow unconstrained, and at the same rate, until the area is filled. The bottom-left image shows the results of the same initial conditions, but with those nuclei representing industrial areas constrained to follow either the river or the road. The bottom-right image shows the result of the same constraints as for the previous image, but with the growth rates changed so that industrial nuclei grow faster than commercial, parkland and suburban areas.

## 5 Conclusion

We have introduced the GEN system for generating rich 3D databases for visual simulation applications. The novel approach taken, which exploits both declarative and procedural programming styles has proved successful, and output from GEN has been ported onto a flight simulator.

The use of more than one programming paradigm can therefore be advantageous, particularly in the application area described. The development environment, although rich, requires refinement of the programming interfaces between the various methodologies supported—more work is needed in the development of tools to support multi-paradigm programming environments. The GEN system has, however, several advantages over traditional approaches to 3D database generation. These include,

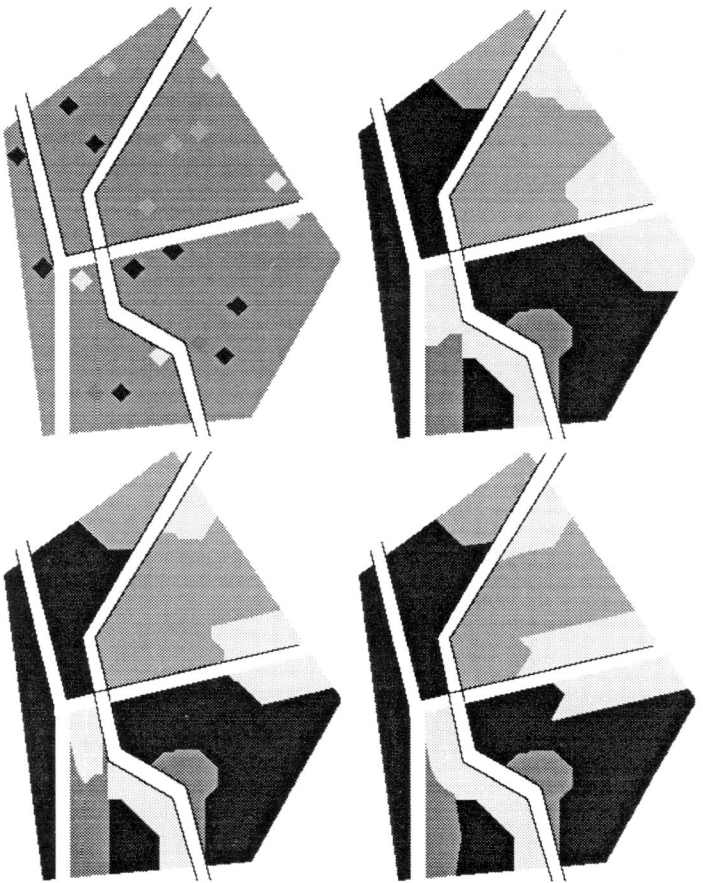

Fig. 3: Allocation of land in an urban area

- real world data can be combined with synthetic data to generate rich databases. Straightforward addition of features such as bridges and electricity pylons reduces the manual effort required.

- where no real world data is available GEN can generate databases for completely virtual worlds. This is of particular value in animation and virtual reality applications, where a backdrop may be required.

- the flexible development environment adopted allows users to change parameters at a high level (such as the texture representing a particular crop) and see significant changes in the database as a consequence. Databases can be generated faster than traditional methods.

- rule sets can be built for many different scenarios and application areas without the need to learn a traditional programming language. Relations, rules and constraints can be expressed in a natural, high level way.

Example databases can be seen in Figure 4 (see Appendix).

# 6 Acknowledgements

The GEN project was funded by the Engineering and Physical Sciences Research Council (UK), and the Department of Trade and Industry (UK). Partners are the Centre for VLSI and Computer Graphics at the University of Sussex, Thomson Training and Simulation (Crawley, UK), and the Defence Research Agency (Bedford, UK).

# References

[1] N. I. Badler. Artificial intelligence, natural language and simulation for human animation. In N. Magnenat-Thalmann and D. Thalmann, editors, *State-of-the-art in Computer Animation: Proceedings of Computer Animation '89*. Springer-Verlag, 1989.

[2] Michael Batty and Paul Longley. *Fractal Cities*. Academic Press, 1994.

[3] Pietro Alessandro Brivio and Daniele Marini. A fractal method for digital elevation model reconstruction and its application to a mountain region. *Computer Graphics Forum*, 12(5):297–309, 1993.

[4] F. Stuart Chapin and Edward J. Kaiser. *Urban Land Use Planning*. Univeristy of Illinois Press, 1979.

[5] J. Hagger K. Ch. Graf, M. Suter and D. Hüesch. Computer graphics and remote sensing - a synthesis for environmental planning and civil engineering. *Proceedings of Eurographics '94*, 13(3):C–14–C–22, 1994.

[6] Robert Laurini. Introduction to expert systems in town planning. *Systemi Urbani*, 11(1), 1989.

[7] Robert Laurini and Derek Thompson. *Fundamentals of Spatial Information Systems*. Academic Press, 1992.

[8] Integrated Solutions Ltd. *Poplog 14.1 User Guide*, 1991.

[9] G. S. P. Miller. The definition and rendering of terrain maps. *Computer Graphics, Proceedings of SIGGRAPH '86*, 20(4):39–48, 1986.

[10] M. Minsky. A framework for representing knowledge. In P. H. Winston, editor, *The psychology of computer vision*, pages 211–277. McGraw-Hill, 1975.

[11] US Department of Defense MIL-STD-1821. Standard simulator data base (SSDB) interchange format (SIF) design standard. Technical report, US Deptartment of Defense, June 1983.

[12] Joeseph O'Rourke. *Computational Geometry in C*. Cambridge University Press, 1993.

[13] Michael J. Papper and Michael A. Gigante. Using physical constraints in a virtual environment. In M. A. Gigante R. A. Earnshaw and H. Jones, editors, *Virtual Reality Systems*, pages 107–118. Academic Press, 1993.

[14] A. D. Radford M. Balachandran R. D. Coyne, M. A. Rosenman and J. S. Gero. *Knowledge-Based Design Systems*. Addison-Wesley, 1990.

[15] Thomas W. Calvert Sang Mah and William Havens. Nsail plan: An experience with constraint-based reasoning in planning and animation. In *Computer Animation '94*, 1994.

[16] Hanqui Sun and Mark Green. The use of relations for motion control in an environment with multiple moving objects. In *Graphics Interface '93*, 1993.

[17] D. Thalmann and N. Magnenat-Thalmann. Artificial intelligence in three-dimensional computer animation. *Computer Graphics Forum*, 5(4):341–238, 1986.

[18] P. Vasey and D. Westwood. *Flex Expert System Toolkit*. Logic Programming Associates Ltd., 1992.

[19] John Vince. Virtual reality techniques in flight simulation. In M. A. Gigante R. A. Earnshaw and H. Jones, editors, *Virtual Reality Systems*, pages 135–141. Academic Press, 1993.

[20] M. Visvalingam and J. D. Whyatt. Cartographic algorithms: Problems of implementation and evaluation and the impact of digitising errors. *Computer Graphics Forum*, 10:225–235, 1991.

[21] Josie Wernecke. *The Inventor Mentor*. Addison-Wesley Publishing Company, 1994.

**Editors' Note: see Appendix, p. 172 for coloured figure of this paper**

# Appendix: Colour Illustrations

Slusallek and Seidel, Fig. 3: Image of a glossy reflection in the metal plate on the table calculated with Monte-Carlo path tracing.

Donikian and Rutten, Fig. 9: One example of obtained simulation: the viewpoint is located in a praxicar driven by a virtual driver whose actual task is to form a platoon with empty praxicars (blue vehicles parked on the right).

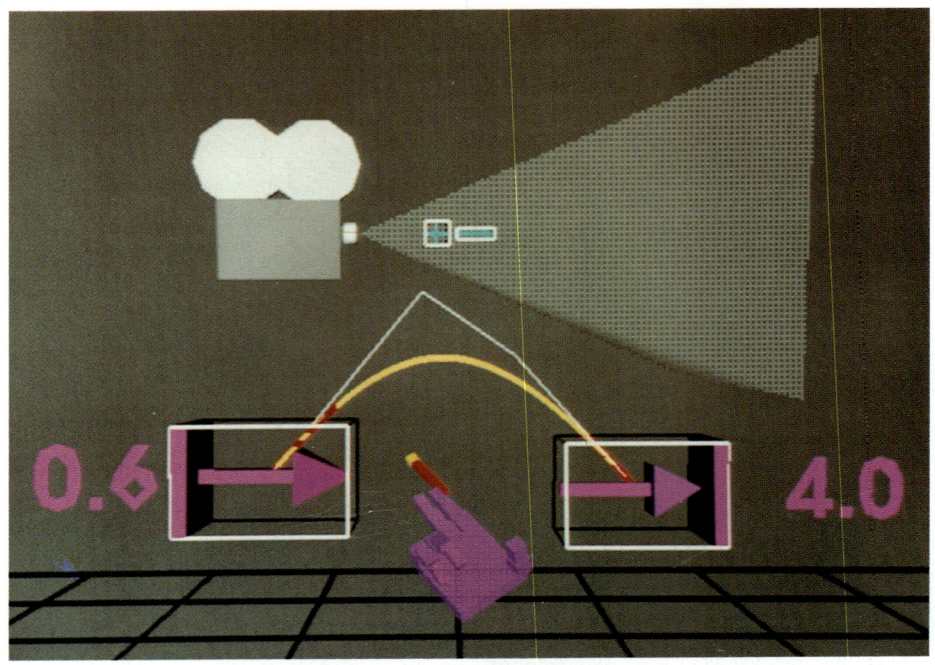

Balaguer and Gobbetti, Fig 7: Camera tool and camera position track.

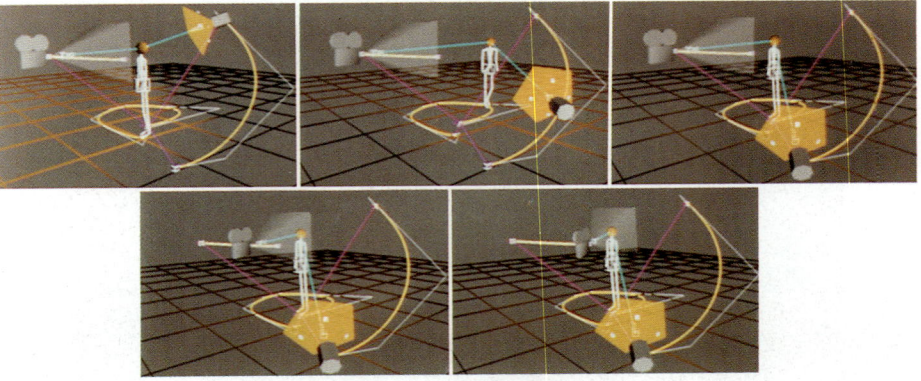

Balaguer and Gobbetti, Fig 8: The scene is composed of a character, a light and a camera.

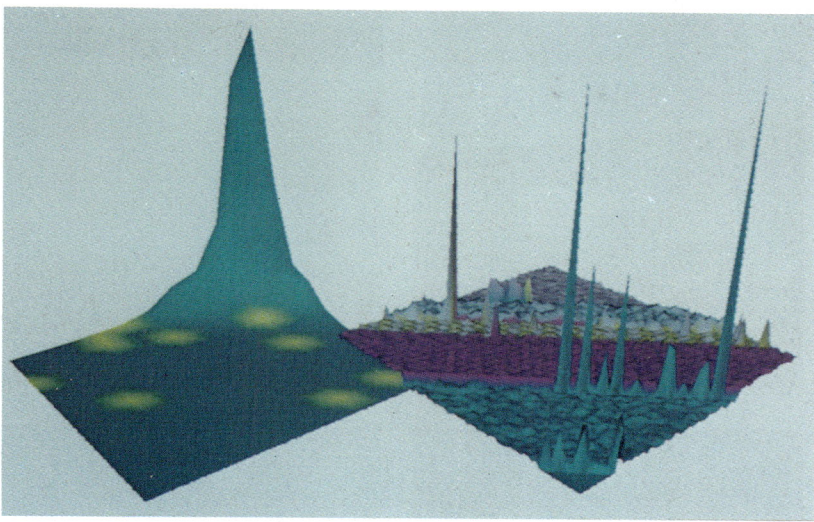

Blake and Goosen, Fig.4: Chiron source and object cost view.
The left surface represents the memory reference overhead incurred by each source line, while the right represents the memory reference overhead of each object used in the program. The left surface shows source lines that reference a particular object selected on the right surface.

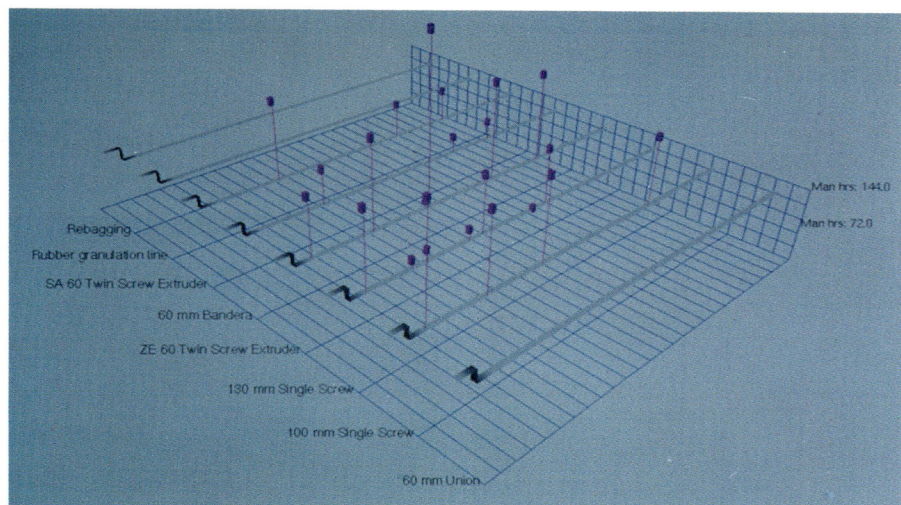

Blake and Goosen, Fig. 5: Manufacturing visualization.
The rough-cut capacity planning module. The ribbons represent the capacity of each work center, while the cubes represent work centers where orders exceed capacity.

172

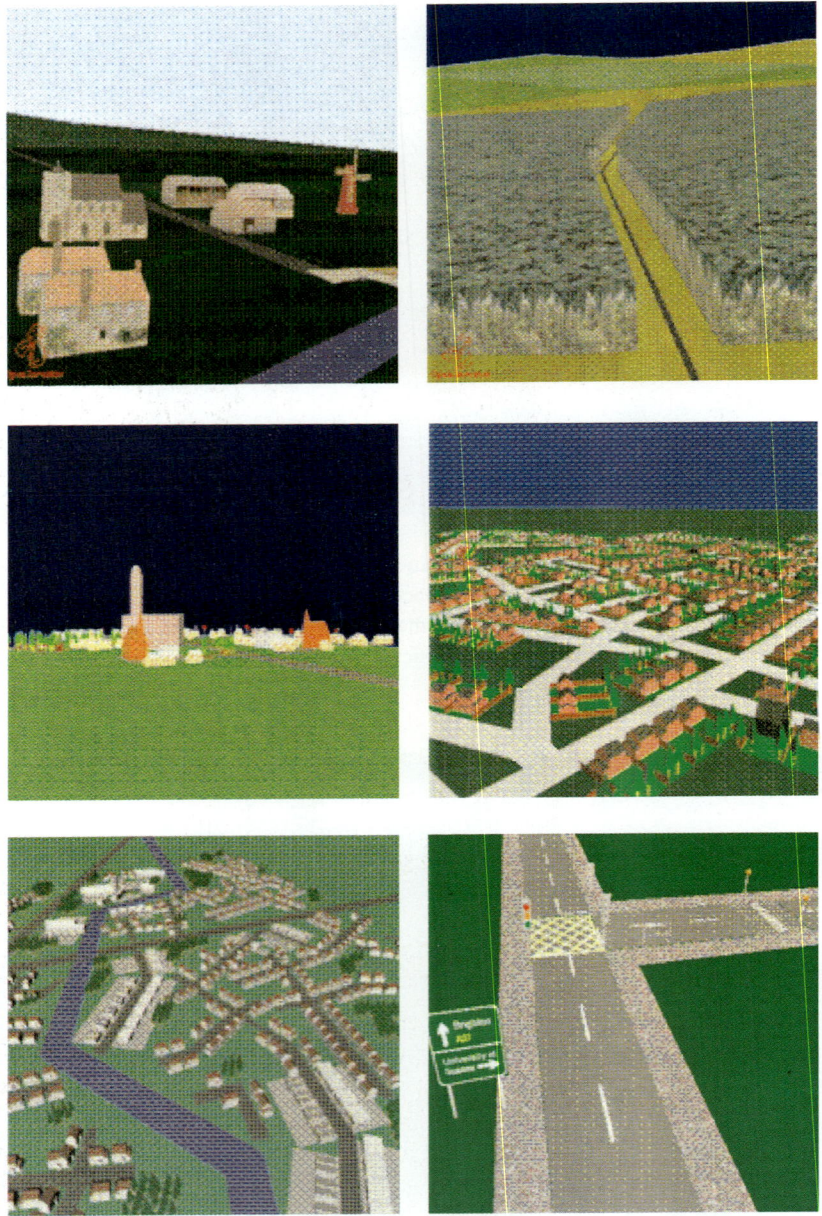

McNeill et al., Fig. 4: Sample databases from the GEN system.

# SpringerEurographics

Philippe Palanque, Rémi Bastide (eds.)

## Design, Specification and Verification

## of Interactive Systems '95

Proceedings of the Eurographics Workshop
in Toulouse, France, June 7–9, 1995

1995. 153 figures. X, 370 pages.
Soft cover DM 118,–, öS 826,–
ISBN 3-211-82739-0

Twenty-one contributions cover the different aspects of interactive systems, from formal user modelling to formal techniques for prototyping, and describe the state-of-the-art on these topics, also giving new directions for future research.
The book is an obligatory piece of literature for all scientists working in the formal aspects of the interactive systems field, but it is also valuable for the practitioner involved in the design of reliable interactive systems.

Martin Göbel (ed.)

## Virtual Environments '95

Selected papers of the Eurographics Workshops
in Barcelona, Spain, 1993, and Monte Carlo, Monaco, 1995

1995. 134 partly coloured figures. VII, 307 pages.
Soft cover DM 108,–, öS 756,–
ISBN 3-211-82737-4

The book contains 22 selected and revised papers that have been presented in EG workshops in Barcelona and Monte Carlo. The areas covered are visual presentation aspects, gesture and speech interaction issues, applications and VE system, demonstrating very clearly the emphasis and the results of various research activities in the field.

 SpringerWienNewYork

P.O.Box 89, A-1201 Wien • New York, NY 10010, 175 Fifth Avenue
Heidelberger Platz 3, D-14197 Berlin • Tokyo 113, 3-13, Hongo 3-chome, Bunkyo-ku

# SpringerEurographics

Demetri Terzopoulos, Daniel Thalmann (eds.)

## Computer Animation and Simulation '95

Proceedings of the Eurographics Workshop
in Maastricht, The Netherlands, September 2–3, 1995

1995. 156 partly coloured figures. VIII, 235 pages.
Soft cover DM 89,–, öS 625,–
ISBN 3-211-82738-2

The sixteen papers in this volume present novel animation techniques and
animation systems that simulate the dynamics and interactions of physical
objects (solid, fluid, and gaseous) as well as the behaviors of living systems
such as plants, lower animals, and humans (growth and metamorphosis,
motion control, locomotion, etc.). The book vividly demonstrates the con-
fluence of animation and simulation, a leading edge of computer graphics
research that is providing animators with sophisticated new algorithms for synthesizing dynamic scenes.

Riccardo Scateni, Jarke J. van Wijk, Pietro Zanarini (eds.)

## Visualization in Scientific Computing '95

Proceedings of the Eurographics Workshop
in Chia, Italy, May 3–5, 1995

1995. 110 partly coloured figures. VII, 161 pages.
Soft cover DM 85,–, öS 595,–
ISBN 3-211-82729-3

13 contributions cover a wide range of topics, ranging from detailed algorithmic studies to searches for new metaphors. The reader will find state-
of-the-art results and techniques in this discipline, which he can use to
find solutions for his visualization problems.

 SpringerWienNewYork

P.O.Box 89, A-1201 Wien • New York, NY 10010, 175 Fifth Avenue
Heidelberger Platz 3, D-14197 Berlin • Tokyo 113, 3-13, Hongo 3-chome, Bunkyo-ku

# SpringerEurographics

Patrick M. Hanrahan, Werner Purgathofer (eds.)

## Rendering Techniques '95

Proceedings of the Eurographics Workshop
in Dublin, Ireland, June 12–14, 1995

1995. 198 partly coloured figures. XI, 372 pages.
Soft cover DM 118,–, öS 826,–
ISBN 3-211-82733-1

Martin Göbel, Heinrich Müller, Bodo Urban (eds.)

## Visualization in Scientific Computing

1995. 150 figures. VIII, 238 pages.
Soft cover  DM 118,–, öS 826,–
ISBN 3-211-82633-5

Wolfgang Herzner, Frank Kappe (eds.)

## Multimedia/Hypermedia

## in Open Distributed Environments

Proceedings of the Eurographics Symposium
in Graz, Austria, June 6–9, 1994

1994. 105 figures. VIII, 330 pages.
Soft cover DM 118,–, öS 826,–
ISBN 3-211-82587-8

 SpringerWienNewYork

P.O.Box 89, A-1201 Wien • New York, NY 10010, 175 Fifth Avenue
Heidelberger Platz 3, D-14197 Berlin • Tokyo 113, 3-13, Hongo 3-chome, Bunkyo-ku

## Springer-Verlag
### and the Environment